ZÓBEL READS LORCA

POETRY, PAINTING, AND *PERLIMPLÍN IN LOVE*

To Benjamin,
I hope this one-act hiddengem is a satisfactory first taste of García Lorca's work, and that this slender volume makes a worthwhile addition to your erudition.
Happy reading!

Blessings,

[illegible]

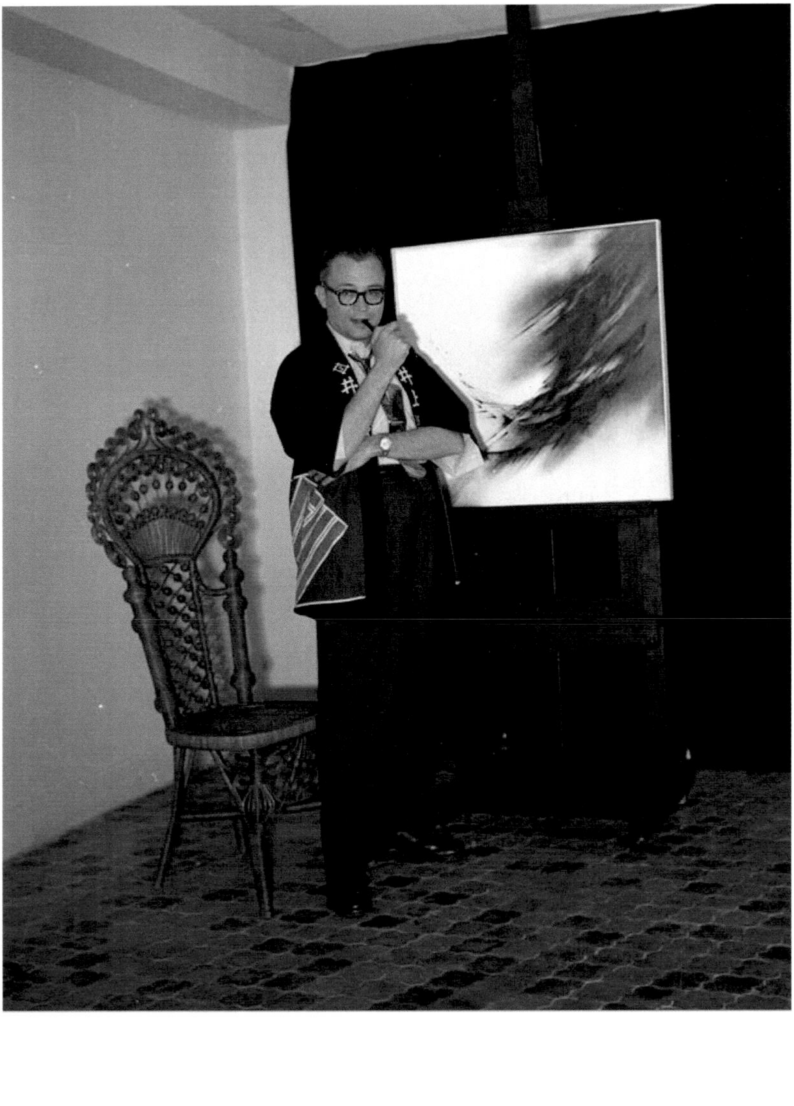

FEDERICO GARCÍA LORCA

FERNANDO ZÓBEL

ZÓBEL READS LORCA: POETRY, PAINTING, AND *PERLIMPLÍN IN LOVE*

SWAN ISLE PRESS

CHICAGO

Fernando Zóbel (Fernando Zóbel de Ayala, 1924–1984), born into a Spanish family in Manila, educated at Harvard, and trained in the U.S. as a painter and scholar, is one of the most complex and cosmopolitan figures of the 20th-century Spanish avant-garde.

Federico García Lorca (1898-1936) was one the most widely read and beloved poets and playwrights of twentieth-century Spain and one of the world's most influential modernist writers.

Swan Isle Press, Chicago 60628

First Edition
26 25 24 23 22   1 2 3 4 5
ISBN-13: 978-1-7361893-3-7

Swan Isle Press gratefully acknowledges Laura García Lorca and the heirs of Federico García Lorca, and with special thanks and acknowledgment to Georgina Padilla Zóbel and Alejandro Padilla Zóbel, heirs of Fernando Zóbel de Ayala, for their respective permissions to use Zóbel's art and translation of Lorca's *Amor de Don Perlimplín con Belisa en su jardín.*

Library of Congress Cataloging-in-Publication Data:
Names: Fernández Cifuentes, Luis. | Mateo, Marta. | Maurer, Christopher. | Pereda, Felipe, 1968- | Currie, Lincoln Son. | García Lorca, Federico, 1898-1936. | Zóbel, Fernando. | García Lorca, Federico, 1898-1936. Amor de don Perlimplín con Belisa en su jardín. English.
Title: Zóbel reads Lorca : poetry, painting, and Perlimplín in love / Federico García Lorca ; [translated and illustrated by] Fernando Zóbel; [essays by] Luis Fernández Cifuentes, Marta Mateo, Christopher Maurer, Felipe Pereda, Lincoln Son Currie.
Description: First edition. | Chicago : Swan Isle Press, [2022] | Includes bibliographical references.
Identifiers: LCCN 2022037727 | ISBN 9781736189337 (trade paperback)
Subjects: LCSH: Zóbel, Fernando--Criticism and interpretation. | García
Lorca, Federico, 1898-1936. Amor de don Perlimplín con Belisa en su jardín. | BISAC: ART / Individual Artists / Essays | DRAMA / General | LCGFT: Essays. | Drama.
Classification: LCC N7329.Z6 Z63 2022 | DDC 759.9599--dc23/eng/20220817
LC record available at https://lccn.loc.gov/2022037727

Swan Isle Press also gratefully acknowledges that this book has been made possible, in part, with the support of grants and funding from the following:
Observatorio de la Lengua y las Culturas Hispánicas en los Estados Unidos – Instituto Cervantes at Harvard University
Boston University Center for the Humanities
Faculty of Arts and Sciences, Harvard University
Literary Arts Emergency Fund: Administered by the Academy of American Poets, Community of Literary Magazines & Presses, and National Book Foundation, supported by the Mellon Foundation
Illinois Arts Council Agency
Europe Bay Giving Trust
Other kind donors

This paper meets the requirements of ANSI/NISO Z.39.48.-1992 (Permanence of Paper).

CONTENTS

Preface
Marta Mateo *vii*

Zóbel Reads Lorca: The Painter's Early Years in New England
Felipe Pereda *1*

Zóbel's Harvard and the 1940s Crisis in Higher Education
Luis Fernández Cifuentes *41*

American *Perlimplín*
Christopher Maurer *63*

About the Translation
Christopher Maurer *81*

Federico García Lorca
Don Perlimplín in Love
Translated by Fernando Zóbel *83*

Federico García Lorca
Music to *Amor de Don Perlimplín con Belisa en su jardín*
Arranged by Gustavo Pittaluga *123*

From Stage to Page: A *Perlimplín* Chronology
Christopher Maurer and Lincoln Son Currie *127*

Illustrations *141*

Notes *145*

Bibliography *165*

Acknowledgments *171*

MARTA MATEO

PREFACE

It is a special honor to present this volume on such an interesting and relevant figure as Fernando Zóbel from the perspective of two themes so closely linked and dear to its three contributors: Harvard University and Federico García Lorca.

Zóbel's life and work are well documented and have been widely studied. Born in Manila in 1924 into one of the richest and most influential families in the Philippines, Fernando Zóbel would become a leading representative of Spanish avant-garde painting in the 20th century—especially the abstract art movement—as well as an acclaimed photographer, printmaker, art collector and art patron. When he died in Rome in 1984, after suffering a heart attack, his works already hung at major museums in various parts of the world and had been the object of important exhibitions in the Philippines, Spain, and the United States. A year earlier he had been awarded the Medalla de Oro al Mérito en las Bellas Artes (Gold Medal for Merit in the Fine Arts) by King Juan Carlos I of Spain.

This book aims to extend our knowledge of Zóbel's complex and fascinating personality as an artist and a scholar by delving into his Harvard and New England years, from 1946 until the mid-1950s, which, though mentioned in numerous studies on the artist, have not yet been the object of in-depth research.

Harvard marked the start of Zóbel's career and of his close and lasting relationship with the United States—particularly with Cambridge, Boston, Rhode Island and New York. We can recall some landmark moments of this connection: his student years at Harvard University, including his internship at Houghton Library; the highly promising beginning of his painting and printmaking career, particularly after enrolling at the Rhode Island School of Design (RISD) in Providence; his first exhibitions, in Boston and at the RISD Museum of Art; major exhibitions featuring his work, such as *Before Picasso; After Miró* at the Solomon R. Guggenheim Museum (1960) or his solo exhibition at the Bertha Schaefer Gallery in the same city (1965). In the US, Zóbel met or discovered the painters that would be most influential in his art, like the Bostonians Reed Champion Pfeufer and Hyman Bloom; Mark Rothko—whose work, which he discovered at the RISD Museum, prompted him to explore an entirely new style of painting— or Ronald Binks, who guided him in his early exploration of photography. In New York he witnessed the early days of the American Abstract Expressionism movement, which would strongly impact his work.

Zóbel's student years at the oldest university in the United States would also deepen his artistic relationship with Spain, a country with which he already had a personal connection through his ancestors and through his mother tongue, Spanish (English was his second language.) During his Harvard years he would relate to Spain both as artist and as scholar, hand in hand with Federico García Lorca (1898-1936), first through his English translation of the play *Amor de Don Perlimplín con Belisa en su jardín*—which he did for a class in Comparative Literature, going far beyond what was probably expected of him by illustrating it with his own drawings (1946)—and then through his senior thesis, a dissertation on "Theme and Conflict in Lorcan Drama" (1949).

Spain would eventually become the artist's permanent abode. After some stays in the country in his thirties, he would finally settle in Madrid in the early 1960s. Zóbel had both Filipino and Spanish nationalities and had even been appointed Honorary Cultural Attaché of the Spanish Embassy in Manila before moving to Spain. Once settled there, he devoted himself entirely to his artistic career in all its manifestations. He soon became a leading figure of Spanish abstract painting and established close connections with prominent painters from this movement, like Gerardo Rueda, with whom he developed a lifelong friendship and shared a studio. A mentor to Spanish painters of his generation, in the late 1950s and early 60s, Zóbel was already taking part in solo exhibitions in galleries in Madrid—such as his well-known *Saetas* series and *Serie Negra*—and in important group exhibitions representing Spanish 20th-century modern art, both in Spain and abroad, as in *Modern Spanish Painting* at London's Tate Gallery. He also developed his career as an art collector, starting his collection of Spanish abstract painting with which he would later found his arguably most important work, the Museo de Arte Abstracto Español, which he opened with the so-called Cuenca Group of avant-garde Spanish artists in the Casas Colgadas of Cuenca in 1966. The beautiful Spanish town would later inspire his *La vista* collection of drawings. In Spain, Zóbel also cultivated his photography, the object of an exhibition in Madrid the year before he died. [1]

These are all well-documented achievements. The present volume unearths valuable information relating to those early years at Harvard, seminal for Zóbel's later career as an artist and a scholar. The book took shape around his unpublished translation of Lorca's play, which Zóbel illustrated with four pen and watercolor drawings, but a more ambitious and comprehensive project soon developed, and I am pleased to say the *Observatorio de la Lengua Española y las Culturas Hispánicas en los Estados Unidos*—this research center of Spain's Instituto Cervantes at Harvard University—opened a dialogue, in person and virtually, between the three contributors.

Felipe Pereda, who is Fernando Zóbel de Ayala Professor of Spanish Art at Harvard University, an expert on Spanish medieval, Golden Age and early modern art as well as on art theory, and the originator of the whole project, opens the volume with a chapter on Zóbel at Harvard—a brief intellectual biography of the artist as a student, an intern and a researcher, from the perspective of his university years. This contextualization is followed by a chapter devoted to Hispanism and the Humanities at Harvard—and in US academic institutions in general—in the 1940s with attention to Lorca's presence in the curriculum and a brief discussion of Zóbel's senior thesis on the great Spanish poet and playwright. There could hardly be a better writer for this chapter than Luis Fernández Cifuentes, Robert S. and Ilse Friend Professor Emeritus of Romance Languages and Literatures, a specialist, among other research areas, in contemporary Spanish literature and with a long and distinguished academic career at Harvard University. After these essays on Zóbel at Harvard and on Harvard in Zóbel's time, Christopher Maurer, Professor of Spanish at Boston University, highly acclaimed translator of Spanish-language poets, among them García Lorca, edits Zóbel's translation, situates it in its American context, and, with Lincoln Son Currie, co-authors a chronology of *Perlimplín's* genesis and key performances.

The three authors have based their chapters largely on valuable unpublished material such as Zóbel's diaries, his class notes and ample correspondence, together with relevant documents from archives and other cultural institutions in Cambridge, Madrid and Manila, including reproductions of some important early works Zóbel created during those crucial Harvard years.

The bond between Zóbel and Harvard would not weaken over time. A collection of ink and watercolor illustrations by the artist would be published by the Harvard College Library Department of Printing and Graphic Arts in 1970—*Cuenca. Sketchbook of a Spanish Hill Town*. And Spain has celebrated the artist in various ways. Important art galleries and museums in Madrid have devoted major monographic exhibitions to him; for example, the Fundación Juan March in 1984 and, more recently, in 2017, the Museo Nacional Reina Sofía. The Museo del Prado, too, pays special tribute to the artist with an exhibition entitled *El futuro del pasado. Zóbel y la historia del arte* [The Future of the Past. Zóbel and the History of Art] which opened in November 2022. The present volume joins in the homage to this fascinating artist and scholar, with the reconstruction of those crucial years in his life and work by three leading exponents of today's Hispanism in the United States.

Instituto Cervantes at Harvard University

FELIPE PEREDA

ZÓBEL READS LORCA: THE PAINTER'S EARLY YEARS IN NEW ENGLAND

"In a world of fugitives,
the person taking the opposite direction would appear to run away."
—T.S. ELIOT
(AS CITED BY ZÓBEL, *SKETCHBOOK* #56)

I will begin with a dream:

> DR[EA]M. Showing Spanish painters through the glories of Harvard. Houghton Library in particular. Phil [Hofer] enters. I can't introduce X, my painter, because I have forgotten his name, but mention to Phil that his work is in the library. No response. Phil is polite, but not really listening; wanders off with vaguely charming expressions.
>
> I tell X how Houghton once blinded me (*me deslumbró*) with its gorgeousness. I list a variety of things that I wish him to admire.
>
> Instead of seeing them, we find ourselves sitting in the backyard of the Fox Club. Warm late spring or early fall evening. A huge round moon in the sky surrounded by whole clouds of brilliant stars. Seven of us, including one girl, sit elegantly sipping drinks. X, Bruce, myself–the others are vague. The girl has something to do with Bruce. Bruce and I tell X of the delights of Harvard.

X leaves momentarily. Bruce and I switch the conversation to calamities that have befallen some of our fellow club members, ruins, bankruptcy, embezzlement, divorce, perversion. X returns and I give a very vague explanation of what we are talking about.

As I do, the stars surrounding the moon seem to give a slight twitch, a movement like that of a live oyster receiving a drop of lemon juice. I think my eyes are playing tricks. The stars twitch again. I tell the others. We all look. Every star in the sky joins in the twitch. Over and over again. The twitches turn into jerks; then the stars begin to clot. Finally they go out, in bunches. The moon seems to shrink, loses its luminosity, fades into a leaden hue.

I, to the others who sit in stunned silence: "Could our dear old world be going out?"[1]

Fernando Zóbel was in Madrid. It was June 13, 1965. The dream was still neat and clear in his memory when he awoke, and he sat down and wrote it out in one of the diaries in which he had methodically recorded thoughts, anecdotes and observations since 1949, the year he graduated from Harvard. The diaries are fundamental to his thought and to Zóbel's biography, and dreams like this one tell of his character: orderly, detailed, extremely attentive and perceptive and, as in much of his work, systematic.

The protagonists of his dream, of no little relevance, carried him from Madrid back to America, New England, Cambridge. The "Phil" in the dream is Philip Hofer, librarian and first curator of the Department of Printing and Graphic Arts at the Houghton Library, a great bibliophile and Zóbel's old mentor in the art of book collecting. By 1965 he had known him for almost twenty years, and while their lives had taken very different paths, they still corresponded frequently. Hofer had visited Zóbel in Madrid, and Fernando did not fail to drop by his office every time he returned to Cambridge. On his final visit to his alma mater, in the Spring of 1964, he spent some time at the Houghton Library, looking "page by page" at Dunoyer de Segonzac's *Géorgiques*. On that occasion, he donated some contemporary abstract drawings to the Fogg, Harvard's museum of art, in an effort to promote the work of the Spanish masters. Consistency, or—better said—fidelity, was another of his character traits.

The scenario of Zóbel's dream is no less precise and local than his daily accounts of the days he spent in Cambridge. Everything happens in the Fox Club, in the back yard of the building on John F. Kennedy Street in Harvard Square,

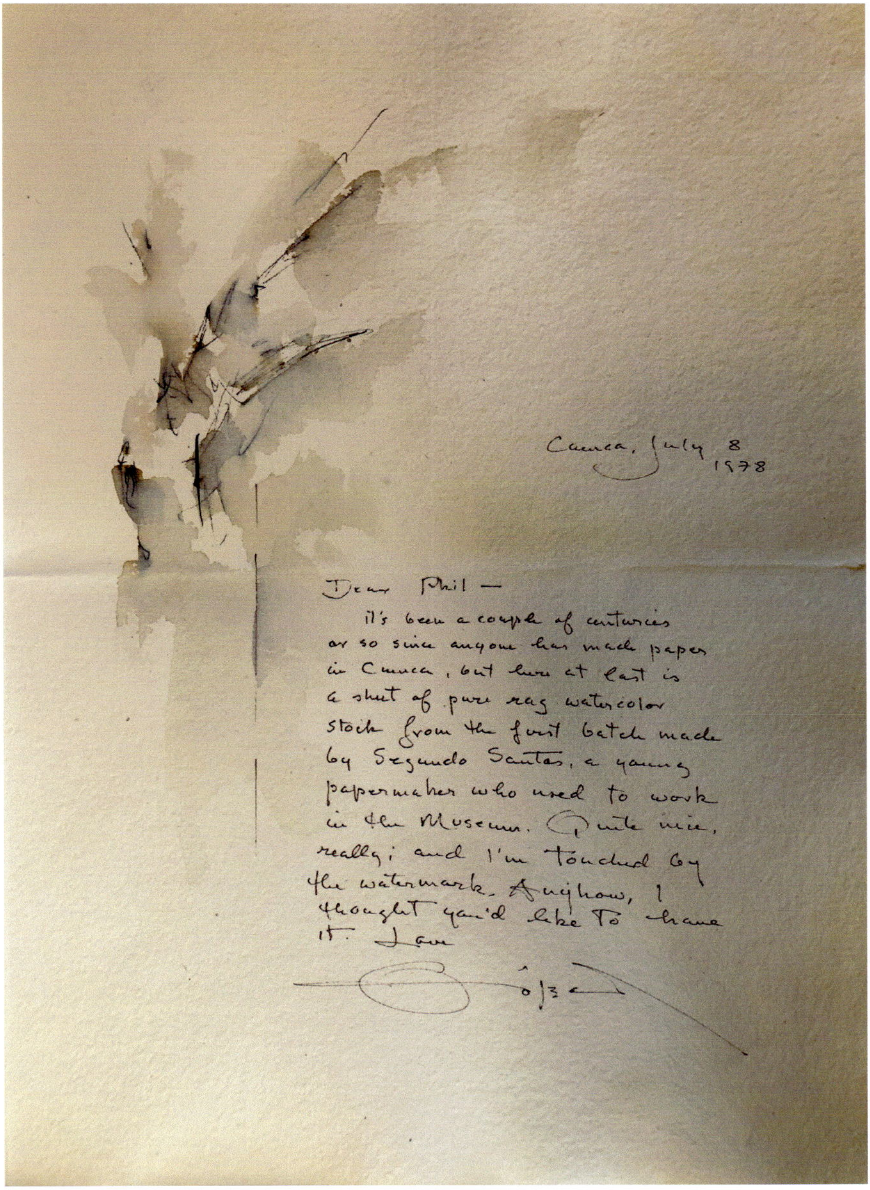

Cuenca, July 8
1978

Dear Phil —

it's been a couple of centuries or so since anyone has made paper in Cuenca, but here at last is a sheet of pure rag watercolor stock from the first batch made by Segundo Santos, a young papermaker who used to work in the Museum. Quite nice, really; and I'm touched by the watermark. Anyhow, I thought you'd like to have it. Love

Zóbel

1.1 Letter of Zóbel to Philip Hofer (Cuenca, July 8, 1978).

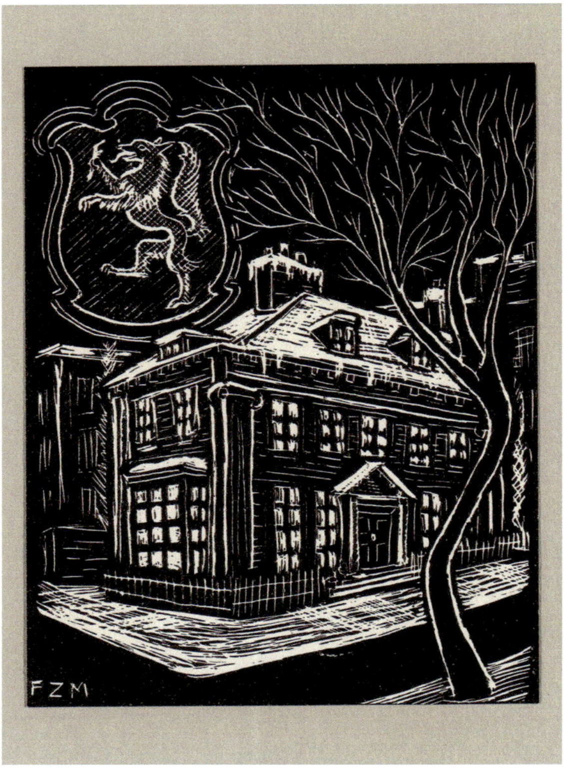

1.2 Fernando Zóbel, Undated print of Fox Club, Cambridge MA.

where it is still standing, little changed. Zóbel had joined the Fox Club as a sophomore and recorded his memories in the form of drawings and mural paintings. His humorous murals still decorate the bar and the entrance but there are many others hanging framed on the club's walls. Innocent and somehow naïve, they betray the little we know about him when he arrived in Cambridge, a place which brought him good memories, tinged by distance and melancholy.

The artist had spent the summer of 1965 in Madrid, but the day of his dream he had just returned from two weeks in New York and an exhibition of his work in the Bertha Schaefer Gallery. It wasn't the first time his paintings could be seen in the city, but it was his first (and only) solo exhibition. Five years before, his paintings had been selected for an exhibition at the Guggenheim Museum. *Before Picasso; After Miró* had been planned with the support of the Spanish Ministry of Foreign Affairs, to promote the new generation of Spanish "informalist" artists in dialogue with the international avant-garde, as

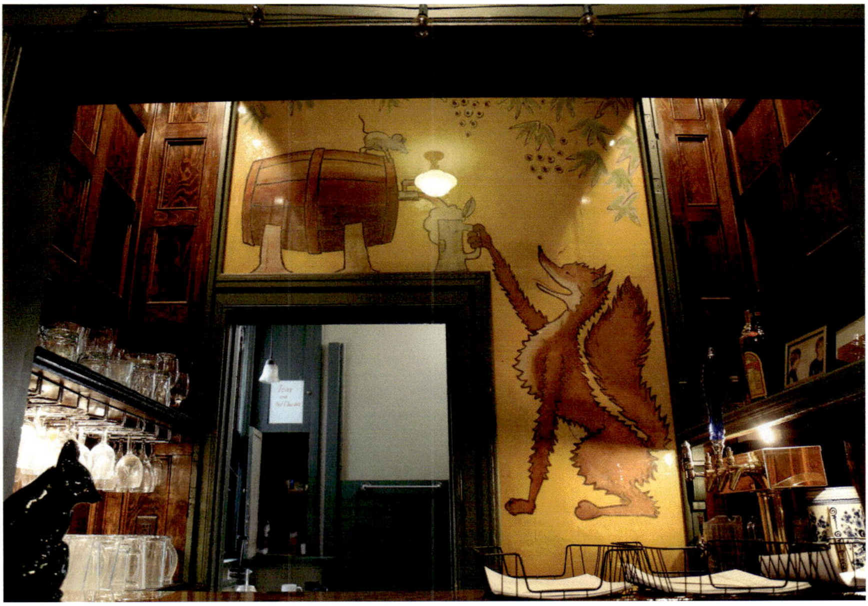

1.3 Fernando Zóbel, mural paintings at the Fox Club, Cambridge MA.

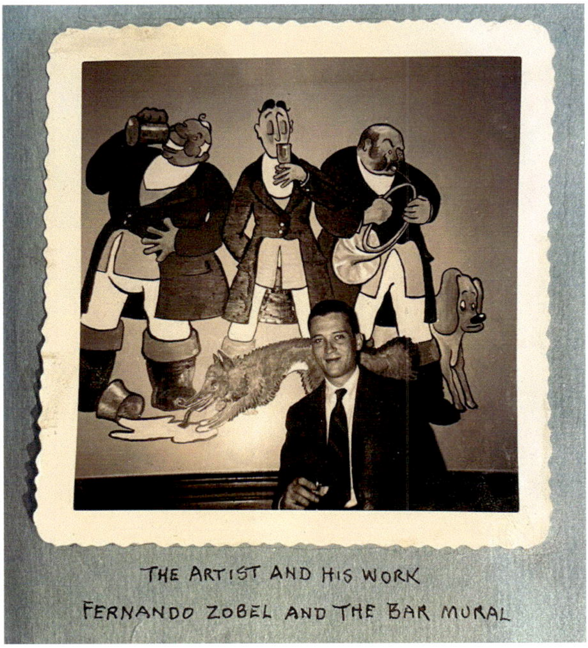

1.4 Fernando Zóbel and Fox Club mural.

a sign of Spain's democratic normality (a propagandistic strategy which did not escape the notice of local art critics).[2] The Guggenheim exhibition had aimed at presenting the "*continuing* vitality of painting in Spain" (my emphasis), from the art of these painters back to that of Goya, Velázquez and the Spanish Baroque, and even further back, to the caves of Altamira (!), an argument that echoes contemporary readings of the Spanish avant-garde in terms of its tragic, expressionist identity.

Fernando Zóbel, who had recently settled in Spain, consistently challenged this tortured narrative, which exoticized this pictorial tradition, and explicitly rejected his identification with it. The three paintings he had shown at the Guggenheim (with somewhat esoteric titles: *Histonium, Illici, Oscum*) were three large almost completely white canvases painted with surgical syringe, a technique he had discovered as he entered abstraction in the late 1950s. The use of the syringe produced what Zóbel would call "great oil-painted drawings," paintings where sparks of black color cross the canvas as the fleeting shadow left on its surface by the painter's gesture. These *grandes dibujos al óleo* chal-

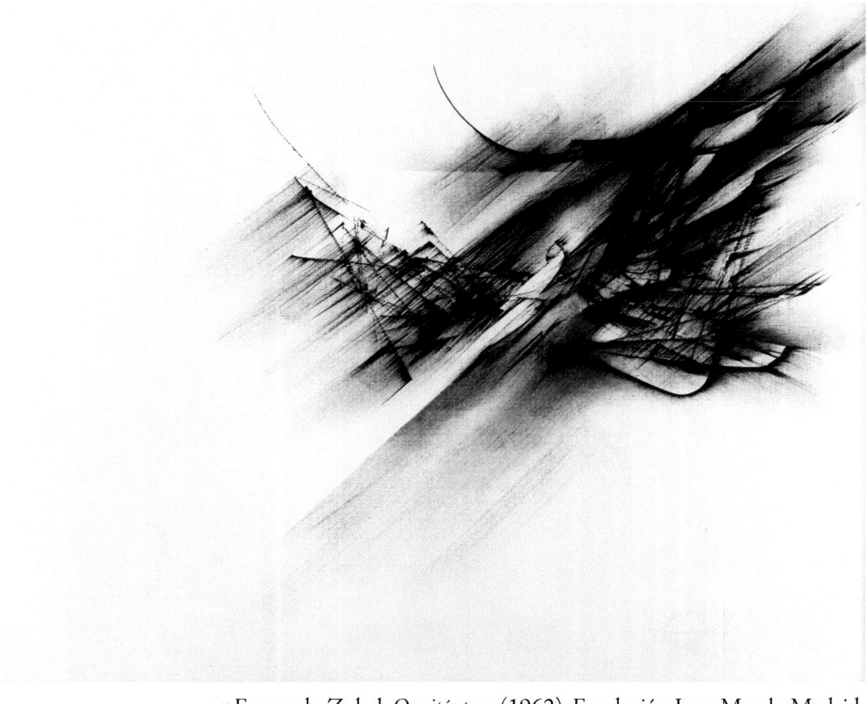

1.5 Fernando Zobel. *Ornitóptero* (1962). Fundación Juan March, Madrid.

lenged any possible distinction between the media of painting and drawing, a lesson very much indebted to his study of Chinese painting.

The exhibition at Bertha Schaefer Gallery was the natural development of those previous experiments. Zóbel was now introducing color for the first time, in an ultimate effort to analyze and capture the effect of movement. Following poetic terminology, the artist repeatedly called his style lyrical.[3] The *New York Times* laconically recorded the event: "Nonobjective paintings done in a velvety austere fashion have luminous black-and-white foggy effects whose parsimony of color and emphatic shape lead to unexpected richness of effect."[4] Zóbel had flown in from Madrid for the opening on March 16, where he met friends and artists. The abstract painter José Guerrero, who was living in New York, was among them, and the one who made the greatest impression was an unexpected visitor, Mark Rothko. Zóbel had long admired Rothko's painting, and—from the moment when he first came across it in the mid-1950s—considered it decisive for his move towards abstraction.[5] As usual, Zóbel's diaries document the encounter (written this time in English; Zóbel switched between Spanish and English indiscriminately and almost haphazardly):

> Mark Rothko appears. Big, wrapped into himself like into an overcoat. Awed, I have nothing to say but offer a few banalities: Cuenca, his 1954 RISD [Rhode Island School of Design] show, when I would much rather hug him, shouting his greatness to the four winds. I think he gets the drift of things because he sticks it out with every appearance of friendliness and people later wonder about the profundities we must have said to each other.[6]

As we learn a few pages later, Rothko returned the following week to visit the exhibition more calmly, "spent a long time looking," —as Zóbel would be told—and "said he liked the show very much."[7] We will never know what interested him in Zóbel's paintings, but it matters little, or not at all. The paintings shown at the New York gallery represented a recent shift in Zóbel's work but continued the line of experimentation that had begun with the *Black Series*: calm, meditative, even analytical pictorial gestures, often rooted ("translating," is the term that the artist would probably have used) in the remembered impressions of particular landscapes.

Ironically, but probably tellingly, the most interesting comment that I have found on how the painter conceived the paintings shown at the Bertha Schaefer

Gallery—and the value he thought they had—comes from an unexpected source: a letter Zóbel wrote (Manila, January 5, 1965) to the New York typographer Joseph Blumenthal, who was to print the invitations for the exhibition. (Zóbel had a deep knowledge of, and a personal obsession with, the arts of typography and calligraphy.) The letter explains the script that was to be used, the conditions of the design to be followed, and the relationship of these elements to the quality of his paintings.[8]

> My paintings, though abstract in subject, are highly traditional in technique and execution. I would like to convey this sense of tradition (and restraint) by means of the invitation. A roman typeface strikes me as ideal for the purpose, though you may have a better idea of the subject. However, we must avoid a sense of "quaintness." For instance, the use of block letter would not be suitable, though a good italic might be.

The remarks express "restraint," certainly not modesty, but they do point to a crucial component of Zóbel's painting, that "sense of tradition," the connection of his art to history—tradition not in the sense of a transcendental *Geist* (Spanish or any other kind) that his paintings would share but, quite differently, a continuity in his way of seeing and, also, in his way of making. Seeing and making: "I believe to have found a way to see and to make," Zóbel told a journalist in 1964 with unconcealed irony—a way "flexible enough to have me occupied without repeating myself for the rest of my life."[9] Such an attitude gave Zóbel's art a unique personality in the context of the artists of his generation, whether American, Filipino, or Spanish. That he was able to carry out such an idiosyncratic plan speaks first and foremost of his privileged economic position.

A member of one of the most prominent clans of Filipino society, Fernando was the oldest son of Enrique Zóbel de Ayala's second marriage (to Fermina Montojo, the Cádiz-born daughter of the admiral of the Spanish squadron that confronted and was defeated by the American navy at the Battle of Manila Bay, or Battle of Cavite, in 1898). Fernando's father was the president of Ayala y Compañía, founded during the colonial period and one of the largest companies of the Philippines, and also a cultural philanthropist, having supported the impressionist Filipino painter, Fernando Amorsolo, arguably the strongest pictorial referent for Zóbel before he left the Philippines in 1946.[10]

Like his father, Fernando had completed his high school education in Europe (in Spain and in Switzerland), but these privileges would develop, much later, into one of a different quality: the freedom to pursue his artistic convictions. The letter to Blumenthal, the typographer, gives a hint of his singular personality:

> It is currently the fashion to make invitations to art shows very aggressive, eye-catching, gaudy, "clever," and what-have-you. I wish to do exactly the reverse. In other words, I wish to attract attention by restraint. The things I paint are the very opposite of a circus act—they are quiet, carefully thought-out and carefully executed. No attempt is made to surprise the spectator, or to capture his emotions by storm. *The tone is a conversational one.* [my emphasis]

Modern painting, in the eyes of Fernando Zóbel, entailed not a rupture with the past, but a new beginning, a new mode of continuity. Or perhaps better said, the "revolt" of modern art against tradition gave him the chance to rediscover and even reinvent it. This was not only a different way of making, but also a new way of looking. Such an attitude placed him at polemical odds with the "Modernism" deployed by such critics as Clement Greenberg. As early as 1964, Zóbel expressed his disagreement when Greenberg wrote that "artistic excellence resided in opening new technical visual horizons." For Zóbel, giving such agency to technical innovation—in this particular case, the introduction of color—was simply erratic.[11]

Not surprisingly, in those same years, Zóbel would enthusiastically embrace non-linear, or even anti-historicist proposals developed by art historians such as George Kubler, which opened the possibilities of a new form of anti-historicism (as I write this, Kubler's words seem almost prophetic). Kubler's short but provocative *The Shape of Time* invited the artist to explore anachronistic narratives and also—what would have been of particular interest for Zóbel—to trace all kinds of multi- or transcultural artistic exchanges: "The history of art," the Mesoamerican art specialist had written in 1962, "resembles a broken but much-repaired chain made of string and wire to connect the occasional jeweled links surviving as physical evidences of the invisible sequence of prime objects."[12] Kubler's chains extended both diachronically and transnationally. Zóbel would transcribe those words, and many other quotes from *The Shape of Time*, in one of his sketchbooks. It is no wonder that it was precisely in

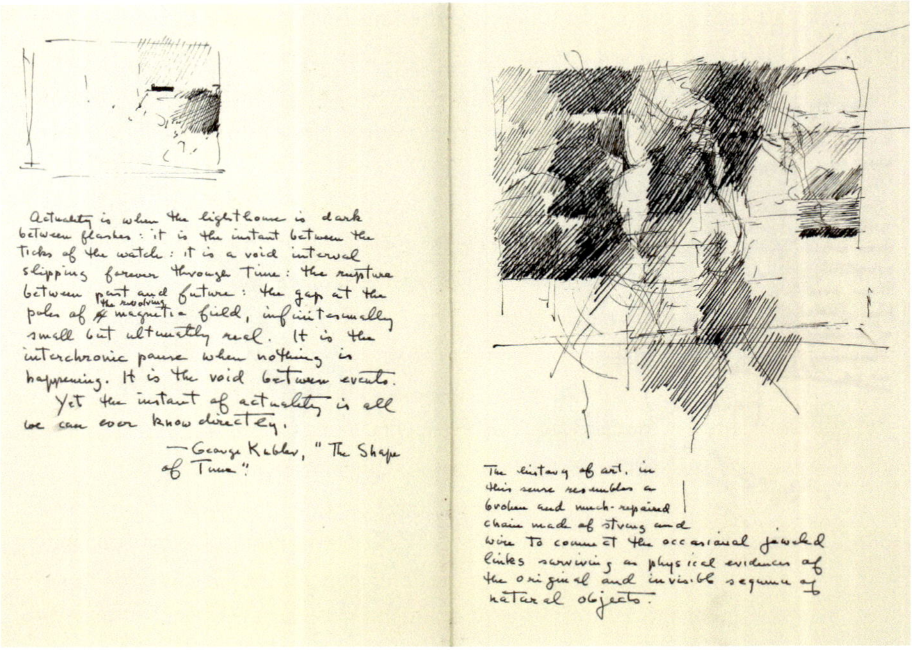

1.6 Zóbel's notes on George Kubler's *The Shape of Time*, from Sketchbook #56, 1965-66, f. 1. Fundación Juan March.

these years that Zóbel's painting embarked more consistently on the study and reinvention of paintings of the Old Masters, exploring, one might say unveiling, some of those imaginary chains envisioned by Kubler; paintings that Zóbel described most frequently in terms of pictorial "dialogues."

My brief summary above has intended nothing more than to introduce a singular personality that combined the proficiency—and the manner of looking—of a modern painter with the erudition and the intuition of a historian. My only claim is that in order to correctly understand his work, those two sides should not be taken separately. Otherwise, his life work runs the risk of being simplified or rendered unintelligible.

In some of the most brilliant pages of *The Shape of Time*, George Kubler compared the historian to an astronomer gazing at the signals sent across space and time by stars that could well be dead by the time their light reaches the human eye: "any work of art is actually a portion of arrested happening, or an emanation of past time," he wrote.[13] Kubler's reflections remind us of the Zóbel dream that opened this chapter: the artist and his friends looking at the skies in the backyard of the Fox Club, contemplating their last twitching tremor as they all fade slowly into the night. I believe this is more than a coincidence. Zóbel's peculiar sensibility for the perception of time has deep roots, stretching as far back as his early years as a student in Cambridge. I will devote the rest of this chapter to exploring those years of his formation and training—which until now, have been very much ignored.

The different faces of Modern Art.

"'The sheer blessedness of civilian life.'
I think I know what you mean.
It probably means the way I felt after
three and a half years of Japanese occupation.
I won't itemize. How easily one forgets."
—F.Z. TO PAUL HALDEMAN, DECEMBER 6, 1955

February 1946. Zóbel was already twenty-three years old when he arrived in Cambridge, Massachusetts. Only his family's political and economic influence had enabled him to flee the country. A long, painful illness and left him bedridden for almost three years, and his former studies in the School of Medicine in Manila had been dramatically interrupted by World War II. When the young Fernando had boarded in Manila, the city had been not much more than a mountain of ruins: the skirmish between the Japanese forces and General MacArthur's artillery had left the city completely ravaged (Manila was liberated on March 3, 1945). As Zóbel writes several times in his diaries, when he returned to Manila after years of studying abroad, he could not find the city he remembered from his childhood: in a certain way, Manila had become a place in his imagination.

There is not a word about the devastation he left behind in his early letters to his friend at the American Consulate in Manila, Paul Haldeman—the person who helped him get his visa, a Harvard graduate himself, and a close friend for over thirty years, as we can see from their abundant correspondence. Not a word about the destruction of the city from which he had fled at the beginning of the war, finding shelter at a farm in Calatagan, 100 miles from the capital.[14] Written in fluent English, the letters (kept today at the Houghton Library, to which Haldeman wisely donated them) recall only excitement and gratitude for the opportunity to begin a new life. In caricatures Zóbel shared with his friend in Manila the upheavals of the ship voyage to Seattle, and soon after, his accommodations in Cambridge. In the years following, Fernando would continue to practice the burlesque art of cartooning, publishing his works occasionally in *The Advocate* and later in the *Harvard Alumni Bulletin*. There are dozens, startlingly proficient in execution for a self-taught amateur.

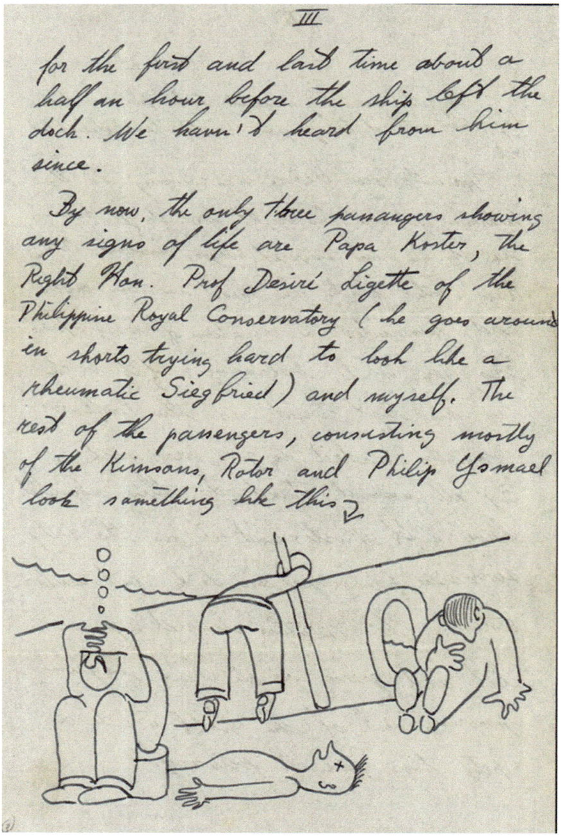
III

for the first and last time about a half an hour before the ship left the dock. We haven't heard from him since.

By now, the only three passengers showing any signs of life are Papa Koster, the Right Hon. Prof Desiré Ligette of the Philippine Royal Conservatory (he goes around in shorts trying hard to look like a rheumatic Siegfried) and myself. The rest of the passengers, consisting mostly of the Kimsons, Rotor and Philip Ysmael look something like this

1.7 From a letter to Paul Haldeman, January 23, 1946, written aboard the *Longview Victory* en route from Manila to Seattle, and mailed from the Olympic Hotel, Seattle. Houghton Library.

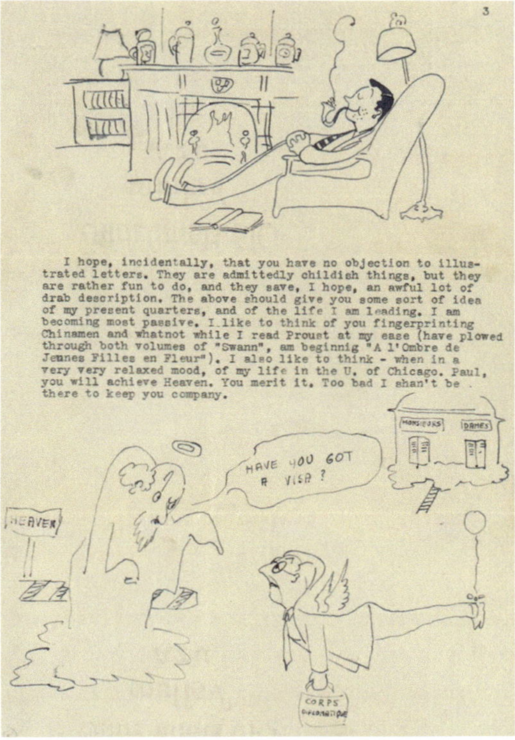

3

I hope, incidentally, that you have no objection to illustrated letters. They are admittedly childish things, but they are rather fun to do, and they save, I hope, an awful lot of drab description. The above should give you some sort of idea of my present quarters, and of the life I am leading. I am becoming most passive. I like to think of you fingerprinting Chinamen and whatnot while I read Proust at my ease (have plowed through both volumes of "Swann", am beginnig "A l'Ombre de Jeunes Filles en Fleur"). I also like to think - when in a very very relaxed mood, of my life in the U. of Chicago. Paul, you will achieve Heaven. You merit it. Too bad I shan't be there to keep you company.

1.8 From a letter to Paul Haldeman, June 5, 1946. Houghton Library.

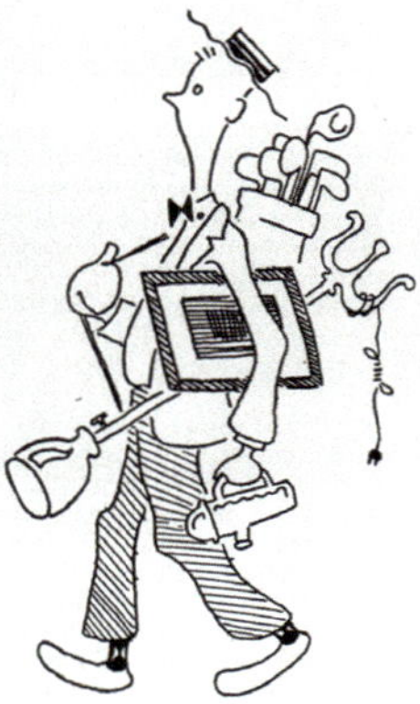

1.9 Caricature by Zóbel for *Harvard Alumni Bulletin,* October 14, 1950.

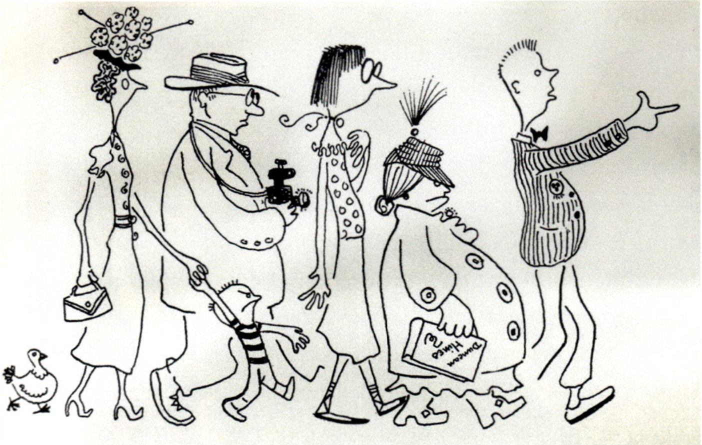

1.10 A Harvard student guiding tourists; Zóbel caricature from *Harvard Alumni Bulletin,* November 11, 1950.

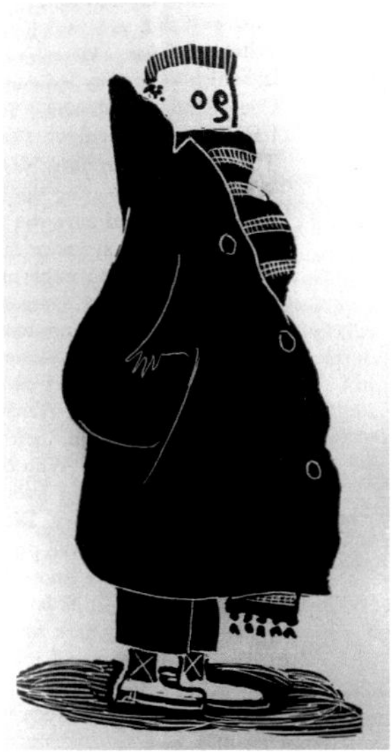

1.11 Caricature,
Harvard Alumni Bulletin,
March 24, 1951.
Photo: author.

The possibility of becoming a painter does not seem to have entered his mind. That germ of an idea would grow slowly, only after he graduated—but we are still four years away from that. The young Filipino had a hunger for anything related to culture, art, and in general, the humanities. In his first semester, he took classes in English (Composition and Public Speaking), European History (Michael Karpovich), Modern Philosophy (Raphael Demos), and Modern Painting.[15] The latter was taught by Frederick Deknatel, a specialist in medieval art who taught the introductory course on modern painting for several years.[16] Paul Sachs' famous and influential graduate seminar Fine Arts 15a: Museum Work and Museum Problems, was taught until 1948—a year after Zóbel entered Harvard—, but his diaries make no comment on it.[17] We don't know if Sachs' teachings from this course affected him, but I find it interesting to recall that Zóbel would later create and found two important contemporary art museums (the Ateneo de Manila and the Museum of Abstract Art, Cuenca), and that the latter, would one day receive the visit and applause of a significant student from that seminar, Alfred H. Barr. More on this later.

The department offered only one other class on modern painting (plus one on modern architecture by K.J. Conant), and Fernando would take it only in his last semester: a class on American Art From the Revolution to the Present Day, taught by Benjamin Rowland, who was a specialist on East Asia, not on modern art. Zóbel's notebooks from that class ended up in the hands of Philip

Hofer and were deposited at the Houghton Library. Their pages are filled with drawings sketched from the black-and-white images projected with the large glass slides of a camera lucida, as if he could only understand what he was seeing when he was drawing it. The slides themselves are still in the archives, with the date they were borrowed for their projection.

It is more than anecdotal that Zóbel decided to write for that class on *String Quartette* (1937, Metropolitan Museum, NY), by Jack Levine (1915-2010), a painter from Boston and one of the most visible representatives of the local

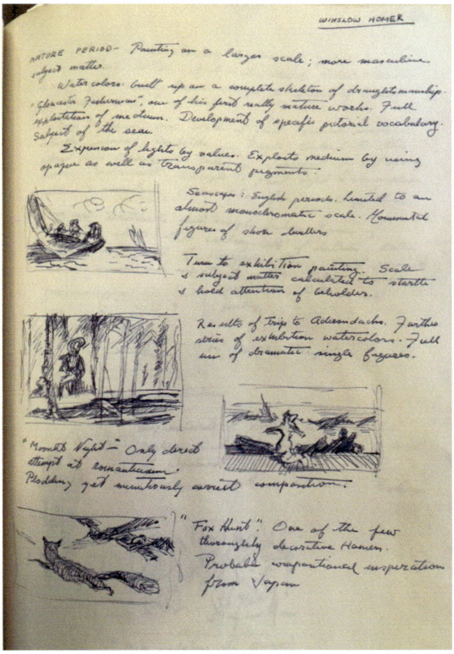

1.12 From Zóbel's class notes on Winslow Homer, 1946. Houghton Library.

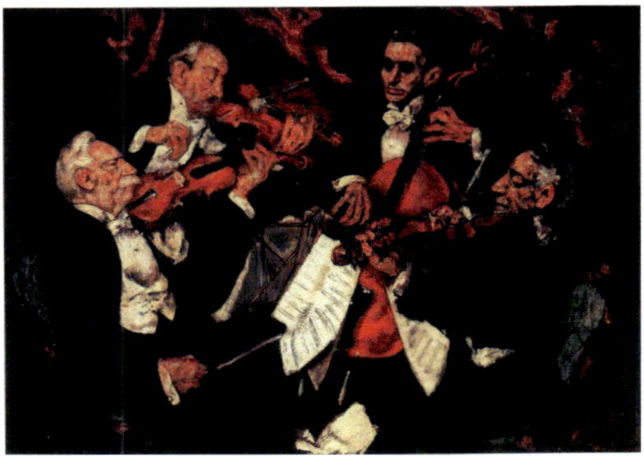

1.13 Jack Levine, *String Quartette* (1937). Metropolitan Museum of Art.

school of Expressionism. Unlike another prominent member of that school, Hyman Bloom, to whom he turned when he started to think of becoming a painter, Zóbel doesn't seem to have met Jack Levine yet; he would do so later, in 1955, on occasion of one of his exhibitions in Boston. The painter from Manila would have seen *String Quartette* at the exhibition in the Institute of Contemporary Art (ICA), which had opened earlier that year in Boston on the waterfront. The exhibition catalogue included a short presentation by Lloyd Goodrich, from the Whitney Museum of Art, that celebrated how, finally, "from the provincial backwaters of 1900, [American art has] entered the main stream of world art."[18] The ICA show privileged realism, post-cubist and expressionist tendencies, failing to represent some of the most dynamic creations of those years, the masters of Abstract Expressionism that Zóbel would discover during a visit to New York the year after, in 1956.

At the ICA exhibit, Jack Levine was grouped in the catalogue under the heading of "social comment" together with Ben Shahn and George Grosz. Fernando Zóbel's paper on Levine's work for Deknatel's class was praiseworthy but, oddly, far from enthusiastic: the painting was described as the work of an "American satirist," "a painting [that] is American without being provincial, modern without being 'French,' personal without being obscure [...] maybe not a magnificent masterpiece, but [...] certainly [...] an extremely fine piece of painting."[19] Levine's *String Quartette* would figure again in the controversial show at the Metropolitan Museum, *American Painting Today* (New York, 1950), just a year later, an exhibition that Fernando also visited, and commented on. By then, however, the emergence of Abstract Expressionism could no longer be ignored and Zóbel's response, as we will later see, reflected it.

There is little question that Zóbel's interest in caricature had a lot to do with his choice of Levine's composition of a jazz concert: "The real plastic art of our age, and of the downfall of our civilization is caricature," he wrote in his diaries in 1950.[20] While Zóbel's work is known today only as that of an abstract painter, the latter is not the only language that he mastered and practiced. In fact, he did photography and caricature throughout his lifetime, and it is no coincidence that his work in these two forms would proliferate after his discovery of abstraction and his encounter with the work of Mark Rothko. And Zóbel is certainly no exception. Other artists of the 20th century avant-garde were similarly "bilingual": Lyonel Feininger, an American who had been Gropius' first appointment at the Bauhaus (and who had also been included in the 1955 ICA exhibit), or Ad Reinhardt, to name just two artists whom Zóbel especially admired. A more exceptional case is that of one of the most prominent artists of the German *Neue Sachlichkeit*, the New Objectivity, George Grosz, and the latter now deserves closer attention.

In 1950, Fernando Zóbel finished two small projects thematically and iconographically connected to his life as a student. *Letabundus rediit* ("Joyously Return Again"), as it reads on the cover of the manuscript, illustrates the Latin verses from the medieval *Carmina Burana*, reflecting its jubilant lyrics, while emptying them of their originally-intended sardonic nature[21]. The other one is more strictly satirical. Taking as a point of departure Sebastian Brandt's 15th century *Ship of Fools*, a heavily illustrated incunable (*Das Narrenschiff*, 1494), Zóbel composed a charming critique of the academic world, including students as well as professors. The book was conceived as some sort of pre-typographic experiment. Over the summer Zóbel went to visit Arno Werner, a German-born bookbinder, in Pittsfield, Massachusetts who was responsible for the most delicate work at Houghton Library, and who was credited for keeping alive

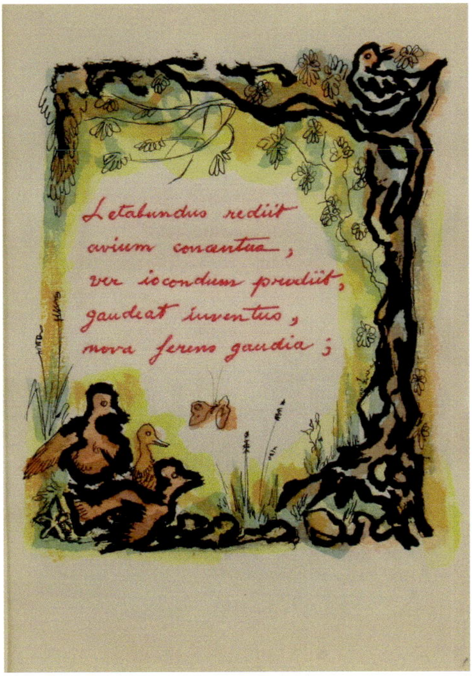

1.14 Zóbel, *Letabundus Rediit, ex Carmina Burana* (1950). Fundación Juan March, Madrid.

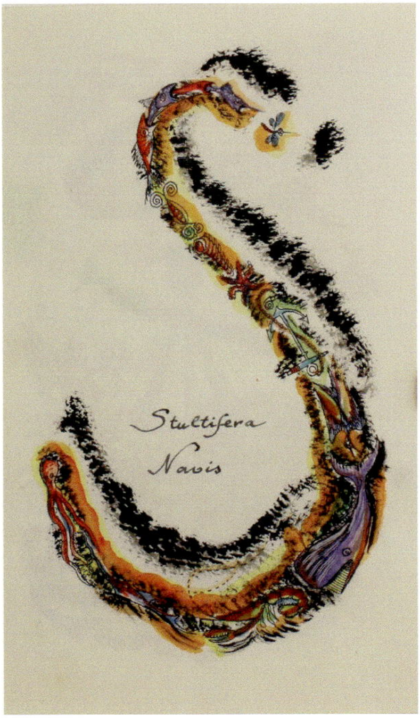

1.15 Zóbel, *Stultifera Navis* (frontis), 1950. Fundación Juan March, Madrid.

the most traditional binding techniques.[22] Each page of Zóbel's manuscript contains a caricature, opening with the inevitable fool holding the mirror on which the scholar sees (or should be able to see) the reflected image of his own vanity.[23] The satires betray, most probably, Zóbel's anxiety about his future—which at the time was very much uncertain. These preoccupations included his desperate desire to stay in America instead of returning to the Philippines, and in visual terms, bear the clear influence of the work of one of the most accomplished artists in the art of graphic caricature of the day: George Grosz, whom Fernando had recently met.

The master of political satire of the Weimar Republic, Grosz had left Germany in 1932, finding refuge in New York, his residence for over twenty-five years (he would die only a few months after his return to Germany in 1959).[24] The encounter with America, which was frightening and promising in equal parts,

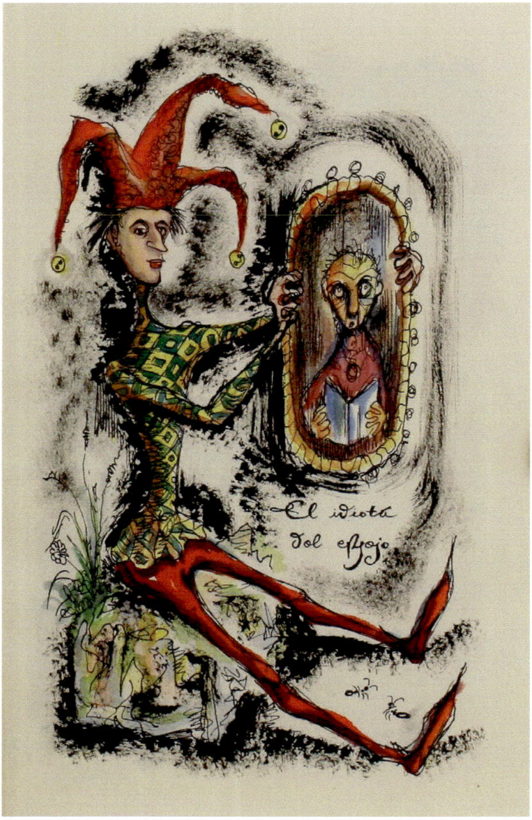

1.16 *El idiota del espejo* (The Fool in the Mirror), in *Stultifera Navis*. Fundación Juan March, Madrid.

had made the painter from Berlin completely transform his art, "rediscover the joy of painting," and—as he would write in his 1946 autobiography—"deliberately and carefully burn part of my past."[25] Grosz's art had turned to watercolors of landscapes, although he had continued to provide book illustrations.

The details of Grosz's meeting with Fernando Zóbel escape me (Fernando's diary entries for the years 1946-49 provide only occasional anecdotes), but in 1949 the German painter gave and dedicated a copy of his recently published autobiography with a full-page watercolor: "To Fernando Zóbel-Montojo, with best greetings, George Grosz, May 7, 1949." Although he doesn't mention it in the book, Grosz's autobiography had been published in 1946, months after he learned of the death of his mother as a result of an air-raid bombing in Berlin (a different, but telling coincidence with Zóbel's silence about his traumatic memories of a razed Manila). Despite all efforts, however, memories of his past

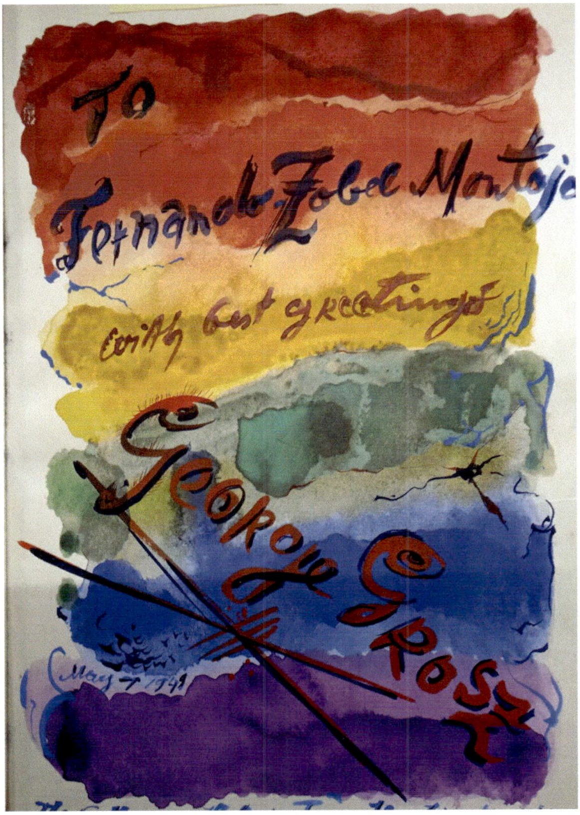

1.17 Dedication to Zóbel by George Grosz in a copy of *A Little Yes and A Big No: The Autobiography of George Grosz* (New York: 1946). Fundación Juan March, Madrid.

continued to haunt Grosz. In Spring 1948, the painter in exile had presented an exhibition in New York of what he called "stick men," emaciated Kafkian figures living in some kind of apocalyptic landscape: "men who are called by numbers, and not by names—men who wear slave collars—grey men in a grey world following empty meaningless banners," as read the invitation for the show.[26] Harvard's Germanic Museum had hosted his work almost since his arrival—for the first time in 1935, and then again in 1942—but the largest show opened in Cambridge in 1949: *Grosz. A Piece of My World. Social Satire*, Nov. 14-Dec. 20.[27] The museum's director Charles Kuhn had written in a private letter that the exhibition wanted to "emphasize his most recent works which I think will forever scotch the rumor that Grosz has become soft as a result of his enjoyment of the flesh pots in America."[28] The exhibit in Cambridge showed some of his most recent and brutal antimilitarist manifestos, including his famous work, the *Painter of the Hole*,[29] representing the artist with his easel in

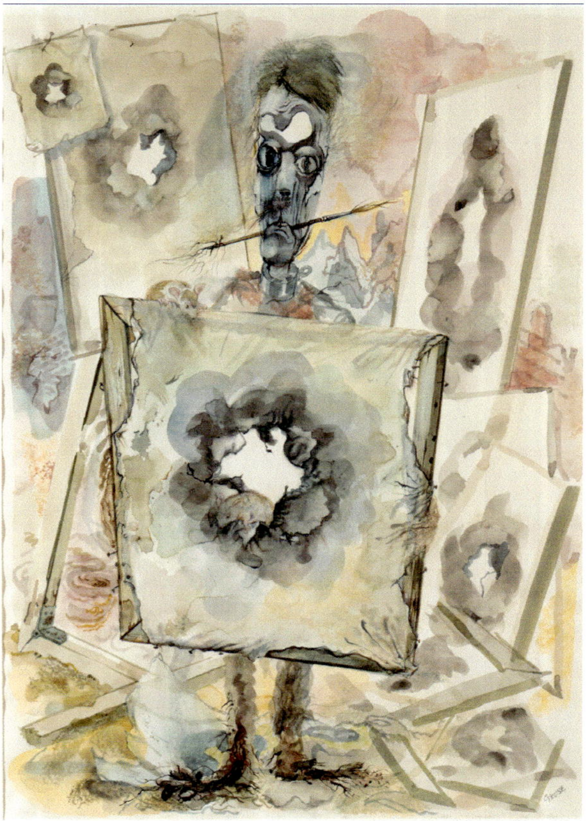

1.18 Georg Grosz, *Uprooted. The Painter of the Hole* (1948). Harvard Art Museums.

the middle of a landscape of complete destruction. A later version of the same motif would later enter the collections of the Fogg Museum, then directed by John P. Coolidge, a member of the History of Art Department.[30]

Zóbel's burlesque caricature of the "critical eye," unequivocally reveals that he had seen Grosz's most recent satires. Grosz's watercolors turn the hole in the middle of the canvas into a metaphor of the existential emptiness which his art found impossible to fill (at the time Grosz had serious drinking problems). In Zóbel, on the contrary, the hole on the canvas becomes a parody of the art critic's blindness. Unable to really "see" the painting, the critic—or the art historian—looks through it hoping to find its meaning written in the text of the book that he is holding with his hand right behind the canvas. Charming but somehow trivial, it is nonetheless one more symptom of Zóbel's struggle, despite his erudition and literary background, to confront painting within the limits of its own purely visual language.[31]

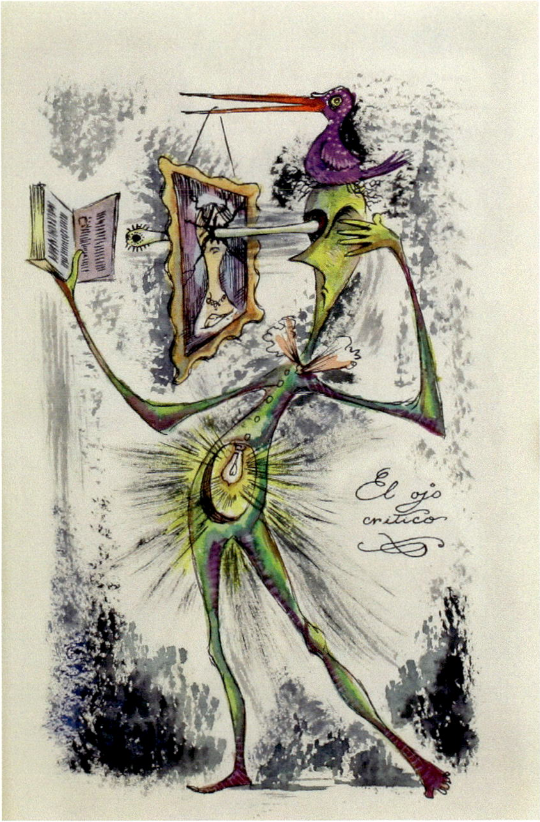

1.19 Fernando Zóbel, *El ojo crítico* (The Critical Eye), from "Stultifera Navis" (1950). Fundación Juan March, Madrid.

From Lorca to the Bauhaus

"Me sobran riquezas, se me llenan las manos y se me desparraman. Quiero guardar algo para esa mañana de paredes secas y al ir a cerrar el puño,todo, absolutamente todo se cae al suelo. *Quién fuera un escritor de acero fino como Lorca.*"
(I have plenty of riches, my hands are full to overflowing. I would like to keep something for that morning of dry walls and, when I am about to close my fist, everything, absolutely everything, falls to the ground. I wish my pen were as refined as Lorca's.)
—DIARY #2, OCTOBER 3, 1950

At the outset, it was literature, and not yet painting, that most attracted Zóbel. On March 27, 1951, his diary records a list of the books to be taken to "Tibet or a desert island." The list includes lots of poetry: Thomas Wyatt, Gerard Manley Hopkins ... e.e. cummings (whom he met in Cambridge) and T.S. Eliot among the living; and, of course, also novels, like Stendhal, Gide, Kafka, or the *Quijote* which, as argued elsewhere in this book, he probably had read under the guidance of Harry Levin. The list was put together after what had been an intense year in Cambridge. Having graduated in June 1949, Fernando had resisted a return to Manila by enrolling in Harvard Law School. After quitting law school in the spring (he confessed to finding the study of law excruciating), his good relationship with Philip Hofer and the director of the Houghton Library, William A. Jackson, resulted in the offer of an internship there. It was a crucial year, granting him a total immersion in the culture of the book, and giving him time to develop more serious interests, first in the practice of engraving, and immediately after, in painting.

Not surprisingly, the books listed for his forced retirement included some of the art texts that were shaping and would continue to shape his visual interests: Delacroix's *Diaries*, which inspired him to write his own, he once confessed ("Anything is possible for a lover of Delacroix," as he wrote to his friend Haldeman in 1946); Paul Klee's *On Modern Art*, and Malraux's *Voices of Silence*, an emblem, in itself, of the invention of a "portable library" (his words, again) at a time when image reproductions were breaking down all historical and geographical frontiers, allowing for new historical dialogues between the past and the present, a phenomenon acknowledged by George Kubler, that would, a few years later, become a major motif of Zóbel's work.[32]

Yet Zóbel's imaginary library opened with a quite different text, that of a Spanish author that he probably had discovered in Cambridge: Federico García Lorca. The first work on his list was Lorca's *Poemas y Canciones*. And also, *Doña Rosita la soltera*, "que sirve para alegrar murciélagos" ("that would make even bats laugh"). Fernando's encounter with Lorca's theater and poetry is better addressed elsewhere in this book, but I will here remind the reader of the chronology: it was in 1946 that Zóbel wrote his "free translation" of one of García Lorca's best plays, *Don Perlimplín in Love*, as a paper for a class taught by Harry Levin. Three years later, as he was preparing for graduation, he decided to write his Undergraduate Honors Essay on "Theme and Conflict in Lorcan Drama," advised once more by Harry Levin, and read and graded also by Renato Poggioli, two key figures of their generation in comparative literature.[33] It is revealing of Zóbel's personality but also of the quality of the friendships he built throughout his life that these two papers from his student years have been preserved. The translation, at the Houghton Library, had remained in the hands of Paul Haldeman, and the senior thesis, in a bound copy from his personal library, is in Madrid at the Fundación Juan March.

Surprisingly the translation of *Don Perlimplín* was illustrated by four full-page pen and watercolor drawings (figs. 4.1 to 4.4). Lorca himself had made costume sketches for some of his own plays, but these were not published until much later. The edition on which Zóbel based his translation was not illustrated, and the inclusion of his own illustration—surprising in an undergradate paper—deserves some comment.

Lorca is known for having practiced drawing throughout his life, and his drawings are simple, unpretentious and exquisite. Although they were shown at two exhibitions during his lifetime (the first one in the Galerías Dalmau, Barcelona; the second, in 1932, in a small show at the Ateneo Popular, Huelva), they received scholarly attention only much later. His poetry completely overshadowed his work as a figurative artist.[34] When Zóbel decided to illustrate his thesis, he probably would not have seen many of Lorca's drawings. Only in the years immediately following the thesis would Lorca's drawings be given some recognition. Gregorio Prieto published a few the same year Zóbel was doing his translation (*García Lorca as a Painter*, London, 1946); and two more studies came out in 1949, one by Prieto (*Dibujos de García Lorca*, Madrid, 1949) and another with 13 drawings from the personal collection of Hans Gebser (*Lorca poète-dessinateur*, Paris, 1949). Most probably, Zóbel was more familiar with the

Lorca drawings included in the first illustrated edition of *Poeta en Nueva York* (Mexico, 1940), based on the manuscript Lorca himself had left with José Bergamín and which the latter had miraculously spirited out of the country during the Civil War. But these were only four drawings, and only two in full color. Lorca's drawings betray the clear influence of Surrealist poetics. Zóbel's, while probably inspired by them, are more elaborate, "cleaner," more abstract and less allegorical; but no less delicate and beautiful. That Zóbel would recognize this aspect of Lorca's creativity, so little known at the time, speaks both of his lyrical sensibility and of his early migration from the textual towards the visual.

Each of Zóbel's watercolors vaguely illustrates one moment of the play: first, Don Perlimplín spying on his bride as she is dressing for her wedding; second, a flying heart sprouting cuckold's horns with white flowers—Perlimplín's, of course (remember, Belisa would betray Don Perlimplín on their wedding night with five different men, of five different races); third, a man dressed in green, standing with a sword on his waist—Don Perlimplín as he promises to defend his honor; and fourth, the tragic finale, Don Perlimplín dressed in blue with a red cape, "*como su sangre*," falling dead into the arms of Belisa who now realizes, too late, that the man she loved, the man in the red cape that she had met in the garden, was actually Perlimplín.

Zóbel's compositions rely on the drawn line but are carefully modeled with fine brushes. Somehow ingenuous—"childish," to use a term Paul Klee had introduced in his writings—they are executed with a playfulness and economy of design that recall Lorca's own drawings and occasional illustrations of his poems. The four illustrations for *Don Perlimplín* are, however, much more elaborate in design than the poet's, revealing the influence of the European avant-garde that Fernando had had the opportunity to study while in Cambridge, and more precisely of the Bauhaus. It is hard to determine what exactly Zóbel had seen in these years. We know he was reading Paul Klee—a teacher at Dessau almost since its opening until 1931—but we know less of what had made him develop a form of drawing so distinct and so different from the skillful, but still amateurish caricatures he had been doing (Oskar Schlemmer's drawings of dancers come to mind as maybe the closest reference).

The connection to a Bauhaus aesthetic is anything but random. Founded in Weimar, Germany, in 1919 by the architect Walter Gropius, the Bauhaus school encapsulated a revolutionary artistic and educational experiment: an academy of fine arts merged into a school of applied arts, dissolving the distinction between the artisan and the artist and declaring the seamless con-

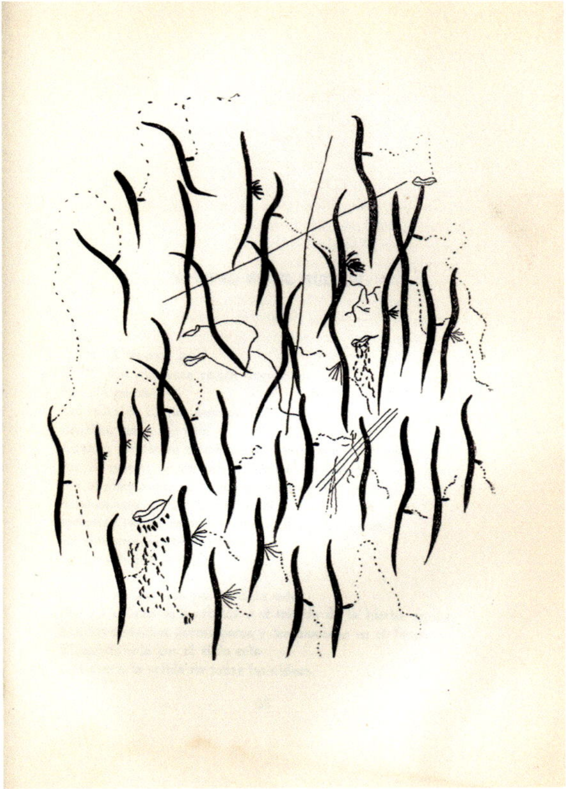

1.20 Federico García Lorca, illustration from *Poeta en Nueva York* (México: Séneca, 1940). Mario Hernández, editor of the catalogue raisonné of Lorca's drawings, titles it *[Bosque sexual]*.

tinuity of industrial design with modern art. The Bauhaus's activities had been followed and admired from the other side of the Atlantic long before the municipal government of Dessau, controlled by members of the National Socialist Party, forced the school to close on September 30, 1932. It had been in Cambridge, in 1930, that the "Harvard Society for Contemporary Art," founded two years earlier, had started exhibiting the work of German avant-garde artists (Feininger, Itten, Kandinsky, Klee and Schlemmer).[35] This was only a year after Alfred H. Barr had transplanted the Bauhaus' plan into the departmental design of the newly created Museum of Modern Art, anticipating the big exhibition Barr would devote to the history and living influence of the legendary school (*Bauhaus, 1919-1928*, MoMA, 1938).[36] Alfred H. Barr would later be consulted when Harvard's Graduate School of Design searched for a modern architect to chair the Department of Architecture. The name of Walter Gropius was shortlisted.[37]

When Zóbel arrived in Cambridge, the activities of the Germanic Museum (today the Busch-Reisinger) were slowly starting to take off after having been closed for several years. Under the impulse of its curator, Charles L. Kuhn, the support of John Coolidge (director of the Fogg Museum) and of Walter Gropius (who became director of the architecture department in 1937), the Germanic Museum launched an ambitious program of exhibitions: Käthe Kollwitz (Fall, 1948), Max Beckmann (1948), Mies van der Rohe (Spring 1949), *Bauhaus Graphic Design* (Spring 1949), *Grosz. A Piece of My World. Social Satire* (Fall, 1949)—where Zóbel, as discussed earlier, would have had occasion to meet the artist again; *Black Mountain Textiles* (1950); Laszlo Moholy-Nagy (1950), Anni Albers (1950) and of course Paul Klee (1950). As Zóbel was about to return to Manila, the Museum opened an exhibition devoted to the work of the artists involved in the decoration of the Graduate Center (Albers, Miró, Bayer, Lippold, Arp), to which I will return shortly.[38]

Walter Gropius had been chairing the Department of Architecture for almost ten years when Fernando Zóbel arrived at Harvard, but Gropius' first and most important architectural intervention on campus took place the year after Zóbel graduated, in a building belonging to the Law School, with which Zóbel was affiliated at the time. Harvard's commission to Gropius and the firm TAC (The Architects Collaborative) to build the new Graduate Center had been received in the press with a mix of curiosity and surprise: "Harvard, the oldest university in the United States, has decided to 'build modern.'" (*The New York Times*, October 25, 1948). The Graduate Center was a compound of seven residential blocks organized around courtyards and connected through covered walkways leading to a dining hall called "Harkness Commons" (now Caspersen Student Center), a building showing some of the trademarks of his personal style: a floating façade supported by circular-shaped piers, a flat roof, and continuous steel-framed windows running along its concave exterior. Harvard did its best to explain the nature and novelty of the building, completely surrounded by historicist constructions. In an article published in the *Harvard Alumni Bulletin*, October 14, 1950, "Tradition and the Center," Gropius told the community that it was "an anachronism to express the spiritual functions [of buildings] borrowing a historical shell from the past" and that the concept of beauty had changed along with that of technique, for architecture "must move or die."

The opening of Harkness Commons was celebrated as a seminal event.[39] "The tradition, I believe, is [the] result of constant growth. Its quality must be dynamic, not static." With this declaration, Walter Gropius inaugurated the new

Graduate Center (October 6, 1950). Harvard commissioned modern painters and sculptors for the interior. Joseph Albers, former member of the Bauhaus now teaching at Black Mountain College, made a brick relief, Herbert Bayer, a mural, *Verdure*, for the refectory; Hans Arp created two *Constellation* murals; last, but not least, Joan Miró contributed a six-foot-long mural for the cafeteria (today at the MoMA, replaced in 1960 with a tile panel of the same design made by the artist himself).[40] Finally, the American sculptor Richard Lippold (1915-2002) created a stainless-steel sculpture for the courtyard, *World Tree*, on which Gropius and other members of TAC were portrayed in a now famous photograph. Zóbel, as we are about to see, actively participated in the bewildered reception of *World Tree* on campus.

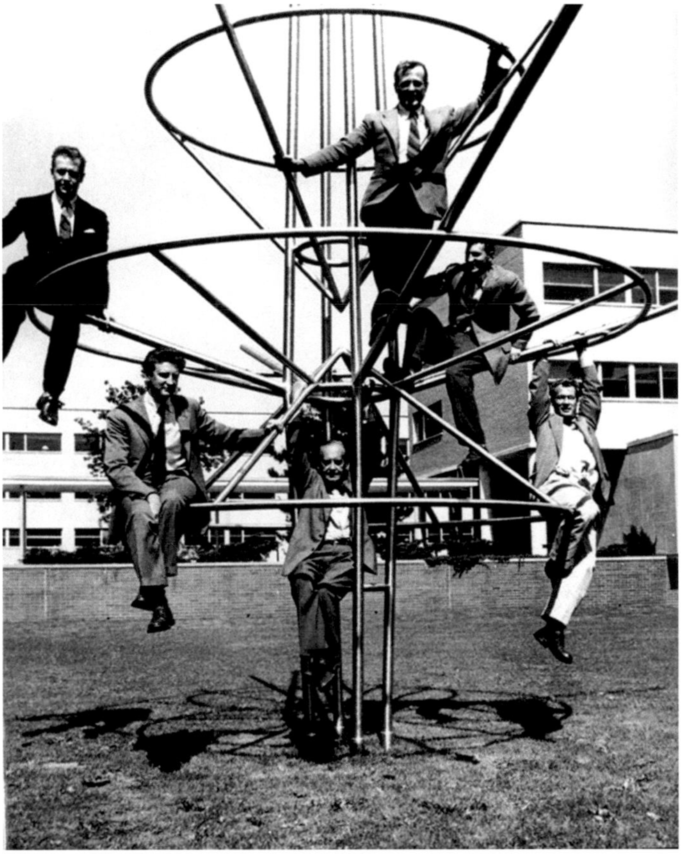

1.21 Walter Gropius and the members of TAC (The Architects Collaborative) climbing at Richard Lippold's *World Tree*, 1950.

Lippold, who had studied industrial design in Chicago and would later move to New York, spent the Summer of 1948 with his family at Black Mountain College, among other things collaborating with John Cage on the staging of Satie's *The Ruse of Medusa*, with choreography by Merce Cunningham.[41] This recently founded (1931) experimental art college had brought Josef and Anni Albers, former Bauhaus teachers, to North Carolina. (Zóbel remained enthusiastic about Albers's work and donated to the Houghton a copy of his *Interaction of Color* (1963), a portfolio of 80 of Albers's illustrations.) John Cage brought Lippold to the attention of Albers and it was probably Albers who enlisted Lippold in the Graduate Center project.

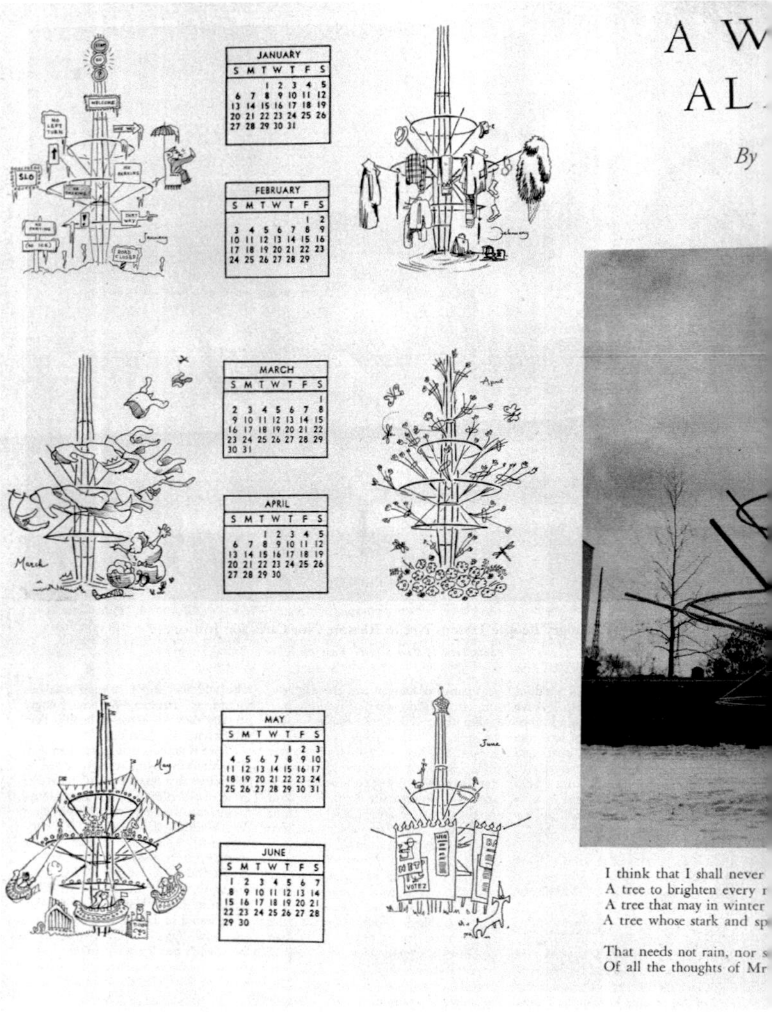

1.22
Fernando Zóbel. "A World Tree Almanac." *Harvard Alumni Bulletin*, January 12, 1952.

World Tree is a 22-foot tubular stainless-steel structure, made to resemble more an antenna than a living organism, its centrifugal metal rods looking more like cables than branches. Conceived to evoke those artifacts of the modern landscape which "make the quickest communication with all points of the earth" (Lippold, 1951), *World Tree* was met with confusion and irony, if not sarcasm. Fernando Zóbel had collaborated with the *Harvard Alumni Bulletin* as a caricaturist in the past and did not miss the opportunity to enter the fray. A big double-page drawing was published in the January 12, 1952 issue of that magazine, an "almanac" with 12 different drawings of Lippold's steel sculpture, the details of which would continue to be published in the following months.

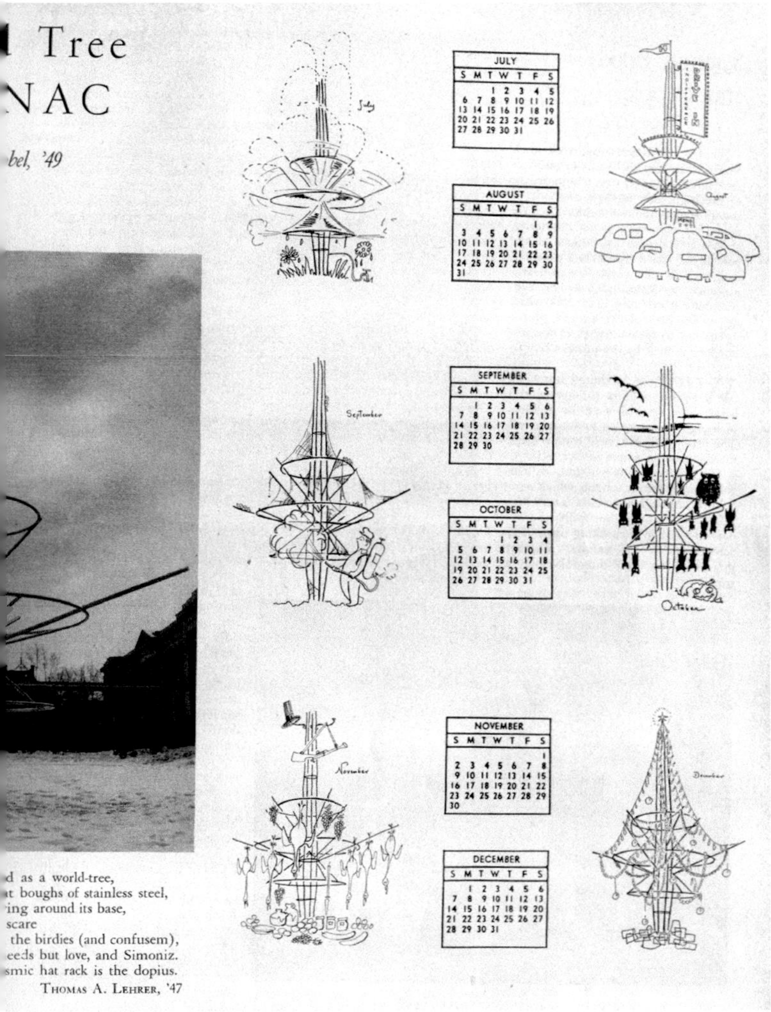

A poem by the budding songwriter, singer, and satirist Tom Lehrer (Thomas A. Lehrer, '47) was included at the bottom:

I think that I shall never see
A poem weird as a world-tree,
A tree to brighten every meal
With fragrant boughs of stainless steel,
A tree that may in winter grace
A skating rink around its base,
A tree whose stark and spikèd busem
Will scare the birdies (and confusem),
That needs not rain, nor sun to rise,
That needs but love, and Simoniz.
Of all the thoughts of Mr. Gropius
This cosmic hat rack is the dopius.

Zóbel's drawings turned mockery into innocent humor, each month imagining the *World Tree* as transformed into a different object, every time more ingenious: a coat-rack full of winter-coats (February), a parking lot, a kiosk (June), a Halloweenesque bat shelter (October) and, inevitably, a Christmas tree (December). For the presentation of his sculpture, Lippold had written: "The piece would enjoy an annual polishing (with Bon Ami cleanser), probably as a rite at the vernal equinox [...] and it will not resent being inhabited by one or two contemplative beings, Enjoy it!" (*The Harvard Crimson*, January 4, 1951). We don't know if the sculptor ever got to see Zóbel's cartoonist commentary on *World Tree*, and if he did, what he thought about it, but I am inclined to think that he would have found it more than amusing.

To Become an Artist

"Para un experimento como este, lo que mejor pega es verso;
sobre todo lleno de colorido, como lo es el de Lorca. 'El diván de Tamarit';
el nombre solo ya es un poema.
Se escribe solo."

—DIARY #2, AUGUST 25, 1950

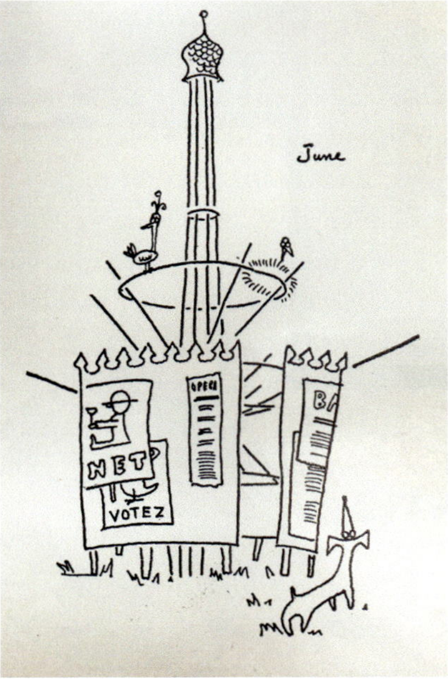

1.23 Fernando Zóbel. "June," from "A World Tree Almanac." *Harvard Alumni Bulletin,* January 12, 1952.

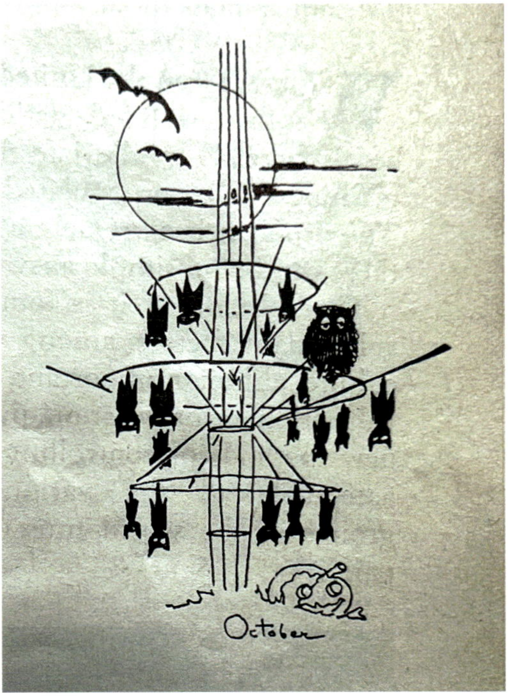

1.24 Fernando Zóbel. "October," from "A World Tree Almanac." *Harvard Alumni Bulletin,* January 12, 1952.

Our protagonist (not yet an artist) did not return to Manila in the winter of 1950. He spent Christmas in Cambridge with two friends, Reed Champion and Jim Pfeufer, painters from the Boston area, with whom Zóbel was to build a strong and in a certain way, life-changing friendship.[42] He admired Reed's determination to become a painter, but also learned from the technical advice of her husband Jim, who, as already mentioned, in a few years would convince his younger Filipino friend to study for a semester at the Rhode Island School of Design (RISD). It was under Jim's guidance that Zóbel had started to make some woodcuts with old engraving instruments that Phil Hofer had lent him (they might have belonged to Ruzycka, he wrote; they were blunt enough and worn enough to have belonged to Dürer).[43] In these first prints, Zóbel used popular Spanish subjects, a bullfighter's *cuadrilla* that, as he would write in his diary, he expected to look a little like Lorca when finished.[44]

As he would continue to do for the rest of his life, Zóbel approached art-making at RISD in a very reflective, almost scholarly way: "As of this moment I have read some ten books on wood engraving. No one would tell me how one clears out a nice and big white space. A great XIX expert will go only so far as to say that only the hacker engraves a 'white-line' design. I stand not only ignorant but corrected." It was a time of intensive seeing and hours of reading and long evenings talking about literature (once more on Lorca, this time with the composer and pianist Gordon Binkerd (1916-2003), on the musician's plans to compose an opera on *Bodas de Sangre* (*Blood Wedding*); which, as far as I know, he never did.[45]

As the Harvard Graduate Center was inaugurated in September 1950, US forces invaded northern Korea. It was the beginning of the Korean War to which the Philippines was to send a major force. Zóbel's diaries betray his fear and anxiety, but also his amazement with the muted reception of the news coming from the Pacific: "People do not talk about Korea; it would show a lack of politeness; like talking about death ..."; and a bit later down the same page: "The world is becoming liquid before our eyes," though people seemed not to notice.[46]

At the end of the year he took a train to New York to pick up a painting he had commissioned from the Filipino painter Alfonso Ossorio, his distant relative, also a Harvard graduate a few years older than him, of the class of 1938. Fernando knew Ossorio well and in many ways their lives ran parallel: both Filipinos, they had many shared acquaintances even if they had not actually met in the Philippines; and they were both members of the few Spanish fami-

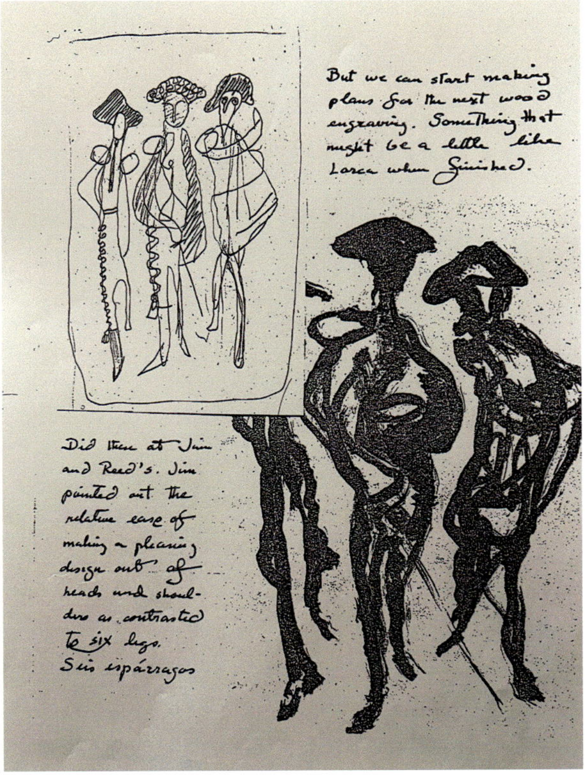

1.25 In Diary #2 (August 6, 1950), fol. 12, Zóbel anticipates his "next wood engraving. Something that might be a little like Lorca when finished." Fundación Juan March, Madrid.

lies that had made their fortunes in the colonial period (sugar for the Ossorios; trade, insurance, and real estate for the Zóbels). They both went to Harvard, the two of them were somehow destined to become artists and, finally, both became important art collectors, significantly investing in the art of their contemporaries, who also frequently happened to be their friends. It is telling that the painting Fernando had commissioned from Alfonso Ossorio was one representing Thomas Aquinas, painted according to an iconography pervasive in Filipino colonial art (most probably the painting today in the Ateneo Museum, Manila; a painting that treated an old "medieval" subject with a new "primitivist" expressive language.

Arriving at Ossorio's apartment in Manhattan, Zóbel found, to his surprise, that it was occupied, also, by another artist, a good friend of Ossorio, a serious man, *the* painter (his emphasis), Jackson Pollock, as well as Lee Krasner,

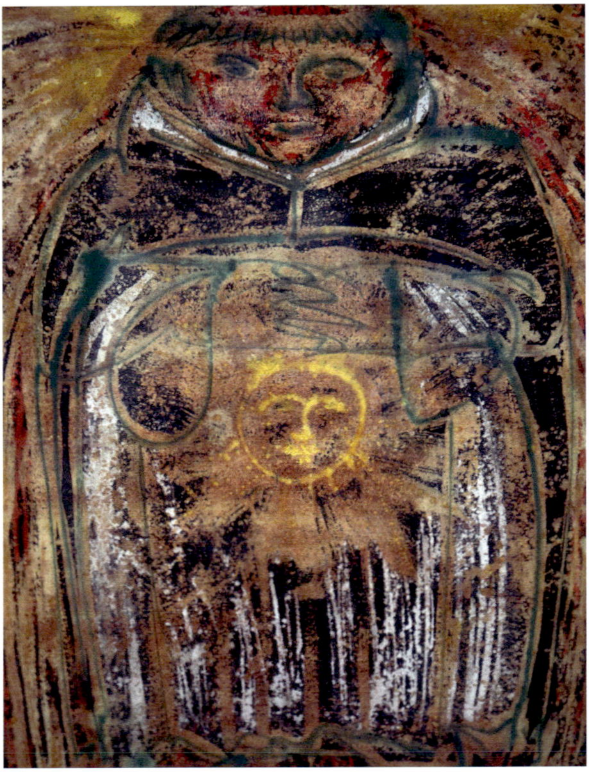

1.26 Alfonso Ossorio, *Thomas Aquinas*, 1952. Ateneo Art Gallery, Manila. Gift of Fernando Zóbel.

Pollock's wife, who had completely filled the apartment with their paintings.[47] Ossorio had met the Pollocks in February of the previous year, becoming one of his first supporters and clients (he bought the first "drip" painting for $1,500, almost twice the highest amount that Pollock had made for any of his works).[48] Ossorio became their friend, collected Pollock's paintings (he ended up with as many as twelve over the next few years) and even wrote for his catalogue, *15 Americans*, MoMA, April-July, 1952.[49]

The Pollocks had been taking advantage of Ossorio's invitation to use his apartment in the Village (9 MacDougal Alley) when Alfonso moved back to the Philippines in December 1949 to paint the the murals of a chapel in Victorias known as *The Angry Christ*. Pollock and Krasner had stayed for three months before returning to their house in Hampton, but something had made them return to New York only a few weeks before Zóbel found them in Ossorio's apartment: the invitation from *Life* to pose for Nina Leen, in what was to become a very famous photograph of "The Irascible group," to illustrate the article on the American abstract painters excluded from a show in 1950 at the Metropolitan Museum of Art, *American Painting Today*. The photograph was taken on November 26, 1950 (it would not be published until January 1951), but the scandal had been growing since *The New York Times* echoed their protest in May. It had not only been the "most prolific" year of Pollock's life; it had also been that of his public launching.[50] No surprise, then, that Fernando Zóbel had introduced Pollock as *the* painter.

They must have had a short conversation (Zóbel remembered in his diary him not only as serious, but also as dull, just "like his paintings"). A third person was with them in the house, "a certain Smith," the sculptor Tony Smith, with whom the Pollocks spent a lot of time in those days.

The exhibition at the Met that had prompted the response of the "Irascibles" had been put together by its conservative director Francis Henry Taylor, and excluded all of the emerging proponents of Abstract Expressionism. The Met show was still open when Zóbel visited Ossorio, and met Pollock, in late December 1950. He went to see the exhibit and didn't like it. His comments, in Spanish this time, reveal an anxiety for artistic, if not cultural identity, that was to follow him all his life.

> With Paul to the Metropolitan to visit the exhibition on contemporary American painting. 300 paintings out of 6,000 that had been presented. The 300 all 'modern' and something worse than boring. Imitations of the French style, each with its original, [but] minimal contribution: one because it scratches copper [*araña cobre?*], another because it uses plastic colors; the third because instead of using sand it uses grass, etc. Dummies. First prize, as expected, a work of compromise; a bouquet of violets, cubist, without any depth, impressionist without any color, realistic without drawing [referring to Karl Knaths, *Basket Bouquet*]. *Mélange adultère de tout.*
>
> We came out exhausted, looking at old archaic bronzes, well made, anonymous.[51]

"Adulterous mix of everything" *Mélange adultère de tout.* The final sentence comes from the first verse of a poem by T.S. Eliot, one of his favorite poets (a Harvard graduate, too, and also, by a dazzling coincidence, a member of the Fox Club) and one with whom he shared, at least at that moment, the same desperate, confusing search for belonging: writing in French in a foreign land, even adopting different personalities in each country (*"En Amèrique, professeur;/ En Anglaterre, journaliste/ [...] En Yorkshire, conférencier; A Londres, un peu banquier"*). Something similar happened with Zóbel: writing sometimes in English, sometimes in Spanish, but never in the place where the language corresponded (in English when in Spain, and mostly in Spanish when he was in America). Zóbel had been born into a Spanish family in the Philippines, went to an American school in Manila, and to college in Cambridge, Massachusetts, all of which contributed to this sense of displacement ("I feel like a foreigner," *me siento extrangero,* he once wrote in his diary).[52] In the last twenty years of his life, while returning frequently to the Philippines, Zóbel became a resident and citizen of Spain, a country he visited in the summer of 1951, in his late twenties, and struggled to reconcile with memories from his youth, when he studied at a boarding school in Spain's capital.

Fernando Zóbel established his residence in Madrid only in 1959, at the age of 35, and in his diaries, he refers to Spain as his "home," adding "in spite of my ease with English prose," an observation that I myself find telling.[53] The important question is less about Fernando Zóbel's national identity and more about how the cosmopolitanism that nurtured his immense, voracious curiosity—inextricably and inevitably dependent on the colonial history of his family—was experienced both as a privilege but also as a curse, the condition of some sort of a permanent exile.

Self-portrait as an artist

> "I don't like being an artist. The role bothers me.
> I like to paint, being an artist interferes with painting."
> —DIARY #14 [1971]

Another question—how or when Fernando Zóbel decided to become a painter—is much more difficult to answer, probably even *mal posée,* but still interesting to pursue. The dense intellectual itinerary on which we have been following Fernando Zóbel on his way to becoming an artist shaped something of a split personality: a painter, on the one hand, a collector and a scholar on the other. There were obvious overlappings between the two but, ultimately, I believe, they were distinct, even separate, like two ways of thinking and making. This becomes particularly clear in the language in which they would be expressed: figurative in one case and abstract in the other. Figurative for thousands of drawings, studies of ethnographic quality and caricatures kept in over 140 sketchbooks in which he continued to work until the moment of his death; and figurative also for the drawings that he used to investigate and illustrate his extensive early art-historical writing on Filipino colonial art.[54] Abstract, on the other hand, for his work as a painter.

It is for abstraction, as seen at the beginning of this chapter, that Zóbel would later acquire his recognition as an artist, and his name today is indissolubly tied to the Museum of Abstract Art, the *Museo de las Casas Colgadas,* that he designed and founded in 1966 in the city of Cuenca with less than forty paintings and sculptures from his own private collection ("the most beautiful small museum in the world," wrote Alfred H. Barr after his visit on the occasion of its opening). Zóbel would escort Barr on his visit to the museum, carefully taking note of his reactions.[55]

Zóbel's itinerary to become a painter, however, had started years before, in a quite unusual way, in Cambridge. None of his earliest works exist—he probably destroyed them—but according to his own testimony in 1953, he had been painting "seriously" for the last "eight years" (which brings us back to his first year of college). This is what he wrote to his old friend Paul Haldeman, as he was completing, from memory, his portrait—a work of which there exists a beautiful preparatory drawing [56] And we have to take his word for it.

In June 1949, Fernando graduated. One of the last classes he took was on contemporary American art for which he wrote the not-too-enthusiastic paper on Jack Levine already mentioned. He had not yet met Levine but, introduced by Reed and Pfeufer, he had already begun to frequent the haunts and hangouts of Bostonian bohemia in the form of galleries of modern art, and informal salons. Particularly impressed by the personality of Hyman Bloom (Zóbel writes with admiration of his works and technique, and speaks eloquently of their conversations), in 1950 he had started to paint in Bloom's style (a "careful multitextured" one as he would later describe it)[57] and had even considered asking Hyman to become his mentor.[58] The impression that abstract expressionists left on Zóbel interfered and he soon abandoned Bloom's style. Personal commitments in Manila would also force him to leave America and put some necessary distance between him and the shadow of his friends and mentors.

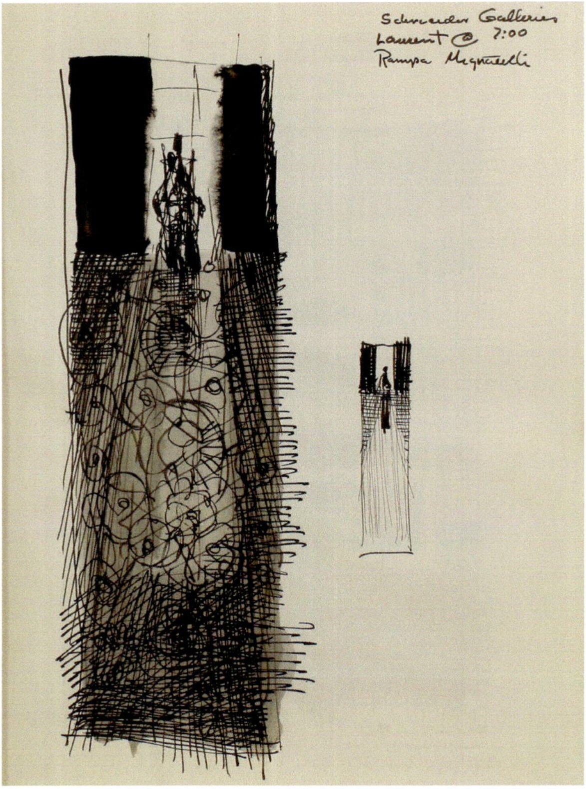

1.27 A preparatory drawing for Zóbel's portrait of Paul Haldeman. Fundación Juan March, Madrid.

Perhaps because of his slow, late start, it was clear to Fernando that he was learning to paint, not to become an artist. Slowly, the latter overtook the former, a process that, as shown in the epigraph introducing this section, was never fully completed—another aspect of his mutifaceted personality.[59] Fernando Zóbel left Cambridge in May 1951. Some of his friends (he refers to Dave Perkins) insisted it was a mistake, but he knew he had no choice. He would return briefly, as in the fall of 1954, when he attended the classes at RISD, but his full immersion in painting only started when he left his obligations at the family company in Manila in 1960. For a long decade Fernando struggled to combine his diverse obligations, that of a painter and that of a businessman, a struggle reflected in his letters with a mixture of excitement and frustration.[60] Particularly revealing are the notes Fernando prepared for a class on contemporary painting that he taught at Ateneo University in Metro Manila, from 1954-55.[61] The syllabus describes the class as "experimental," a seminar on "how to look at paintings," an "experiment in how to *see* things" (my emphasis). The syllabus includes instructions such as the following:

> You should look at these objects for a sufficient period of time. Less than 10 minutes is hardly adequate. Do not look at them passively but actively. Ask yourself questions: what is the artist trying to do? Does this look like anyone else's work? If something disturbs you, what is it? How well has he accomplished what you think he is trying to do?, etc.

I believe this quote encapsulates a mantra I have brought up before in these pages: that making is also a way of seeing, and *vice versa*, a distinctive characteristic of his training as tentatively described in this essay. His classes at the Ateneo also included an Alfred-Barresque diagram on the history of modern art, now continuing into the 1950s (Barr's famous one stopped in 1935), citing some of the names of the artists he had encountered in the previous years. Significantly, the diagram is labeled "A Road Map of Modern Art."

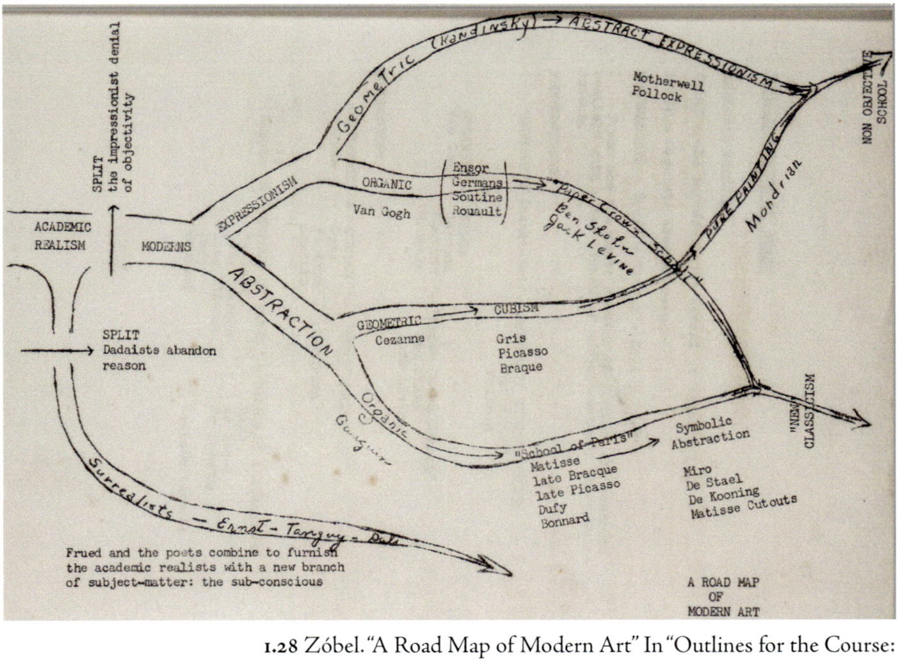

1.28 Zóbel. "A Road Map of Modern Art" In "Outlines for the Course: Introduction to Contemporary Painting."

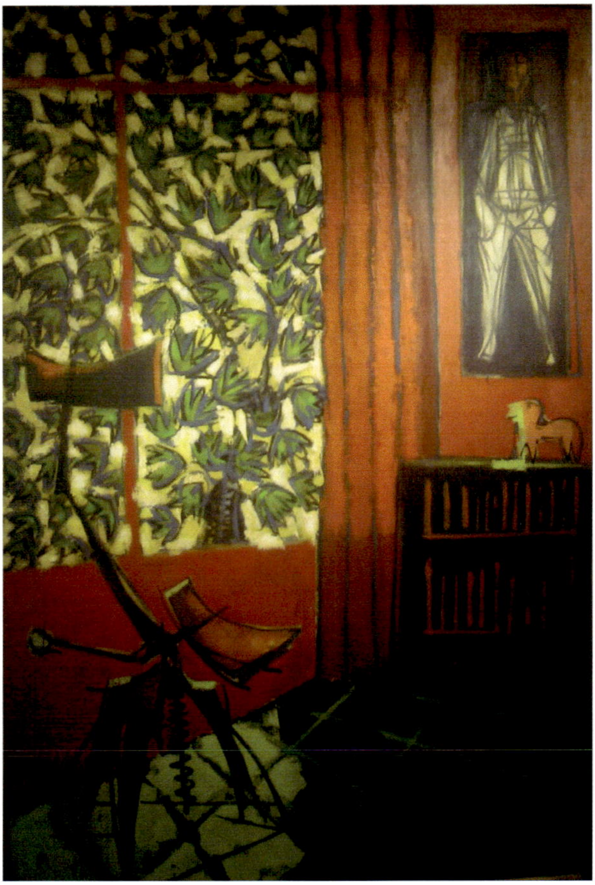

1.29 Zóbel. *Self Portrait in a Mirror* (1954).
Private collection.

The evidence that Zóbel fabricated that map by thinking about how to travel along its roads comes not in a text, but in a painting. A self-portrait. executed in Manila and exhibited in a small solo show (June, 1954, *12 Paintings by Fernando Zóbel*). The painting represents him reflected on the back wall while in the foreground there is an empty chair, the metaphor for a ghostly presence. The chair, however, is not any chair, but a swivel chair, a model developed in Germany in the 1930s that Rowac (Robert Wagner Chemnitz) gave Walter Gropius for use at the Bauhaus in Dessau. In other words, the empty chair is a chair for drawing; that is the self portrait.

LUIS FERNÁNDEZ CIFUENTES

ZÓBEL'S HARVARD AND THE 1940S CRISIS IN HIGHER EDUCATION

Fernando Zóbel was a remarkably good student. At a time when there was no grade inflation at Harvard and undergraduates considered C+ perfectly acceptable, he earned mostly A's and felt terribly disappointed with himself when he failed to do so. One memorable instance occurred in the Spring semester of 1949, Zóbel's last. His grades were all A's except for a B in English 181hf, a course devoted to "The study of Fine Books" and "intended for students interested in the collecting of books." Zóbel, always an avid reader ("I read like a glutton"), was also an avid collector of rare and exquisitely bound books. The professor was William A. Jackson, eminent librarian of Houghton Library where Harvard's fabled rare book collection is kept. Zóbel pled guilty in his journal entry of May 6: "me cogió de sorpresa y mal el exámen [sic]. Frito de sacar la nota más baja en lo que más me interesa. Furioso de la opinión que [Jackson] debe haberse hecho de mí" (The exam caught me by surprise and indisposed. Irritated that I got the worst grade in the subject I am most interested in. It makes me furious to think that Jackson may now have a bad opinion of me.) Zóbel worked with Jackson at Houghton for two years after he graduated.

The law does not permit full access to Zóbel's student records until 2064, 80 years after his death. His journals and correspondence, however, provide bits of information that allow us to fathom the kind of student he was. In October 1945, Zóbel, still in the Philippines, sent an envelope with documents and a note to Paul Haldeman, a close friend who worked at the American Embassy in Manila. Haldeman had graduated from Harvard just a few years earlier and was probably helping Zóbel with his application. In the note Zóbel commented: "from my grades you can tell why I never wish to hear of science again." The poor grades in science, not listed in the note, did not prevent Harvard from admitting Zóbel but they did determine his course of study. Following (largely) his interests, he chose to take a rather whimsical variety of courses, mostly in the humanities, considerably fewer in the social sciences, and none in the sciences.[1] In other words, "disinterested curiosity"—as it was called at the time—and never a professional goal guided those choices.[2]

On February 17, 1946, Zóbel—likely aware of debates in higher education that pitted the *futile* humanities against the *useful* sciences—wrote to Paul Haldeman from Harvard: "My courses are magnificent in their futility. English Aa[3], European history [possibly The History of Continental Europe in the Twentieth Century], modern painting [either Modern Art or Introduc-

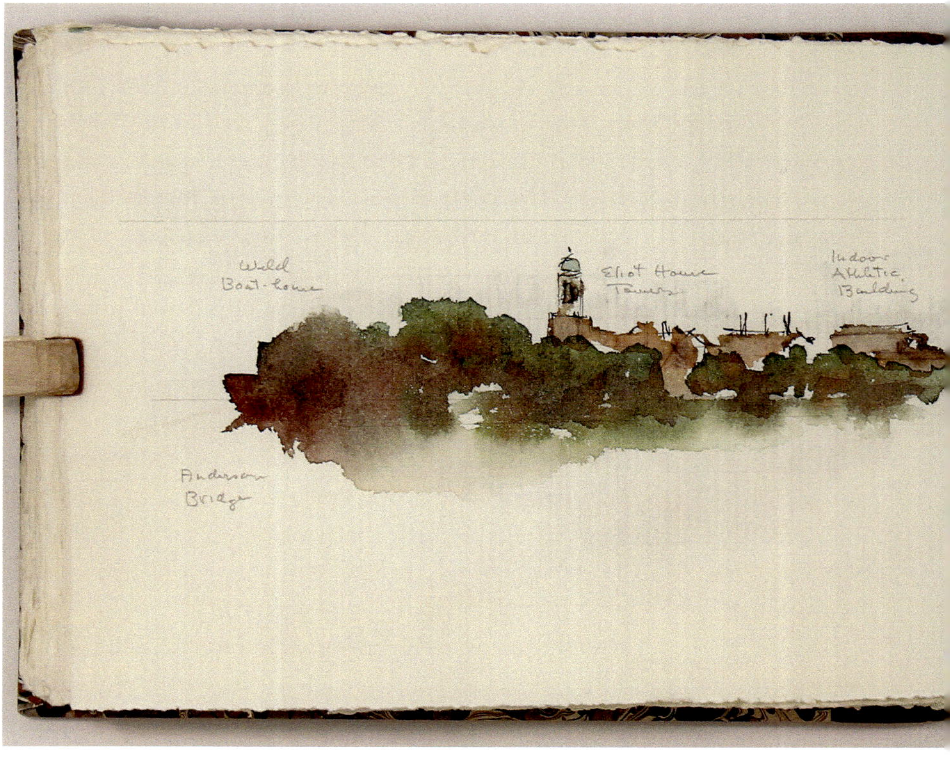

tion to European Painting (High Renaissance to Present Day)] and so-called modern philosophy [most likely History of Modern Philosophy (since the Renaissance)]." On May 6, 1949, Zóbel completed his last semester at Harvard and wrote in his journal: "Revista general para los exámenes. Datos y papeles amontonados. Demasiada prisa. Me estoy envenenando de tragar libros como ostras. Recojo exámenes: Mumford Jones [literature], imbécil perdido, A; Ben Rowland [art], curso espléndido, A con complemento."[4] (General review for the exams. A pile of papers and notes. All too hasty. Swallowing books like oysters is poisoning me. I pick up the results of the exams: Mumford Jones, a complete imbecile, A; Ben Rowland, splendid course, A+.) His third course was Jackson's, with the B grade that infuriated him. Harvard allowed seniors to take only three courses in their last semester—instead of the regular four—when they were writing a senior thesis, as Zóbel was (*Theme and Conflict in*

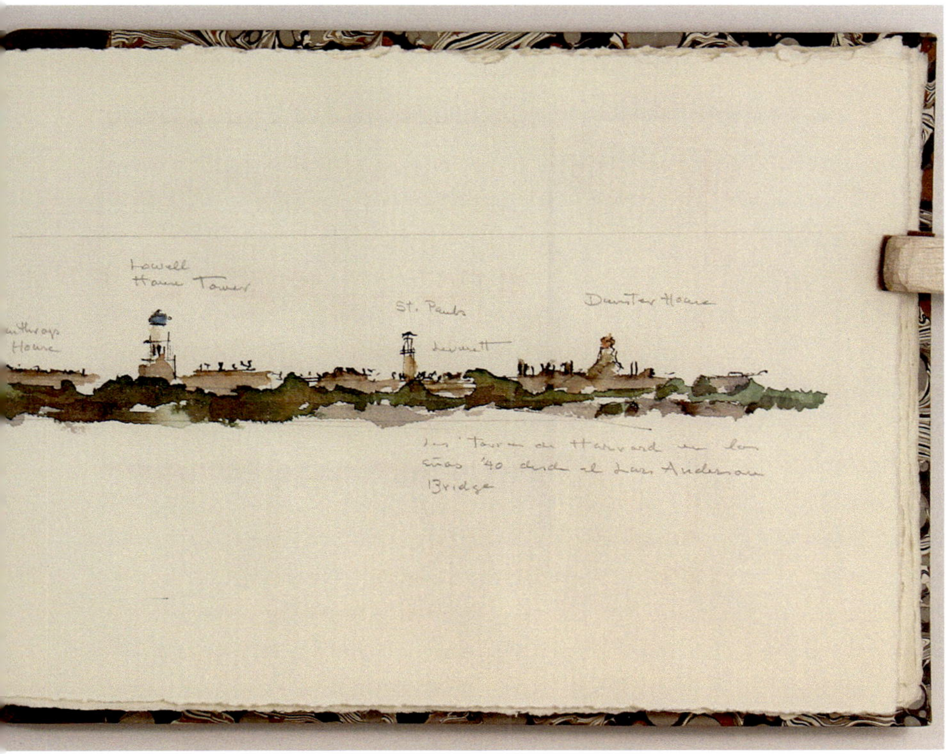

2.1 Fernando Zóbel, "Las torres de Harvard en los años '40 desde el Lars Anderson Bridge", from Sketchbook 83 (1976). Zóbel was working "from a photo, ca. 1948," "before the new buildings changed the skyline." Fundación Juan March, Madrid.

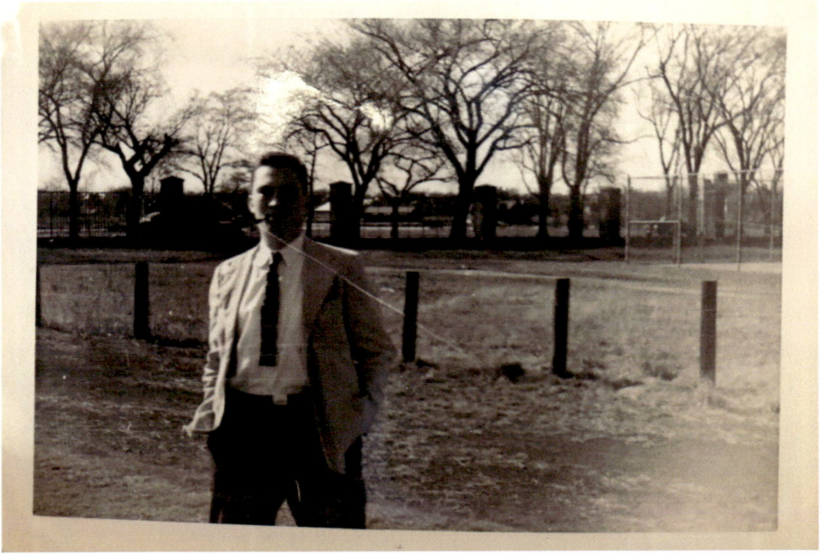

2.2 Zóbel photographed by his friend Dave Perkins, 1947. Fundación Juan March.

Lorcan Drama.) There is no indication that between his first and his last semesters he attended any course in the natural sciences or in the social sciences, other than history.

Zóbel must have done very well in his first college courses because at the end of his freshman year he was accepted into History and Literature, arguably Harvard's most prestigious and exclusive concentration. Peter Prescott, an undergraduate who started at Harvard only two years after Zóbel's graduation and also kept a journal, writes that History and Literature was called "the heavenly circle": "only fifty applicants from Harvard and Radcliffe would be accepted at all, at the end of their freshman year." Prescott describes History and Literature as "a young, small, exclusive and distinctly smug department that gave only honors degrees, with the usual paraphernalia of tutors, especial examinations and a senior paper. One could study the history and literature of a single country [...], but the point was that one could pretty well carve his own curriculum [...]. Nobody not clearly demonstrating a rapacious capacity for honors grades would be accepted."[5] As described in the *Harvard University Catalog 1948,* History and Literature was not a department with its own specific courses; concentrators (majors) in History and Literature could take courses in any department that offered either History or Literature, only "so selected as to come under some general scheme of study of the History and Literature either of a nation or of a period: for example, History and Literature (*a*) of Greece, (*b*) of England, (*c*) of France [...], (*d*) of the Middle Ages, (*e*) of the Renaissance, (*f*) of the Nineteenth Century."[6]

Officially, Zóbel chose the last, Nineteenth Century, With Emphasis on the Romantics, although his true interest was 20th-century Spanish literature, García Lorca, in particular. Significantly enough, the history and literature of Spain is not one of the "examples" listed by the *Harvard University Catalog*; perhaps it was not even an option. It is also significant that Zóbel appears to have shunned the Department of Romance Languages and Literatures (RLL), the traditional home of his field of interest, but a department without tutors in History and Literature. Most of the courses he chose (or we can surmise he chose) were offered in the Core Humanities or were listed by the departments of English, History, Fine Arts, Philosophy and especially Comparative Literature, a department that Claudio Guillén, plurilingual like Zóbel and also interested primarily in Spanish literature, joined as a graduate student at approximately the same time, the fall of 1946. Zóbel and Guillén—the son of poet Jorge Guillén—shared the same eminent mentors, Harry Levin and Renato Poggioli.

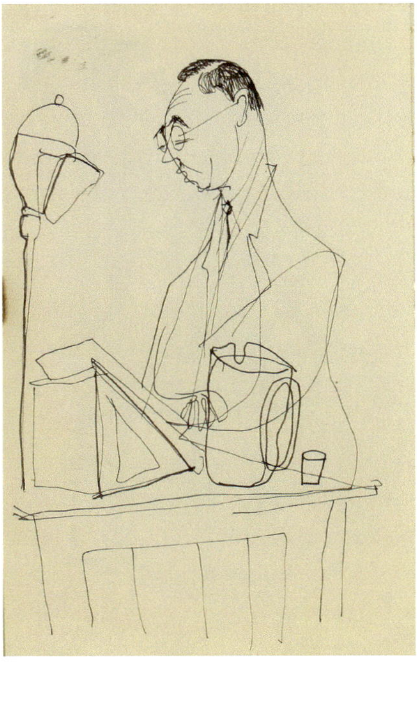

2.3 Fernando Zóbel. Sketch of a professor lecturing at Harvard. Renato Poggioli? Fundación Juan March, Madrid.

Whatever course choices he made, Zóbel excelled as a concentrator in History and Literature. So much so that in 1947, at the end of his sophomore year, he was recognized with the Barrett Wendell Prize.[7] Harvard catalogs specified that the Barrett Wendell Prize "is awarded each year to the member of the Sophomore Class concentrating in [History and Literature] who has made the most notable progress during the year. In making this award, tutorial work, standing courses within the field, and the results of the examinations in the Bible and Shakespeare will be considered." The *Harvard Crimson* added: "only the six most promising Sophomores in the field are invited to compete."[8] Zóbel was proud of the prize, which he mentions in the *1949 Harvard Album*, next to his extracurricular accomplishments: "Art Editor of *Album*, Club Espagnol [sic], Stamp Club, Hasty Pudding, Fox, Phi Eta, Barrett Wendell Award."[9] It was during that sophomore year that Zóbel produced his impressive translation of García Lorca's *Don Perlimplín*: the art of translation was then an important component of language and composition programs, and it is likely to have contributed to Zóbel's qualification for the Barrett Wendell Prize.

And yet, Zóbel's success came without great exertion, as we can infer from his journals, where he pays much less attention to his academic endeavors than to his outings with friends and his commitment to painting and drawing. In 1974 he sent this statement to the annual *Harvard Report for the Class of 1949*: "Perhaps the time has come to confess that what I liked best about working in Cambridge is that it gave me the time and the opportunity to learn to paint. And that, essentially, is what I have been doing ever since."[10]

There is, however, a less glamorous and more troublesome side to Zóbel's experience at Harvard. At some point in the early 1950s, Prescott wrote in his journal: "I live in a world of snobs, and snobbery is nothing but a form of protection for oneself."[11] Zóbel could have written the same in the late 1940s, except that he was, at least to some extent, one of the snobs, and a sarcastic one. Besides shunning RLL—certainly one of the less dazzling and more marginal departments in the College at the time, for reasons I will get to—, boasting about the "magnificent futility" of his courses, declaring book collecting as his main interest, and confessing that his extracurricular activity of painting was the number one benefit of his Cambridge years, he mocked the difficult achievement of being admitted into the clique of History and Literature. In a letter to Haldeman dated September 29, 1946, he writes nonchalantly: "I suddenly find myself in the Department of History and Literature," as if it had been an accident and not the result of a serious trial. And later again, jeeringly (January 9,

1947): "I play with the idea of writing my thesis on the Supernatural Element in Spanish Neo-Gothic poetry." (To my knowledge, no genre called "Spanish Neo-Gothic poetry" ever existed.) Zóbel also alluded, somewhat haughtily and disdainfully, to a general sense of frustration with his Harvard education. On May 19, 1949, when he was about to graduate, vacate his room and leave the college, Zóbel noted (without further elaboration): "En Harvard he tenido de todo menos lo que vine buscando" (At Harvard I've had everything except what I came here looking for.) On May 5, 1951, apparently after reading over the first volume of his journals, he recapitulates: "Cinco años de estudios en Harvard, mal resumidos, pero resumidos al menos por causa del espanto que me produjo ver tanta palabra vana y tanto mal dibujo amontonado a mis pies" (Five years of study at Harvard, badly summarized, but summarized, at least, because of the horror I felt to see so many idle words and bad drawings heaped up at my feet.)

Was Zóbel's disapproval of Harvard—were those sarcastic words and harsh statements—an outburst of snobbish conceit or an indictment of an actual want? If we can assume that what he was looking for (and didn't get) was the highly regarded Liberal Arts education—"the distinctive feature of American education"[12]—then there may be more to Zóbel's disappointment than typical snobbism. A Liberal Arts education meant that, beyond any factual knowledge, the college would provide the student with "a background mentality, a way of thinking, a kind of intellectual DNA that informs work in every specialized area of inquiry."[13] Which raises another question: did Harvard fail to equip Zóbel with that kind of mental hardware? Or did Zóbel fail to make the proper moves in order to obtain it? It was probably a complex and ill-timed combination of the two.

Zóbel arrived in Harvard in the midst of a severe national crisis in secondary and higher education, brought "to a head" by the commotion of World War II.[14] In 1943, Harvard president James Bryan Conant was not only aware of the crisis but eager to have the problem diagnosed and resolved. To that end, he convened a committee that worked for more than two years and produced a 267-page report. It was published in book form in 1945, just as Zóbel was trying to join the first undergraduate cohort of the post-war era. Luminaries like I. A. Richards (English) and Arthur M. Schlesinger (History, later a special assistant to President Kennedy) were part of the 12-member committee; F. O. Matthiessen (chair of the program in History and Literature), Harry Levin (Comparative Literature), and Walter Gropius (Graduate School of Design) served in one subcommittee or another. No faculty from RLL were called to participate in the deliberations. Many universities, colleges and high schools were consulted.

The official title of the document was *General Education in a Free Society. Report of the Harvard Committee* ("free society" being an early reference to the emerging Cold War.)[15] The book was generally referred to as *The Harvard Report* or the *Redbook* (for its binding) and it had an enormous impact in the US world of education. It was reviewed—not always favorably—in innumerable academic periodicals. It was discussed in many a faculty meeting of the nearly 2,000 institutions of higher learning as well as the 27,608 centers of secondary education that existed in the continental US. I have used the eleventh printing of the book, which appeared only a few months after the first. In 1950 it had sold over 50,000 copies. The reforms and innovations it proposed were adopted or adapted most everywhere.

One of the key concepts, perhaps *the* key concept, of The *Redbook* is "unity": "Ours is at present a centrifugal culture in extreme need of unifying forces."[16] The problem of centrifugalism had two different (though intertwined) roots.

2.4 *General Education in a Free Society. Report of the Harvard Committee*. Harvard University Press, 1945.

First, starting in the 1860s, Harvard president Charles Eliot had introduced a curricular system consisting mainly of elective courses: students were handed almost full agency in their own education. Throughout the next 80 years, overspecialization on the one hand and misunderstood diversity on the other slowly eroded the content and function of the once-successful Liberal Arts education. More often than not, Harvard students ended up graduating either with a set of courses limited to a single discipline or with a scattered, "pell-mell" list of courses (Zóbel's case).[17] Overspecialization resulted in another form of disunity: specialists in one subject shared virtually no cultural common ground with specialists in another. As a result, one of the main questions (perhaps *the* main question) the committee was trying to tackle was this: "what then is the right relationship between a specialistic training on the one hand [...], and education on a common heritage and towards a common citizenship, on the other?"[18]

The second root of the problem has been an insidious corollary of higher education's modern inception early in the 19th century. In the high Middle Ages, the first universities organized education in two stages that complemented each other: first the *trivium* as main foundation, second the *quadrivium* as superstructure. The Enlightenment and the Industrial Revolution upended that arrangement, giving the upper hand to the natural sciences when not entirely repealing the humanities. The *Redbook* was not exactly trying to restore the hierarchies of the ancient paradigm; it was trying to find a unifying balance between the new sciences as prime specialty and the old humanities as common "heritage": "The true task of education is therefore so to reconcile the sense of pattern and direction deriving from heritage with the sense of experiment and innovation deriving from science that they must exist fruitfully together, as in varying degrees they have never ceased to do throughout Western history."[19]

The committee decided that there were but three possible ways to achieve that reconciliation. One was to make the study of "the great writings of the European and American past" (the "heritage") the unifying force of General Education. Another, to ground General Education in "actual problems and questions which young people may be expected to meet in mature life—health, vocation, family, social issues, private standards and the like." The third was to find "in science and the scientific outlook this saving unity."[20] All three were given their share in the General Education "Core" program, basically a tripartite set of distribution requirements which "should, in our view, take up about half of a student's time in school."[21] The distribution boiled down to this: "of the sixteen courses required for the bachelor's degree students should be required to take [at least] six courses in general education [...]. Of the six courses, at least one shall be in the humanities, one in the social sciences and one in the sciences."[22] At Harvard, the Core Program—whose different subdivisions were plotted out by subcommittees—was implemented slowly and tentatively, starting in the academic year 1946-1947. Zóbel's discontent would reflect in part the type of disruption and uncertainty that such transition created.

The *Redbook* seems to treat the Humanities—"the arts of reading, writing, thinking and speaking"[23]—somewhat preferentially. Some of the proposed Humanities courses were but variations on the famous Great Books courses launched in the 1930s with considerable success in universities like Columbia, Chicago and Saint John. The selection of "great books" fluctuated only slightly from college to college, which prompted Louis Menand to note later on that "the basic impression is one of canonical stability."[24] Furthermore, "between 1940 and 1995" the total pool of "great books" that humanities courses drew from turned out to be quite small: around 100.[25] Menand explains that "what is important [about that short list of indispensables] is that we live in a society that is shaped to some degree by the ideas of Plato, Rousseau and Mill, just as we live in a society in which we can expect to encounter works of literature influenced to some degree by Homer, Shakespeare and Cervantes."[26]

The Harvard committee disparaged abridgments and stipulated that the texts in the Core Humanities "each must be read completely enough for its parts to help one another to the full." With that objective in mind, they calculated that "eight great books would be trying to do too much" in a single semester, although just eight books was not enough for the Core Education they envisioned. The committee went on to suggest a very structured and rather rigid solution. Three year-long Humanities courses would be offered: 1a/1b, 2a/2b, and 3a/3b. The students would be required to take one but could (or should) take more, only they would have to take them in sequence: Humanities 1 was a prerequisite for Humanities 2, etc. The committee also suggested a list of authors or works to choose from: Homer, one or two Greek tragedies, Plato, the Bible, Virgil, Dante, Shakespeare, Milton, Tolstoy.[27] Intentionally or not, *Don Quixote*, a fixture in most, if not all, Great Books courses across the country and over the years—and the one and only representation of literature in Spanish—is notoriously absent. The subcommittee corrected the oversight: by the time Humanities courses were listed in Harvard's *Courses of Instruction*, *Don Quixote* had its place in the syllabus.[28]

The full range of Core courses was announced for the first time in Harvard's *Courses of Instruction* for academic year 1946-1947, when Zóbel was a sophomore, and he probably didn't take more than two or three of the new courses in the Humanities. The Core apparatus must have mystified him and the entire class of 1949. According to the catalog, all Core courses, designed primarily for freshmen, were taught "on an experimental basis" for the time being (the experiment lasted until the fall of 1950, one year after Zóbel's graduation) and "during the experimental period all of the courses [were] entirely optional," open to sophomores, juniors and seniors in any order they wanted, although with "prior approval for enrolment [...] obtained from the Committee on General Education." Thus, for Zóbel's cohort, Core courses were thinly masked electives, phantom requirements that didn't quite inaugurate a rigorous new order in their education.

Given the options, Zóbel may have chosen Humanities 2b, The Novel, which included *Don Quixote, Candide, Sorrows of Werther, Bleak House, Moby Dick,* and *War and Peace.* The class was limited to 50 students and was taught by Harry Levin. Zóbel did attend Levin's Comp. Lit. 161, Proust, Joyce and Mann, in the fall of 1948. He wrote in his diary on October 6: "Proust por cuarta vez, pero acompañado de conferencias de Harry Levin [...]. Levin es el

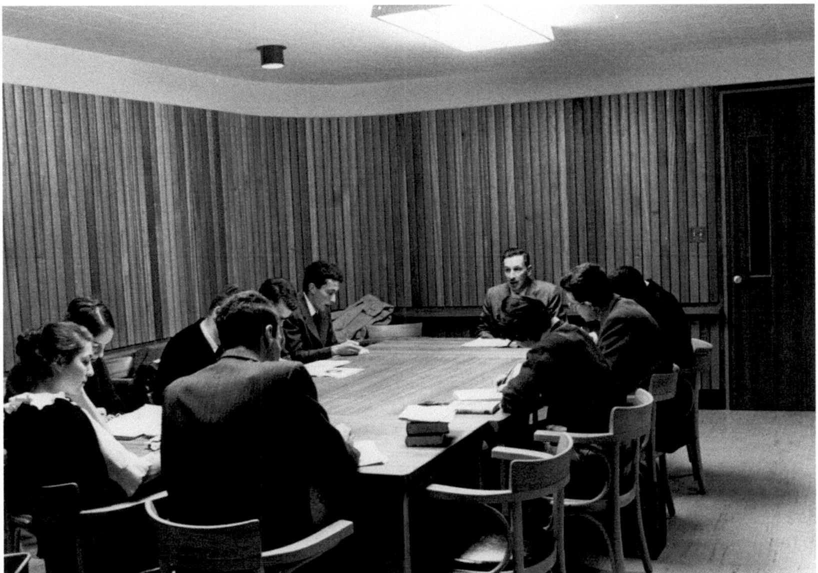

2.5 Harry Levin and students. Harvard University. Radcliffe Archives.

mejor conferenciante que aquí tenemos. Quizá, como dicen, algo superficial, pero no entiendo esa clase de crítica que confunde lo profundo con lo aburrido, serio y frívolo" (Proust for the fourth time, accompanied by lectures by Harry Levin [...] Levin is the best lecturer we have. Perhaps, people say, a little superficial, but I don't understand that sort of criticism, which confuses the profound with the boring, the serious with the frivolous.) Humanities 2b required the students to read about 4,000 pages in 14 weeks, and that for only one of their four courses. Zóbel complained of too much reading in too little time ("swallowing books like oysters"). Isaac Berlin, at the end of his first semester as visiting professor at Harvard (May 1949), observed that most American students "read rapidly, desperately and far too much"; as a consequence, they generally suffered from "intellectual congestion."[29]

Whether Zóbel read *Don Quixote* under Levin's guidance remains a matter of conjecture.[30] He could have read it in a "tutorial," a teaching modality he seems to have admired. History and Literature required that "in addition [to regular courses] the student will pursue a course of general reading with his tutor, both in the principal authors of the country or of the period in question and in the works of standard authorities on cultural and intellectual history." Was Levin his tutor? We only know for certain that *Don Quijote* was in Zóbel's personal library in 1950 (diary entry of March 27) and that he read it *again* in 1963: "*Don Quijote*. Esta vez con gusto. Lo que no entiendo es cómo pudo gustar internacionalmente. Como todo lo nuestro es terriblemente local" (diary entry of September 22.) (*Don Quixote*. This time with pleasure. What I don't understand is how it could please people internationally. Like everything we do, it is terribly local.) The comment runs counter to the principle that justified *Don Quixote*'s inclusion in all Humanities reading lists: prominent American scholars considered *Don Quixote* the one Spanish foundational fiction that deserved a place in the *international* Olympus of Great Books courses.[31] Zóbel's rebuttal, however, may be read as an indirect denunciation of other constraints (or impositions) in the Harvard *Redbook*.

When it came to literature courses, the *Redbook* not only dictated the content (authors or titles) but also, and rather more forcefully, the way those texts should be read. "The aim of such a course [Great Texts of Literature] would be the fullest understanding of the work read rather than of men or periods represented, craftsmanship evinced, historic or literary development shown, or anything else." The *Redbook*, often repetitive, insists: "philology, history of language, history of literature, biography of authors, discussion of literary form, criticism, prosody, and grammar" do not provide a straightforward approach to a text; they are "ancillary studies" that should play a role in the reading of Great Books only "in so far as they are necessary to allow the work to speak for itself [...]. Otherwise they should be left for special, not general education."[32] The mandates and their specificity resonate with the critical principles of T. S. Eliot, *New Criticism* and I. A. Richards' *close reading*. Levin's comparatist approach was also acceptable: relating great books to great books, brokering a conversation among them.[33] Both Richards and Levin taught Humanities courses, but the first (a University Professor) was the leading voice in literary studies in the college at large; the second (an associate professor) less so. Levin had a less restrictive approach, yet without entirely deserting the realm of *close reading*. Outside that realm were the departments that sheltered "ancillary studies"; the Spanish section of the Department of Romance Languages and Literatures was a notorious example.

The *Redbook* committee not only prescribed the authors to be read and the right way to read them; it also treated foreign languages as stocks in the market of General Education. The committee pointed out that "there is probably no educational problem about which there is more confusion and disagreement than the role of foreign languages in secondary education."[34] The war effort, with its peremptory demand for the quick acquisition of foreign languages, only made things worse. To elucidate and resolve the matter, the *Redbook* established the following guidelines for both secondary and higher education. First, the "prime function [of foreign language teaching] is not to give a practical command of the new language; on the contrary, it is to illuminate English in these two respects in which English supremely needs illumination, namely, syntax and vocabulary."[35] Second, there are two types of languages: those that are acquired as working tools—"for instance, German by prospective scientists who will need access to technical writings in German, or Spanish by persons looking forward to a job in South America"[36]—and those that "are studied not just as tools but for the cultural ends"; that is, languages reserved for students "concerned with the very stuff of the humanities, with timeless writings, with other cultures, and the ever changing meaning of words."[37] These languages were primarily Latin and French (which Zóbel knew) "and they should be taught with this intention and this alone. But a word should be said of two other languages, Russian and ancient Greek" (which Zóbel didn't know). Most students read Russian and Greek great books in translation; a select minority could be prepared to read them in the original.[38]

One of Phyllis and Morton Keller's books about Harvard, *Making Harvard Modern*, offers further details (and implicit justifications) of the insignificant role of RLL in General Education: "The traditional raison d'être of the Romance Languages department was not cutting-edge critical scholarship, but undergraduate and graduate instruction in French, Spanish and Italian [...] language and literature. Provost Paul Buck observed in 1944 that 'vital contact with living trends in the field... is something the department has been utterly without during the last decade'." In stark contrast, Comparative Literature was thriving as "an interdisciplinary graduate program of cutting-edge novelty and stratospheric standards under Harry Levin," starting precisely in the late 40s (Levin was chair of the department in 1946) and continuing through the 50s and 60s. The same could be said of Slavic Languages and Literatures, which became a superior department when Poggioli, Jakobson and Lord joined its faculty in the mid to late 40s.[39] The Kellers fail to mention at least one relevant detail: the shortcomings of RLL could not be equally ascribed to all its sections. The general language divide described (or prescribed) in the *Redbook* was also manifest within RLL: two prominent members of the French section—an older one, André Morize, and a younger one, Jean-Joseph Seznec—had at least one foot as tutors in the exclusive corridors of History and Literature, where Spanish, Italian and Portuguese faculty were completely absent.

Zóbel must have found the *Redbook* directives and the general dismissal of Spanish disheartening, but he managed to circumvent them, choosing to study Spanish literature not directly in its specific home, RLL, but indirectly, under a different title, in the more prestigious and updated environments of English and Comparative Literature, the primary contributors to History and Literature. Still, Zóbel's thesis topic brought an additional complication: he did not choose to study Cervantes and his age, which after all had some purchase in General Education, but a 20th-century author, Federico García Lorca, who was gaining recognition in the American literary world, although not quite enough to secure him a place in Comp. Lit. and Humanities courses.

Among the world's literati, Lorca had already become the best-known Spanish writer after Cervantes. In the United States his reputation had been growing exponentially since his assassination in 1936. Multiple translations and anthologies (some bilingual) of his poetry were published between 1937 and 1949. New Directions published a translation of *Bodas de sangre* in 1939, despite its 1935 unsuccessful Broadway production. In 1947 New Directions brought out *Three Tragedies*, with a preface by Francisco García Lorca, which

Zóbel admired and quoted from. Eric Bentley included *Perlimplín* in his anthology *From the Modern Repertoire, Series One* (1949). Lorca is there in lofty company, right after T. S. Eliot and Brecht and right before Cocteau and Yeats. Bentley's anthologies were widely read for years as college textbooks. In Donald Allen's landmark anthology, *The New American Poetry, 1945-1960,*[40] Lorca is revealed as a powerful icon among the so-called New York Poets. Robert Duncan and LeRoi Jones (known later as Amiri Baraka) mention Lorca among their principal influences, along with Eliot, Mallarmé, Pound, Williams, etc. Jack Spicer expounds his poetics in the form of letters to Lorca. Perhaps even more revealing is a poem by Kenneth Koch, "Fresh Air," written in 1955. One of the stanzas starts with this question: "Who are the great poets of our time, and what are their names?" The answer, tortured by question marks, names 17 poets from Auden and Eliot to Pasternak and Mayakovsky, and it contains this line: "Hopkins (is Hopkins of our time?), Rilke (is Rilke of our time?), Lorca (is Lorca of our time?), who is still of our time?" In 1973, Allen published a different kind of anthology, *Poetics of the New American Poetry,* where he included García Lorca's "Theory and Function of the *duende*" (alongside texts by Whitman, Pound, Williams, etc.) as a key reference in the emergence of the new American poetics.[41]

However, for the committee on General Education what mattered wasn't current influence, popularity or even greatness but solid, inveterate, universal significance. Zóbel himself sabotages Lorca's theater in this regard. He writes in the last paragraph of his thesis: Lorca did not live long enough "to create a dramatic character of universal significance." The readers of the thesis, comparatists Harry Levin and Renato Poggioli, mention García Lorca in their own works, but always in passing: Lorca is a name to reckon with but he is never the main focus of their attention (by contrast, Levin wrote at least two lengthy chapters on Cervantes.) It doesn't even look like Lorca's works drew much attention in Harvard's RLL at the time: as happened in most colleges, Cervantes and his age was by far the overriding subject.[42]

The lists of courses offered by RLL in the late 40s give very vague information about authors and readings, let alone methodology. During Zóbel's time, the first indisputable evidence of García Lorca's presence in Harvard classrooms is a hand-written syllabus for Spanish 30 (Spring of 1947) kept in the Harvard Archives.[43] The title of that version of Spanish 30, taught by Professor Pedro Grases, was The Generation of '98 and Their Successors. Readings included Lorca's *Romancero gitano* as well as an anthology of poems by Alberti and

Gerardo Diego. Spanish 30 must have been a staple of the Spanish curriculum because it was repeated every semester. For some reason, it was entrusted at the time to visiting professors. Juan López Morillas taught Spanish 30 in fall 1947 with a new title: Spanish Prose and Poetry of the Twentieth Century. In fall 1948 Antonio Regalado taught Spanish 30 with the same title but a new number, Spanish 122. The content of their courses couldn't have been that different from Grases'. Francisco García Lorca, Federico's brother, finished his Columbia Ph.D. in 1947 with a dissertation on Ganivet directed by Ángel del Río, and was invited to teach at Harvard during the Spring semester of 1948. One of the three courses he taught was Spanish 30, with the same title as López Morillas. It is hard to imagine that his brother's work would not be on the reading list.[44]

And then there was Amado Alonso, much praised by his graduate student Claudio Guillén.[45] Harvard hired Amado Alonso in 1946, possibly with the approval of Harry Levin, who would be officially asked in the 50s to oversee

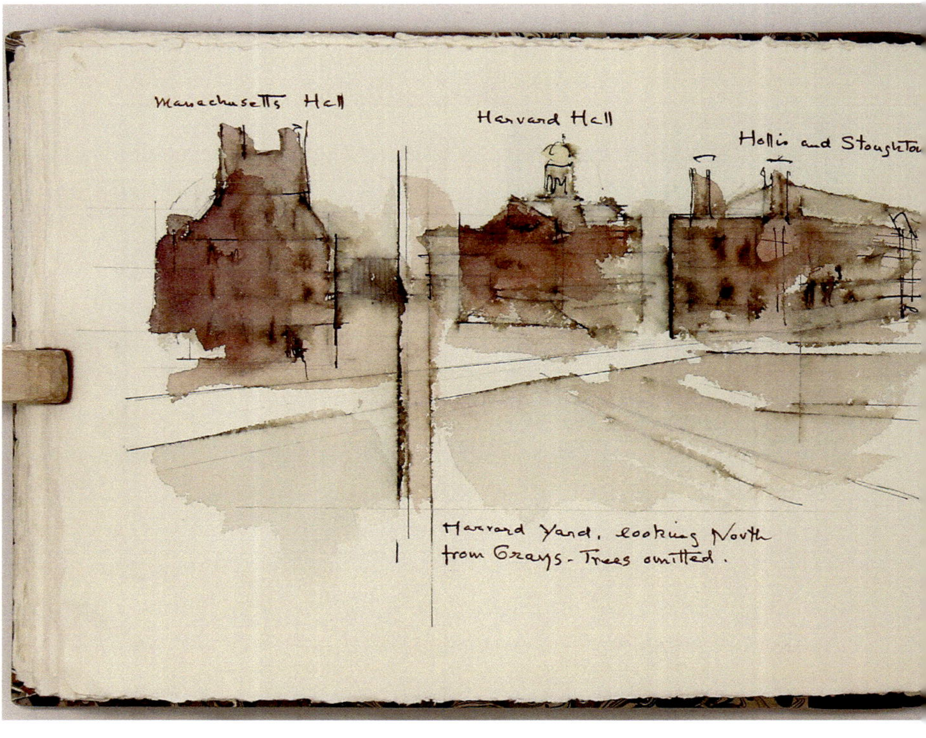

RLL searches and make sure that the newly-hired professors could bridge the theoretical gap between RLL and the other literature departments.[46] Amado Alonso's arrival seemed to inaugurate a new era in the Spanish section of RLL. In Spain and Latin America, Alonso had an extraordinary reputation as a modern linguist (he had translated and annotated Ferdinand de Saussure's *Cours de linguistique générale*), but he was also a skillful literary scholar with a modern (or modernist) approach, stylistics, a form of close reading not so different from that of New Criticism: "I. A. Richards y J. Middleton Murry, cuya crítica tiene estos caracteres que atribuimos a la estilística" (I.A. Richards and J. Middleton Murry, whose criticism has these features which we attribute to stylistics), Amado Alonso wrote to Alfonso Reyes on November 29, 1940.[47]

Alonso did not teach in the Core Humanities, probably because of the limitations of his spoken English. Most of his courses in the department were devoted to the history of the language and to the literature of the Golden Age; for

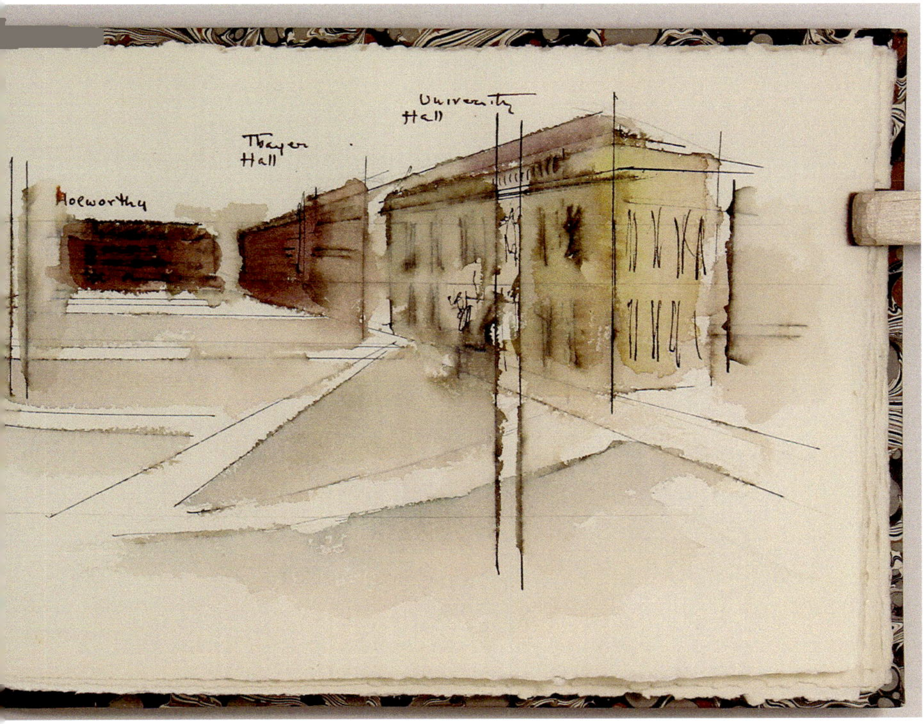

2.6 Zóbel, View of Harvard Yard from Sketchbook 83 (1976). Fundación Juan March.

example, his course entitled simply "Cervantes." However, in the Fall of 1941, when he was a visiting professor at the University of Chicago, he had taught a course on Modern Poetry in Spanish in which he analyzed works by Rubén Darío, Juan Ramón Jiménez, García Lorca and Pablo Neruda. In 1942 he lectured on García Lorca in different US universities. In a letter to Alonso, Jorge Guillén praises his lecture on "Llanto por la muerte de Ignacio Sánchez Mejías." "Studies in Lyric Poetry" was a graduate seminar Alonso offered at Harvard in spring 1947, but the catalog describes it only as "Intensive critical and stylistic analysis of the works of three major poets selected from the classical and modern periods." In the fall of that year one of his undergraduate courses was called The Reading and Interpretation of Poetry in Spanish; again, the catalog discloses neither the content nor the methodology of the course. Harvard's Lamont Library owns a recording of "Poems of Federico García Lorca read by Amado Alonso." Letters from friends and disciples—Ángel del Río, Pedro Salinas, Stephen Gilman, Jorge Guillén—repeatedly urged him to carry out a work on Lorca he had been planning for quite some time.[48] Alonso died prematurely in 1952 (he was 56) and he left no manuscript of such a work. In his publications, Lorca is not much more than a name mentioned regularly, often accompanied with quotations from his poetry.

As far as Harvard was concerned, whether Zóbel took any, all or none of those RLL courses was probably less relevant than the way or ways of reading (Lorca or any other writer) that he was expected to learn and practice in college. What were they? According to Prescott, concentrators in History and Literature aspired to write essays "in the manner of I. A. Richards."[49] It is not clear whether Zóbel ever studied with Richards; it is clear that in his senior thesis—elegantly written and organized, as Levin observed in his reader's report—Zóbel, like the New Critics, strives to treat literary works as autonomous and "self-contained" (Levin's word) artifacts.

He does not resort much to the kind of biographical, social, geographical, and historical context that his Spanish secondary sources deployed as a matter of course. However, what is generally missing in Zóbel's study is the examination of the internal relations that expose complexities and ambiguities in each work. New Critics would have searched Lorca's plays for words and images that worked together to produce and promote ambiguity. It was one of New Criticism's trademarks—"the inevitable ambiguity of almost all verbal formulae," in Richards' dictum[50]—, but it is not to be found in Zóbel's analysis, at least at the more explicit level. His "interpretation" (Levin's word again) is focused instead

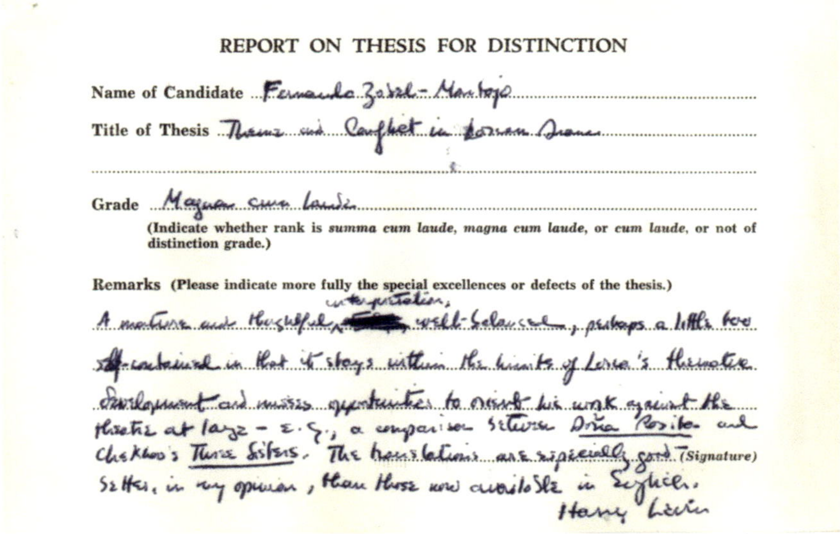

REPORT ON THESIS FOR DISTINCTION

Name of Candidate Fernando Zobel-Montojo

Title of Thesis Theme and Conflict in Lorcan Drama

Grade Magna cum laude

(Indicate whether rank is *summa cum laude*, *magna cum laude*, or *cum laude*, or not of distinction grade.)

Remarks (Please indicate more fully the special excellences or defects of the thesis.)

A mature and thoughtful interpretation, well-balanced, perhaps a little too self-contained in that it stays within the limits of Lorca's thematic development and misses opportunities to orient his work against the theatre at large – e.g., a comparison between Doña Rosita and Chekhov's Three Sisters. The translations are especially good – better, in my opinion, than those now available in English.

(Signature) Harry Levin

2.7 Harry Levin's report on Fernando Zóbel's senior honors thesis. Fundación Juan March, Madrid.

on an unambiguous notion of "conflict" —nature *versus* honor, mostly—that is part anthropology, part moral philosophy, and hardly ever the ambivalent result of an esthetic process.

Zóbel seems particularly concerned with one of the questions that the New Critics asked themselves: what makes a literary work good or bad in any degree? Zóbel makes value dependent primarily on the presence or absence of *humane* or life-like features in the characters: characters in good plays are "human beings" while characters in less accomplished plays are mostly abstractions, "something synthetic and not quite alive." Richards, in his *Practical Criticism*, dismisses this kind of response as based on "preconceptions" and "presuppositions" that the reader brings to the reading: they "hide what is actually present" in the literary work and the result is bound to be a misreading.[51]

Paraphrases of plots and descriptions of characters take up most of the space in Zóbel's thesis. Characters and plots were of interest to the new critics only insofar as the attributes of words, symbols, imagery and the like were mapped onto them. Zóbel hardly ever analyzes the language of the texts and he explicitly rejects stylistics; he allows himself just this kind of isolated statement: "In what we might call the stylistic line, evolution in Lorcan drama tends away from poetry and lyricism towards a prose style of great simplicity and strength."

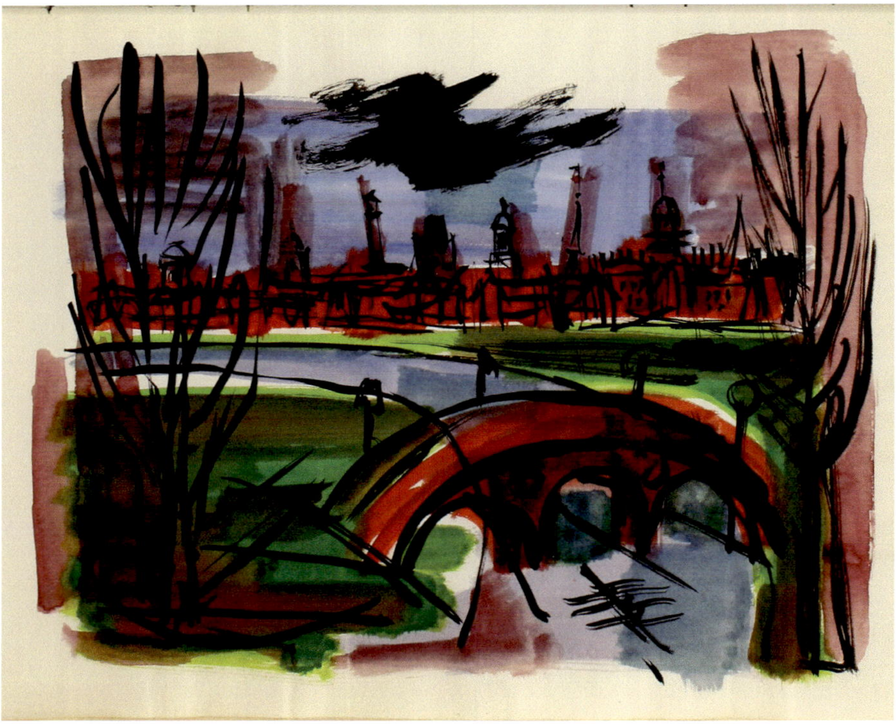

2.8 Fernando Zóbel, study for a painting of the Charles River (1954).

In his best (yet fleeting) moments Zóbel produces sharp close readings and quasi-formal analyses, as when he points out the relevance of "lo cursi" *in* (but not *of*) *Doña Rosita la soltera*, or when he identifies in passing the consistent contributions of the visual elements of the plays. But more often than not Zóbel did not deliver "cutting-edge critical scholarship," only a "critical resumé," as Poggioli defines it in his report. His approach appears largely co-opted by the traditional sensibility of his Spanish secondary sources (mainly Alfredo de la Guardia, whose method he never challenges), in detriment of the reading protocols that he might have learned in the English and Comp. Lit. departments.

Zóbel couldn't have been entirely pleased with the grades (*magna cum laude* and *cum laude*) that Levin and Poggioli gave his thesis, the crowning achievement of his studies; they fell short of the top grade he probably expected (*summa cum laude*). At the same time, he must have been aware that he had never quite mastered the art of writing an essay "in the manner of I. A. Richards," nor, for that matter, in the comparatist manner of Harry Levin (and Levin noted this flaw in his report). Overall, there is little doubt that Zóbel's education was somewhat undermined by the instability of Harvard's "experimental period." Simultaneously, though, it looks like Zóbel's own aristocratic predisposition, colonial hang-ups, and not-quite-conventional priorities conspired to create a certain resistance to some of Harvard's more fundamental demands and expectations.[52]

CHRISTOPHER MAURER

AMERICAN *PERLIMPLÍN*

No one can be quite sure what prompted the Spanish painter Fernando Zóbel to translate Lorca's one-act masterpiece about the power of the imagination and the fatal wounds of love: his "theater of human rag dolls, which begins in burlesque and ends in the tragic."

Unpublished until now, the translation doesn't seem to have been done for any performance in particular, and it is an open question why Zóbel would have preferred what he calls the "rococo humor," "bouncing rhythm," and "comic sensuality of style, décor and characterization" of *Amor de Don Perlimplín con Belisa en su jardín* to the better-known (in 1946) and much darker shades of, say, *Blood Wedding.*

On a deeper level, his motives seem clear. He once remarked that painting is play and explained that idea by quoting the rules of the game according to Desmond Morris:

> 1. You shall investigate the unfamiliar until it has become familiar. 2. You shall impose rhythmic repetition on the familiar. 3. You shall vary this repetition in as many ways as possible. 4. You shall select the most satisfying of these variations and develop these at the expense of others. 5. You shall combine and recombine these variations one with another. 6. You shall do all this for its own sake for an end in itself.[1]

Couldn't those words be directed, also, to a translator, intent on finding "the most satisfying" of variations on an original, combining and recombining them with one another? At its best, translation is always *that*—a hungry exploration of the unfamiliar until it has become familiar.

A number of Zóbel's paintings are "variations," and many are "dialogues" or "conversations" with the painters he found most interesting. His sketchbooks offer *his* part of the exchange: prolonged, attentive meditation on the work of others, through notes, drawings, and color—what he called "the passionate dialogue between painter and painting"—until he felt able to "translate" Rembrandt or Caravaggio, Rubens, Barroci, the landscape or the human body into a language all his own. He was a great reader of poetry, from classical Chinese and Japanese (where word and image come so closely together) to the poets of his own day, and he must have translated Lorca—into word and image—in order to know his language and his aesthetics more intimately. For a painter like Zóbel, translation, like the notes and drawings in his sketchbooks, was creative and recreative, a window into another mind, an enjoyable way of learning and remembering with his hands. In the sketchbooks, translation—both literal and metaphorical—takes a number of forms. On almost every page, paintings by others are "translated" into ink drawings and described verbally. Auden's famous poem on a Breughel painting is transcribed and commented on, along with the painting itself. Poems by Spanish poets like Miguel Hernández or Rafael Alberti are done into English and abstracted into sketches.[2] Even the *copying* of a poem—another form of learning—brought Zóbel closer to Richard Wilbur, flamenco lyrics or John Frederick Nims. Calligraphy and typography were, as Felipe Pereda points out, lifelong obsessions. Impressed with Chinese and Arabic calligraphy, Zóbel spoke of doing an "experiment" that would show the expressiveness of the Roman alphabet:

> probably just letters, but what letters! They must overflow, run over the page, grab the reader by the throat. For an experiment like this what works best is verse, especially verse full of color, like Lorca's. 'El Diván de la Tamarit' [sic]—the name alone is already a poem. It writes itself.[3]

In one of his sketchbooks, Zóbel crosses out the translation of a *waka* by Fijiwara no Toshiyuki and offers his own. Perhaps, in 1946, he was rebelling, as translators often do, against existing versions of Lorca; for example, the lackluster authorized translation, still in circulation today, of *The Love of Don Perlimp-*

lín and Belisa in the Garden by Richard L. O'Connell and James Graham-Lujan.[4] What seems certain is that his rendering of *Perlimplín in Love*—his close reading of a work revealing "Lorca's taste, originality and his vigorous style"[5] —started him down the path to his Harvard senior thesis (1949) on "Theme and Conflict in Lorcan Drama."[6]

One thing that must surely have attracted Zóbel to Lorca, and perhaps to *Perlimplín* in particular, was the poet's way of conjuring word, music, and image into a vision of total theater. Lorca often wanted his plays or his books of poetry to suggest a style peculiar to a visual or musical genre from an earlier historical period. For example, the wedding scene in *Bodas de sangre* (Blood Wedding) seems to have been suggested, in part, by a Bach cantata—a fact not lost on Zóbel[7]—, and the stage settings of Lorca's historical drama *Mariana Pineda*, designed in collaboration with Dalí, were meant to evoke a series of Romantic engravings. In a lecture, Lorca referred to his *Gypsy Ballads* as a *retablo* or reredos—one can imagine a Baroque altarpiece—and he styled *The House of Bernarda Alba* as a "documental fotográfico" (photographic documentary) in black and white. The poet Mario Hernández, author of an excellent book on Zóbel, once remarked that in any given work by Lorca, more than one stylistic suggestion is at play, and the poet's brother Francisco García Lorca observed that although Lorca's art begins with a concrete reality, it is "sometimes a reality at two removes."[8] *Perlimplin*, for example, suggests both an eighteenth-century aesthetic (its "rococo humor"[9] heightened by "frock coats, gowns, powdered wigs")[10] and—given its subtitle, *Aleluya erótica*—the world of the *aleluya*, a sort of comic strip typically printed on cheap colored paper, with crude engravings that narrate a story in images and rhyming octosyllabic couplets, one couplet to each of its 48 frames.[11]

Lorca's title is itself such a rhyming couplet:

> Amor de Don Perlimpl*ín*
> con Belisa en su jard*ín*.

By the time of Lorca's childhood, the *aleluya* was a genre of children's literature sold in different sorts of retail establishments or, like the broadside ballad, in public places: on streetcorners, in kiosks, at the fair, the bullfight, etc. Francisco García Lorca (1902-1976) remembers:

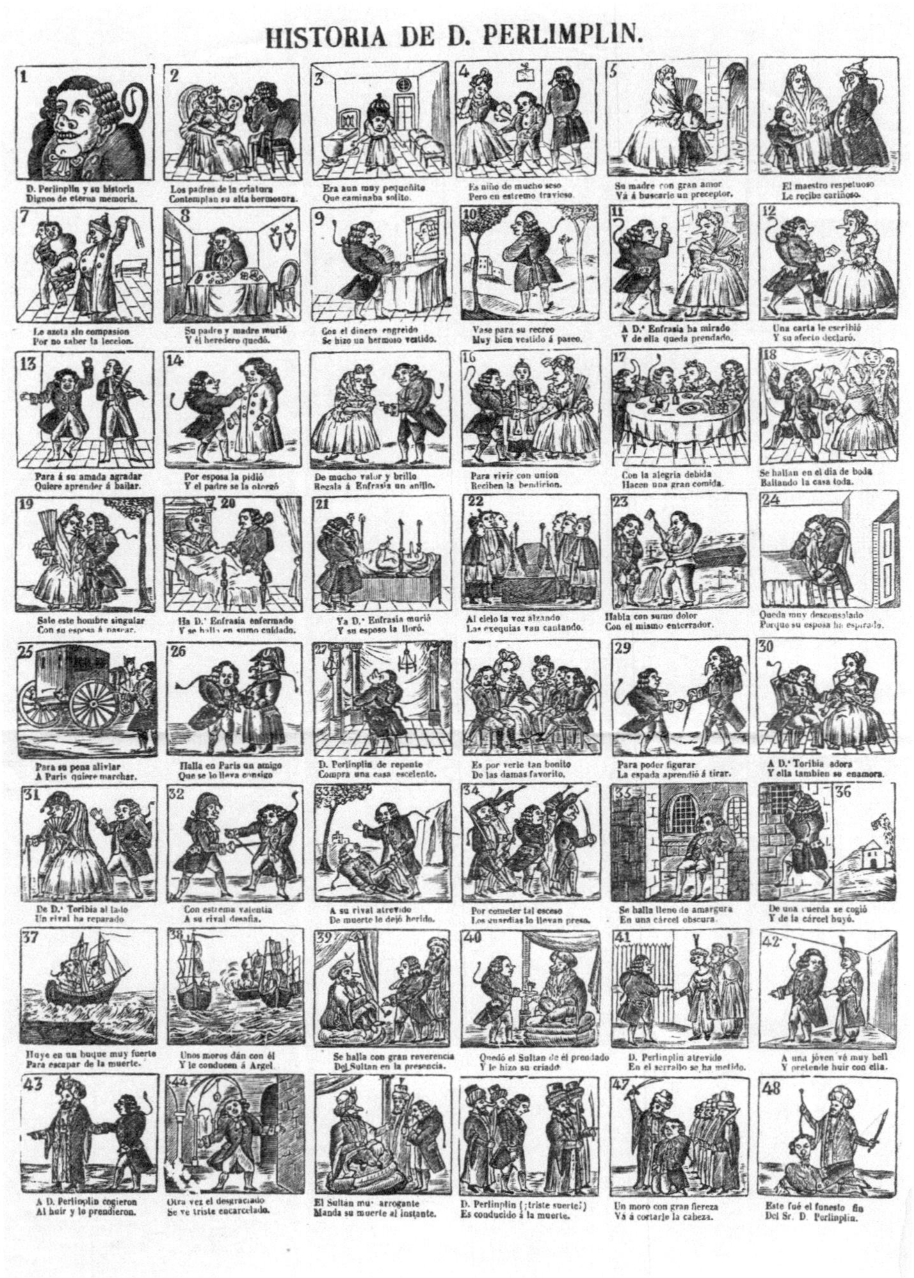

3.1 "Historia de D. Perlimplín." Nineteenth-century broadside. Private collection.

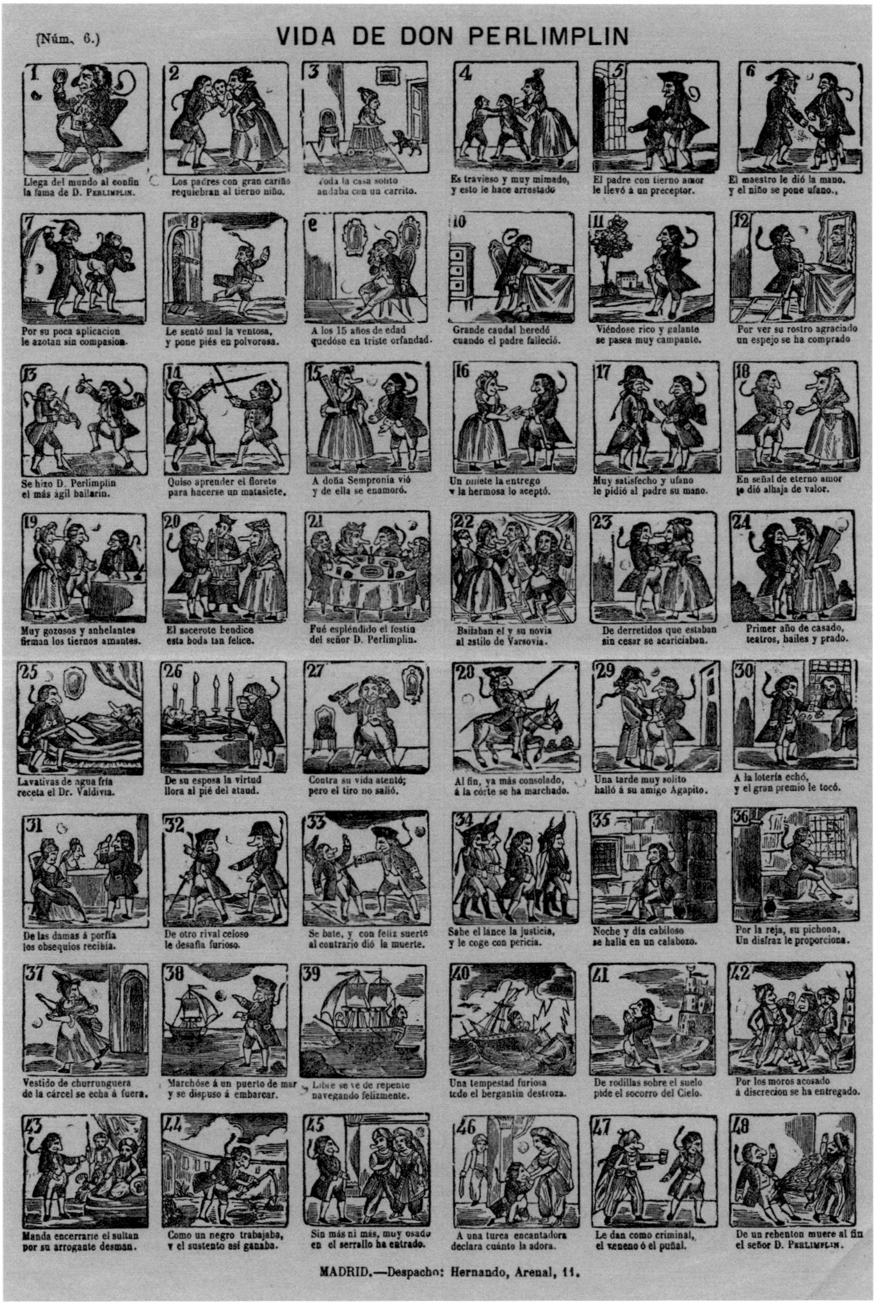

3.2 "Vida de Don Perlimplín." University of New Mexico Center for Southwest Research and Special Collections.

> When we were children (the custom I am about to describe has long since disappeared), one could buy large sheets of cheap, variously colored paper, each with a series of drawings (the oldest were wood engravings) making up a story. Each engraving was-explained by two lines of verse. These broadsides, which fulfilled more or less the same role as do modern-day comics, were called *aleluyas*. The word is now applied to the verses themselves. I remember the "aleluyas and misfortunes" of the tall man, the fat man and the "*Aleluya* of the Land of Milk and Honey."[12]

Cut up into their 48 little squares, *aleluyas* had sometimes been scattered from balconies during religious processions—during Carnaval, Holy Saturday or Corpus Christi processions, for example.[13] But by the early 20th century *aleluyas* with religious themes (for example, the lives of saints) mingled with the more mundane subjects mentioned by Lorca's brother: retellings of current events, *The Life of Don Crispin the Dwarf*, *The Wandering Jew*, the adventures of the bandit Jaime el Barbudo, the foibles of a hunchback, or comic-strip versions of *Don Quixote*, *Don Juan*, or the epic of the Cid.[14] The two versions of the *aleluya* featuring the life and death of Don Perlimplín (pronounced Per-leem-PLEEN), the plots of which are unrelated to that of Lorca, were popular enough to migrate from the broadsheet to the satirical press, children's books and magazines, and even, as a brain teaser, to the entertainment page of the daily newspaper, inviting the reader to combine these four verses in as many different ways as possible:

> El señor don Perlimplín
> vestido de emperador
> declamaba "el Trovador"
> en un teatro de Pekín.[15]

One venue that seemed improbable was music. In a 1910 essay ridiculing Richard Strauss's tone poem *Don Quixote* (which Lorca admired and defended), the musicologist Felipe Pedrell, whose compilation of Spanish folksong he knew practically by heart, warned that it was one small and dangerous step from such productions to something as ridiculous as putting to music "las *aleluyas* de Don Perlimplín."

Touches of the *aleluya* genre—this or that comical rhyme ("¡Don Perlimplín, / marido ruín!"), the mention of the "five races of man" who sleep with Belisa,[16] or the gilded horns worn by the cuckolded Perlimplín—find their way into the "sophisticated foreign air" of Lorca's play,[17] but the playwright was less interested in a story pulled this way or that by jingling rhyme printed on colored paper (which probably suggested the black and green contrasts of his play) than in the challenging tonal mix of the grotesque, the farcical, and the pathetic that emanated from the comic strip: the suggestive aesthetics of a popular, flat, *one-dimensional* artform whose coarse humor reminded Lorca of the puppet theater and other popular forms of children's entertainment.[18] "Un 'grotesco' muy atrevido"—a "rather daring 'grotesque'" (the noun, not the adjective)—is the way he describes *Perlimplín* in the theater section of a Madrid daily newspaper, and as Luis Fernández Cifuentes has shown, critics responded to that mix of the comic, the tragic and the grotesque with bewildered condescension.[19] By the time he began working on Perlimplín, Lorca had experimented with "teatro planista" (a "flat" or "planar" theater using cut-out figures),[20] and at another moment, he muses about a play based on photographic blowups. At least one rough draft of *Perlimplín* seems to have been intended for hand puppets.[21]

More than once during his life Lorca would take up the idea of a stylized popular art of constrained—one might say *flattened*—emotion. Like the poet Antonio Machado, whose poetry was steeped in traditional children's song, Lorca seems to have been struck by the idea of children giving voice to some of the more truculent stories and narrative ballads of the Spanish tradition as though blissfully unaware of what they were singing or hearing, or hearing it at an ironic emotional and temporal remove. In a note titled "Teatro de aleluyas," Lorca asks that the characters speak in something like flattened voices: "en un solo tono y tendrán un eco infantil" (in a monotone, with a childish ring)[22]. The stylization and flattening of tone and emotion were characteristic of the world of the traditional Spanish ballad, and when, in 1933-34, Lorca tried to choreograph some traditional ballads for the stage, he explained that he wanted to reduce their stories to a sort of "plastic algebra"

> What I am trying to do is get at the dramatic depths of the ballad, and set them in action. First of all, assign each line of verse to the proper voice, and then suggest the atmosphere [of the ballad] with lovely figures. This is an extremely stylized evocation

> with only the faintest indication of the action. A distant evocation, in which things are strangely transformed, in the manner of the Mass, which evokes the passion of Christ by means of his original words. This evocation ought to be based on slow movements and motionless faces... it ought to be the plastic algebra of a drama of passion and pain.[23]

For Lorca, the Mass and the *aleluya*—and, one might add, the farce—have a repetitive, ritual component which (as Fernández Cifuentes suggests) Lorca dared to break or interrupt or infuse with discordant poetic mystery.[24] A note titled "Historia de Perlimplín y Belisa en su jardín" (The Story of Perlimplín and Belisa in the Garden), written for an earlier version of the play, dwells on the aesthetics of the *aleluya* and speaks not of "algebra" but of "geometry." The story will be

> emphatically austere and inexpressive. It must appear to have a geometric character and the feeling of being told by children from centuries ago. It is our daily bread. It requires not human emotion, but emotion that is petrified, remote. The story must be gazed at like a frieze, taken in with the eyes. Its *most emotional* scenes will last only a second. The reader or viewer will always have a pitcher of cold water on his head. The beginning and ending will have the very same tension. And yet the effect should be terribly expressive and tragic. The life of the characters should appear to be tied to the rhythm of the world, and they will be seen tumbling to their destiny without being able to pull back. Their only fear is that the *aleluya* will end. The love scenes will have a keen sort of melancholy, but the characters will be unaware of it. The characters ought to be aware of nothing, only the audience. The drama should occur in the audience, not in the characters, who do not know they are being watched and who accept life unthinkingly, as it comes to them. They are part of the world. The spectator, on the other hand, should be fully aware of their passion and pain. The characters explain, without wanting to, what the audience is seeing. They are cold mathematical formulae, and the audience reads the problem they carry inside them. Emotion has to be produced with few elements.[25]

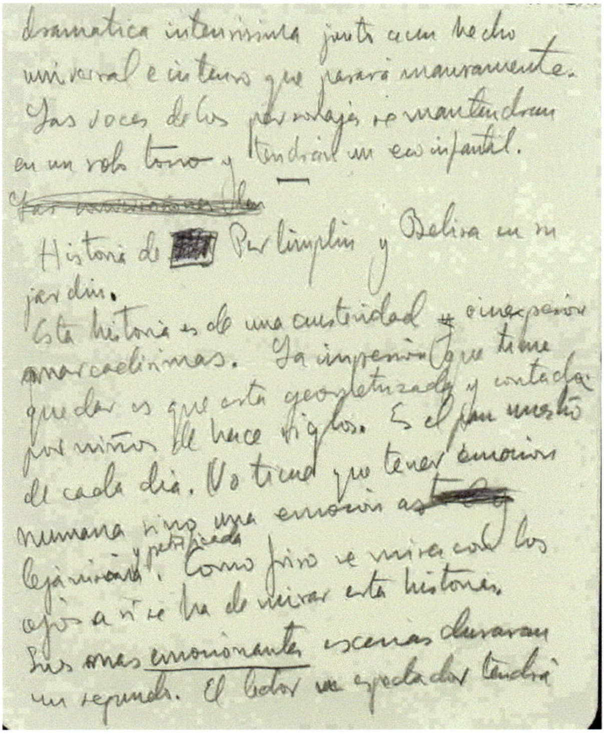

3.3 Manuscript of "Historia de Perlimplín y Belisa en su jardín." Centro Federico García Lorca, Granada.

Translators of the play into English struggled not only with the mix of tragedy and comedy but also with the aesthetic implications of the subtitle, *Aleluya erótica*. The misleading subtitle of the 1963 Graham-Luján/O'Connell translation, which survives even in recent productions of *Perlimplín*, sent viewers and reviewers in the wrong direction.[26] Although Graham-Lujan and O'Connell had subtitled the first edition of their translation (1941) "An Erotic Allelujah in Four Scenes," explaining vaguely and erroneously in a note that "*Aleluya* is the name of a particular kind of decorated papers with flowery couplets printed on them that are distributed among the people on certain festive days" (47), the second, revised edition of their translation, *Five Plays. Comedies and Tragicomedies* (New Directions, 1963), changed the subtitle—without explanation—to "An Erotic Lace-Paper Valentine in Four Scenes." This from a pair of translators who believed—correctly—that Lorca's subtitles were as important and "explicit as the instructions a musician affixes to his score." Lorca called *Perlimplín* an *aleluya* and *Yerma* a "Dramatic Poem" the way "Beethoven might say,

Sonata, quasi una fantasia—or [give] the more usual directions for tempo, mood or spirit—*allegro vivace, diminuendo, adagio sostenuto.*"[27]

Given the erroneously translated subtitle, it isn't surprising that an American production was timed to open on Valentine's Day or that a reviewer could praise Lorca's "tragi-comic vignette, written in the traceries of poetic language."[28] Even Francis Fergusson, the author of one of the best essays ever written on *Perlimplín*, who directed an early production in English, pointed the reader mistakenly toward a Hallmark card rather than a broadside ballad: "An *Aleluya* is something like a valentine; a love-poem decorated with pictures, gilt cut-outs, lace paper and the like: something heroic, overdone, absurd: an extravagant offering to the beloved."[29] Zóbel opted for something entirely different: "An Erotic Play With a Moral."

The "flatness" of the *aleluya*–the genuine one, not the "lace-paper Valentine"–shows up in certain details of Lorca's staging, which must have caught Zóbel's painterly eye—for example, the "flock of paper blackbirds"–probably cut-outs–that crosses the stage (p. 91), or the description of Perlimplín's dining room ("The perspective should be delightfully wrong, and the table should have all the objects painted on, as in a Primitive's 'Last Supper'") (p. 106). No doubt these elements of style changed as the play went through different iterations during Lorca's years of revision (1924-1933) and after his death, but they offer a clue to what he might have meant his subtitle to suggest. The *aleluya* offers a frame in which ritual farce can be transmuted into tragedy in the presence of theatrical archetypes (the clever servant, the mother who hopes to monetize her daughter's beauty, the old man with a young wife, the impossible love akin to Pierrot's) most frequently associated with the world of the *commedia dell'arte* or—in Spain—the *Interludes* of Cervantes.[30] Zóbel was aware of that heady mix, and not entirely convinced of Lorca's success. The play, whose theme, if "seriously handled might have been tragic," was "a light and amusing curtain-raiser, saved from being a pastiche of the *commedia dell'arte* only by Lorca's taste, originality and his vigorous style."[31]

Another element—music—bears out Hernández's remark about the density of stylistic suggestion. A notice in a Madrid newspaper[32] a few weeks before the 1933 premiere announces that in order to avoid "confusion" in "a certain sector of the public" that was "unprepared" for such a play, *Don Perlimplín* will be performed in a "chamber version, exclusively for minorities."[33] The subtitle "Versión de cámara" (chamber version or salon version) affixed to the 1933 Madrid premiere, besides signaling Lorca's intention to develop the play more

EN EL ESPAÑOL

FUNCION DE GALA EN HONOR DE GARCIA LORCA :-: :-: :-: :-:

REPOSICION DE "LA ZAPATERA PRODIGIOSA" Y ESTRENO DE "AMOR DE DON PERLIMPIN CON BELISA EN SU JARDIN", ALELUYA EROTICA EN CUATRO CUADROS

De mucho aliento ha de servirle al Club Teatral de Cultura Femenina la fortuna alcanzada anoche en su primera actuación. Merecido era el éxito feliz, como premio a la calidad del esfuerzo y recompensa a la limpia orientación que supone el haber dedicado la primera velada a destacar y honrar la firma de uno de nuestros mejores poetas jóvenes y su obra teatral, que ya cuenta varios intentos felices y algunas realidades venturosas; obra, en fin, suficiente para situar a Federico García Lorca en la primera linea—frente difícil de larga guerra—de nuestro teatro nuevo.

Nada necesitamos decir de la policroma alegría y la gracia fresca de "La zapatera prodigiosa", farsa violenta estrenada ya por la compañía de Margarita Xirgu con estilo que sirvió de norma a la interpretación de los aficionados del Club, especialmente a la que dió de la "apetitosa talabartera", Pilar de Barcarán. En halagüeña acogida la crítica habló ya de esa obra de Federico García Lorca en ocasión de su estreno.

La aleluya erótica que, como segunda parte del espectáculo de anoche, representó el Club de Cultura, es una obrilla en la que Lorca consigue dar valor musical a una fábula de marionetas, acercándose al tema doliente y dramático de los celos, doblado por la grotesca exaltación del cornudo, caudal de poesía dramática que va desde Shakespeare a Cromemlink y que en Cer-

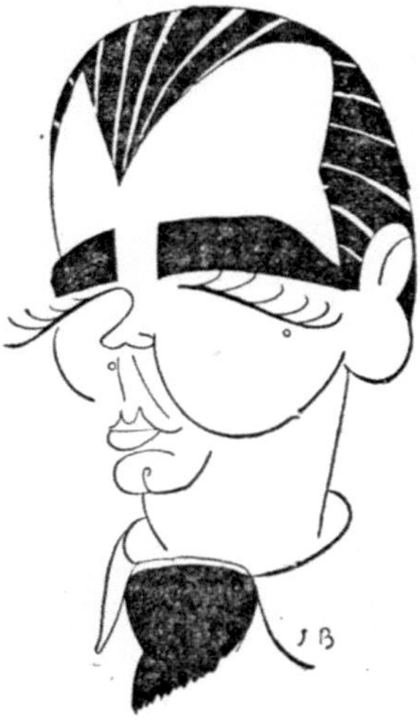

vantes alcanza, con igua ldoblez, la plenitud admirable de "El viejo celoso".

Ese valor musical de "Amor de don Perlimplín con Belisa en su jardín" no nace tan sólo, y externamente, de los comentarios metódicos de Scarlatti, sub-

3.4 From a review of the Madrid premier of *Amor de Don Perlimplín con Belisa en su jardín*, *Luz* (Madrid), April 6, 1933.

fully at a later date—and inadvertently inviting future directors to do so for him—reminds us of his brother Francisco's observation that perhaps "none of Lorca's plays shows with more poetic evidence the musical influence in his theatre. [...] The cast is reduced to four characters, who interweave their voices in a kind of concerto grosso for four instruments."[34] Lorca is said to have directed the pace and rhythm of the 1933 performance—the only one during his lifetime—while seated at the piano, and a reviewer write that "la farsa se desliza con la gracia alada de un minueto" (the farce glides along with the wingèd grace of a minuet).[35] For *Perlimplín*'s first translators—one of whom, Graham-Lujan, was an assistant to Lincoln Kirstein and a budding choreographer—Belisa's serenade (p. 115) had "much the same feeling as De Falla's suite for piano and orchestra called *Noches en los jardines de España*"; "a director would do well to think of the scene in terms of that music." For Nelson Orringer, the "musical

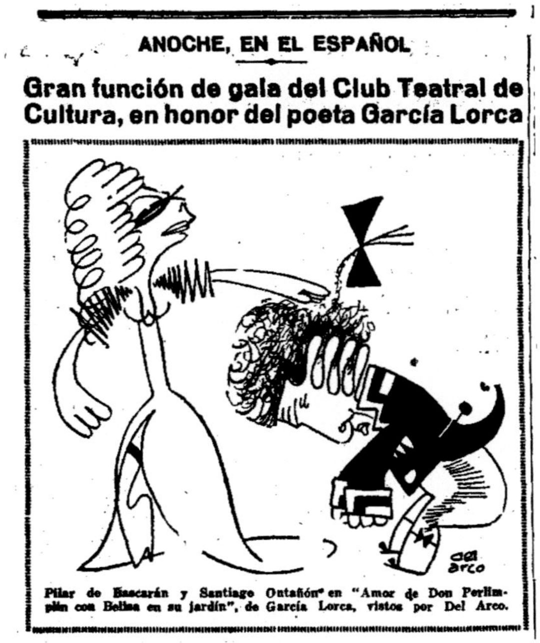

3.5 Cartoon by Del Arco on the occasion of the Madrid premiere of *Perlimplín*, *Heraldo de Madrid*, April 6, 1933.

structure" of *Perlimplín* "resembles the *Vivace* movement of Falla's *Harpsichord Concerto* (1923-6)," and for Luis T. González del Valle, it takes the form of a sonata.[36] The four principal rhythmic and musical voices mapped out by Francisco García Lorca had to harmonize, in 1933, with at least two other strands of music: the songs his brother composed to accompany the poems[37] and five sonatas by Scarlatti[38], played offstage by Pura Lago, a Galician pianist who was no stranger to the fusion of poetry and music.[39] On the eve of the April 1933 premiere, Lorca had told a journalist that his piece "rests on music, as in a little chamber opera. The brief moments between acts are tied together by Scarlatti sonatas," an indication that would orient a number of future directors and composers but would be ignored by others. Gwynne Edwards, one of Perlimplín's most careful translators, reports that, while Lorca's text "called for piano music in relation to Belisa's first appearance, for guitar music as an accompaniment to her sexual longing, and for the garden scene to be a serenade," Joan Littlewood's long-running (1945-1951) English production of the play had a different mix, wild "flamenco underpinning Belisa's eroticism, a grave pavane the dignity and seriousness of Perlimplín, and the music of Manuel de Falla, the tense drama of the final scene."[40] Zóbel himself was vividly aware of the musical properties of Lorca's theater. One of his diary entries, commented upon by Felipe Pereda (p. 32), recalls a conversation about *Bodas de sangre* (Blood Wedding) with one of his friends: "Le interesa la idea de componer una ópera. Discutimos como librito magnífico las 'Bodas de sangre': No solo temenos una gran obra literaria, sino que es un melodrama magnífico, hecho a medida. Lo único que le falta es música."[41] Zóbel uses the same word—melodrama—in his translation of *Perlimplín*, when Perlimplín informs Belisa she is "living in a melodrama" (*drama*, in Lorca's original.)

Like other translators of the play, Zóbel must have struggled to do justice to the lyrical passages sung by Perlimplín and Belisa. The 1941 translation by Graham-Lujan and O'Connell had left much to be desired in songs like this one:

Amor, amor.	Love, love
Entre mis muslos cerrados,	Enclosed within my thighs
nada como un pez el sol.	the sun swims like a fish.
Agua tibia entre los juncos,	Warm water in the rushes,
amor.	love,
¡Gallo, que se va la noche!	Morning cock, the night is going!
¡Que no se vaya, no!	Don't let it vanish, no! (p. 50)

Zóbel's translation seems more supple:

Love, love!
The sun swims like a fish
between my legs.
Warm water laps against the reeds.
Love...
Cockrel, see, the night is leaving!
Don't let it leave! Don't!

When New Directions revised and reissued the 1941 Graham-Lujan/O'Connell translation in 1963, for inclusion in *Five Plays by Lorca: Tragedies and Tragicomedies*, Wolfgang Sauerländer, an editor at the Bollingen Foundation and a "demon for details," was asked to work with Francisco García Lorca to vet the the translation for accuracy and resolve any discrepancies between the *Obras completas* published by Losada (beginning in 1938) and by Aguilar (beginning in 1954).[42] The songs received special attention, as noted by Robert M. MacGregor, New Directions' musically-minded editor in chief: "The [re] translation of the songs was done by me and [the poet] May Swenson, who was on our staff at the time, and [they] were published over the imprecations of O'Connell & Graham-Lujan, who felt that these were too 'modern.'"[43] The result of that collaboration was a more rhythmical—and singable—version.

> Ah love, ah love.
> Tight in my thighs imprisoned
> there swims like a fish the sun,
> warm water in the rushes.
> Ah love.
> Morning cock, the night is going!
> Don't let it vanish, no![44]

Given its musical intensity and rhythmic qualities it is no wonder that *Amor de Don Perlimplín* has given rise to a number of operas, ballets, and other musical adaptations,[45] in at least one of which—the opera by Bruno Maderna (1962)—a flute speaks for Perlimplín and, comically, a saxophone quartet speaks for Belisa's mother.[46]

A passing remark by the theater critic Frank Eng hints at what Lorca must have represented in the U.S.—at least to a knowledgeable theater critic in Los Angeles—when Zóbel was working on his translation and, a few years later, writing his honors thesis. Eng observes in 1947 that Lorca "has, to this point, been mostly a legend and an esoteric cult amongst the avant-garde in this country." The "Palm Springs climate of American tastes [has] something to do with" that neglect, although "why a public that readily accepts a *Wuthering Heights* with all its admitted rough-hewn qualities of style should consider Lorca's larger-than-life dimensions of tragedy outsize is a point we should like to belabor."[47]

A year earlier (1946), Eric Bentley had commented that it was still too early to predict Lorca's place in "the development of drama." He was

> the most gifted playwright of his generation, but the Falangists killed him before his art emerged from the "experimental stage." (Even so, his "experiments" are riper than the "masterpieces" of our acknowledged and anthologized dramatists.)[48]

In Boston, in circles frequented by Zóbel, Lorca's presence on stage was confined to amateur or student theater groups. Reviewing a 1943 student production of *Doña Rosita la soltera* (Doña Rosita the Spinster) at Harvard University a critic remarks that Lorca "is not a complete stranger to the stage in Cambridge": his *Shoemaker's Prodigious Wife* had been presented a season earlier by the Harvard Dramatic Club.[49] In the United States, in the 1940s, among those who could read him only in English, Lorca's posthumous fame often rested less upon his work than upon his assassination in the early days of the Spanish Civil War, and it still seemed difficult to reconcile the "surrealistic" Lorca of *Poet in New York* (published in English in 1940), the Lorca of "folk dramas" like *Blood Wedding*, and the author of a farce like *Perlimplín*, who has "delicately woven together the lyrical and the grotesque, cruelty and tenderness, the world of the flesh and that of the spirit."[50] Reviewing a production of *Perlimplín* by a little theater group in Oakland in 1947, a disoriented and exasperated Theresa Loeb found it "merely an incomprehensible, jumbled string of scenic bits strung together sans much point."[51] Not so, the British-American actor and producer John Houseman and his Pelican Productions, a Los Angeles theatre troupe rumored in 1947 to be planning to stage *Perlimplín* after success with Sartre's *No Exit*, Brecht's *Galileo*, and Thornton Wilder's *The Skin of Our Teeth*. Eng, whose partner was the dancer and choreographer Lester Horton and who was in a position to know, had heard not only that Pelican was going to stage *Perlimplín* but also that "George Balanchine [was] being sought to choreograph a 20-minute ballet sequence to fill out the running time on this almost full-length one-acter."[52] In the end, the group decided not on *Amor de Don Perlimplín con Belisa en su jardín* ("a titular mouthful")[53] but on *The House of Bernarda Alba*, which opened on November 13, 1947, directed by the Hollywood character actor Vladimir Sokoloff (a disciple of Reinhart and Stanislavski who had learned about Lorca through his work with Orson Welles' Mercury Theatre), with a score by Darius Milhaud. The event was billed as "the American premiere" of *Bernarda Alba*, and it looked for a while as though García Lorca might be headed from amateur or semi-professional stages back to Broadway, where a floridly translated *Bodas de sangre* had failed a decade earlier.[54] Interest in *Don Perlimplín* was growing. In May 1948, the Century Theater Group—a little-theater start-up backed by Frank Capra, Bing Crosby, Bette Davis, Clark Gable and others—made plans to stage the play with "lucious" Austrian actress Lenore Aubert in the role of Belisa, only to see her pulled, instead, into *Abbot and Costello Meet Frankinstein*.[55]

Whether in Madrid, in Hollywood or in amateur productions in the U.S. *Amor de Don Perlimplín con Belisa en su jardín* drew part of its meaning not only from audience expectations based on Lorca's "rural tragedies"[56] and from some ferocious stereotypes about the Spanish spirit (one American actress is said to go "shrieking and striding through [Belisa's] part with delightful Latin abandon")[57] but also from the pieces that Lorca's "lusty folk farce"[58] happened to be paired with on the American stage. Too short to provide an entire evening of theater, *Perlimplín* was occasionally coupled with and compared to (as in Lorca's own 1933 production) his other "violent farce," *The Shoemaker's Prodigious Wife*.[59] Over the years, however, *Perlimplín* has had much stranger bedfellows and as many as two at a time: *Lord Byron's Love Letter* by Tennessee Williams, Sean O'Casey's *Bedtime Story*, Synge's *The Tinker's Wedding* (billed as a "folk comedy"), Strindberg's *The Stranger*, e.e. cummings' *Santa Claus*, Chekhov's *On the Harmful Effects of Tobacco* and *The Proposal*, James Broughton's *The Last Word*, Molière's *The Flying Doctor*. In 1979, Frank Lenton's Philadelphia Puppet Theater presented "two off-color Spanish classics," warning that neither was recommended for children: Miguel de Cervantes' *Hook-Nosed Sentinel* (probably *La guarda cuidadosa*) and Lorca's *Perlimplín*.[60] In that checkered company, American reviewers of the 1940s and 50s puzzled over the play's Freudian, moralistic, or allegorical "message." As early as 1944, a Hispanic theatre troupe in Albuquerque included *Perlimplín* in a repertoire meant to show "how Hispanics deal with love and intimacy."[61] For another reviewer, *Perlimplín* was "a horrifying tale of the excesses to which repressed sexuality inevitably drives mankind."[62] Another rooted out a different moral: "in the cracked shell of age, there is always the heart of youth, the ardent, adolescent face of love."[63] When Joan Littlewood's theater company incorporated Perlimplín into its repertory in Liverpool in 1945 (a year before Zóbel's translation), it caused "frenzied controversy." And when the British actress and director staged the play in 1949 at the Library Theatre in Manchester, England, a disgruntled critic pronounced it "as unpleasant a piece as has been seen for a long time on a Manchester stage." If the theater had had a gallery, and had it been full, "the gallery would surely have given [Lorca's] piece a proper greeting, and indeed the only one—the bird."[64] Gwynne Edwards quotes the actor (Howard Goorney) who played the cuckolded Perimplín in that production:

> Some were so disgusted they crossed the street to avoid me . . . .
> I suppose it's not surprising that in that time and place some

> people were disturbed by an old man's obsession for a woman young enough to be his daughter.[65]

In an angry response to the review, Littlewood—a leading figure in British theater—acknowledged that her production of *Perlimplín* had "shocked some of our audiences in Britain," but in a salutary way:

> We have got used to the prose plays of Ibsen and of Shaw which shocked our fathers: Lorca's subtle shafts of poetry disturb our minds rather than our morals. Surely the first impact of any work of art is disturbing and even destructive: we must risk this "unpleasantness" if our culture is not to atrophy.[66]

Lorca's –and *Perlimplín*'s—fortunes in the United States of the 40s and 50s were favored not only by the *Three Tragedies* (1947) and *Selected Poems* (1955) published by New Directions, by Ben Belitt's bold retranslation of *Poet in New York* (1955), and by a couple of key anthologies (e.g., Eric Bentley's *From the Modern Repertoire,* 1949); they were also carried along on the current of music mentioned earlier. As Lorca's brother Francisco once observed, "to Federico words and music were practically the same thing."[67] In Boston or New York, Chicago or San Francisco, audiences might hear and see Lorca choreographed, danced, recited or sung by Doris Humphrey, Valerie Bettis, Pilar López and La Argentinita, Rosario and Antonio, or José Limón. Concerts based on Lorca poems were given at the MoMA in 1941, and Paul Bowles' zarzuela inspired by *Así que pasen cinco años, The Wind Remains,* was staged there in March 1943, choreographed by Merce Cunningham and directed by Leonard Bernstein.[68] A year later, the Ballet Russe de Monte Carlo put on *The Cuckold's Fair,* based on Lorca's *Yerma*.[69] For reasons already mentioned, *Amor de Don Perlimplín,* even in translation, is a work that has always begged for musical adaptation. In 1952, Chicago audiences saw the premiere of Vittorio Rieti's *Don Perlimplin: opera in un prologo e tre quadri,* the first in a long line of musical adaptations extending into our own century.[70] The following year—1953—jazz pianist and composer Billy Strayhorn composed music for a version by the Artists' Theatre in which he hoped to celebrate "black and gay pride."[71] But over the years—between 1959, when New Directions began serving as agents for the Lorca family and 1984, when that arrangement came to an end—requests to create additional versions of *Don Perlimplín* as opera and ballet became frequent enough to constitute a nuisance. By September 1974, MacGregor was writing to Lorca's brother Francisco that "one of the Lorca works that is most attractive to composers (and I must admit it seems a natural for an opera) is *The Love of Don Perlimplín,* and we have turned down flatly a good many composers' requests to do it." He adds that "there is today an enormous amount of activity of people composing operas at least in this country. Part of it is the assignments of professors in universities and graduate schools of music, and we get many requests from students who want to do García Lorca plays as operas for their M.A. and Ph.D. theses. We turn all of these down"[72] in the knowledge that opera contracts were far more complex than book contracts, that such projects were seldom successful, and that a slew of amateur projects would lessen the chances that a play like *Perlimplín* would be produced in a major venue like the Metropolitan Opera. What Lorca—and after him, Fernando Zóbel—had envisioned as an intimate "chamber version" was being reserved for a larger stage.

ABOUT THE TRANSLATION

Zóbel based his "Free Translation" on the text of *Amor de Don Perlimplín con Belisa en su jardín* in volume 1 of Lorca's *Obras completas* collected and edited by the Spanish critic Guillermo de Torre for the publishing house Editorial Losada, Buenos Aires. When that multi-volume *Complete Works* first appeared in October 1938, the Spanish Civil War was raging, the personal archive left by the recently assassinated poet was inaccessible, and, for the text of Lorca's plays, Torre had to rely on copies lent to him by the actress Margarita Xirgu and others. Unauthorized versions of some of Lorca's plays—including texts taken down by ear by audience members—were being published in Spanish America, and Torre made do with the best material at hand. The text of *Amor de Don Perlimplín* published in 1938 and in subsequent editions of the *Obras completas* (1940. 1942, 1944, 1946) was based on an uncorrected, blurry, sometimes illegible carbon copy made in Madrid in 1933 and contains misprints and copyists' errors that seriously altered the meaning of certain lines: "está herido" (*he is* wounded) rather than "estoy herido" (*I am* wounded); "una luz *lógica*" (a *logical* light) instead of "una luz *mágica*" (a *magical* light), etc. The Losada edition divides the play—mistakenly dated 1931—into a "Prólogo" and an "Acto Único" (single act) in three "Cuadros" (scenes), whereas the definitive arrangement is simply "Aleluya erótica en cuatro cuadros" (Ucelay, 251).

Many such errors were detected by Arturo del Hoyo, editor of the first edition of the *Obras completas* allowed to be published in Francoist Spain (Madrid: Aguilar, 1954). Del Hoyo's edition was itself corrected four decades later in a splendid critical edition and introduction (Madrid: Cátedra, 1990) by Margarita Ucelay, who had access not only to all of the extant manuscripts from the Lorca family archives but also to the archive and memories of her mother, Pura Maortua de Ucelay, including the manuscript Pura had retrieved from government censors in preparation for the 1933 Madrid premiere by her amateur theater group, the Club Teatral de Cultura, which Lorca had nicknamed "Anfistora" (see the "Chronology," below). Recent editors and translators have followed the version established by Ucelay, who edited the Spanish text with the utmost care, listing pertinent variants.

There would be no point in reproducing in this book either the inaccurate Losada version (the one used by Zóbel) or Ucelay's corrected text, which would be out of synch with the translation. Instead, in the pages that follow, occasional footnotes indicate where the faulty Losada text led Zóbel astray. I have also indicated passages which Zóbel translated differently in his honors thesis ("Theme and Conflict in Lorcan Drama") and in his translation of the play. Zóbel labeled his version—quite accurately—a "Free Translation," and was probably aware that, for performance, it would need to be revised and adapted. It is presented here not as the best possible translation of *Amor de Don Perlimplín,* but as the verbal and visual homage of one of Spain's most important painters to its most beloved poet.

—C.M.

FEDERICO GARCÍA LORCA

DON PERLIMPLÍN IN LOVE

AMOR DE DON PERLIMPLÍN CON BELISA EN SU JARDÍN

An Erotic Play with a Moral, in Three Scenes
(1931)

A Free Translation from the Spanish Original
By Fernando Zóbel-Montojo
1946[1]

1. Houghton Library, Harvard University, MS Typ 688, (2). TS. with MS. annotation; 1946. 30 sheets

CAST

DON PERLIMPLÍN

BELISA

MARCOLFA

BELISA'S MOTHER

FIRST GOBLIN

SECOND GOBLIN

PROLOGUE

Don Perlimplín's house. Green walls; chairs and furniture painted black. Backstage, an open balcony, from which Belisa's window may be seen.

Perlimplín wears a green cassock and a curly white wig. His maid, Marcolfa, is dressed in a striped servant's smock.

PERLIMPLÍN

Yes?

MARCOLFA

Yes.

PERLIMPLÍN

But why?

MARCOLFA

Because.

PERLIMPLÍN

What if I should refuse?

MARCOLFA

Refuse?

PERLIMPLÍN

Yes, refuse.

MARCOLFA

And tell me, sir, why should you refuse?

PERLIMPLÍN

Tell me then, O insistent menial, why I shouldn't.

MARCOLFA

Twenty and twenty make forty...

PERLIMPLÍN (*Attentively*)

Go on.

MARCOLFA

Plus ten makes fifty.

PERLIMPLÍN

Well?

MARCOLFA

At the age of fifty one can hardly be called a child.

PERLIMPLÍN

Obviously.

MARCOLFA

I may die any minute.

PERLIMPLÍN

Naturally.

MARCOLFA (*Weeping*)

And what will become of you, all by yourself?

PERLIMPLÍN

That's true.

MARCOLFA

That is why you should marry.

PERLIMPLÍN (*Absent-mindedly*)

Yes?

MARCOLFA

Yes.

PERLIMPLÍN (*Uneasily*)

But Marcolfa...why should I? I can remember that while I was a little boy a woman strangled her husband. He was a shoemaker. I can't get it out of my mind. I have never thought of getting married. I have quite enough with my books. What can I possibly get out of marriage?

MARCOLFA

Marriage, sir, has great possibilities. It is not at all what it seems to be at first sight. It is full of hidden things. Things that should not be discussed by a servant...there, you see...

PERLIMPLÍN

What?

MARCOLFA

I am blushing.

(*Pause. A piano is heard. Then* Belisa's *voice, from within, singing.*)

Love, love!
The sun swims like a fish
Between my legs.
Warm water laps against the reeds.
Love...
Cockrel, see, the night is leaving!
Don't let it leave! Don't!

MARCOLFA

Do you see what I mean?

PERLIMPLÍN (*Scratching his head*)

She sings well enough.

MARCOLFA

There is a woman for my master, the pale Belisa.

PERLIMPLÍN

Belisa... wouldn't it be better if...

MARCOLFA

No, follow me

(*Grasps his hand and leads him to the balcony.*)

Say "Belisa"!

PERLIMPLÍN

Belisa.

MARCOLFA

Louder.

PERLIMPLÍN

Belisa!

(Belisa's *balcony opens; she appears, half naked, radiantly beautiful*)

BELISA

Who calls?

(Marcolfa *hides behind a curtain.*)

MARCOLFA

Answer her.

PERLIMPLÍN (*Trembling*)

I called.

BELISA

Really?

PERLIMPLÍN

Yes, really.

BELISA

But, why?

PERLIMPLÍN

Because.

BELISA

And what if I shouldn't believe you?

PERLIMPLÍN

Well, I'd be sorry. . .because. . .we have decided that I want to get married.

BELISA

To whom?

PERLIMPLÍN

To you.

BELISA

But… (*screams*) Mother, Mother, Mamma!

MARCOLFA

All goes well.

(*The* Mother *appears.* She *wears a gigantic Rococo wig, full of birds and ribbons and rhinestones.*)

BELISA

Don Perlimplín wants to marry me. What shall I do?

MOTHER

Ah, good afternoon, my dear little neighbor. I have always told my daughter that you combine the charm and manners of that great lady, your Mother, whose acquaintance, I am sorry to say, I never had the honor of making.

PERLIMPLÍN

Thank you.

MARCOLFA (*Furiously, from behind the curtain*)

We have decided to...

PERLIMPLÍN

We have decided to.

MOTHER

To get married, no?

PERLIMPLÍN

That is right.

BELISA

But Mother, how about me?

MOTHER

You, of course, are delighted. Don Perlimplín will make you a charming husband.

PERLIMPLÍN

This is my fondest desire, Madam.

MARCOLFA (*Calling Don Perlimplín*)

This is almost over.

PERLIMPLÍN

Really? (*They speak together.*)

MOTHER (*To Belisa*)

Don Perlimplín has many estates. On those estates grow many geese and sheep. The sheep are sent to market. In the market they are exchanged for money. With money you can buy beauty. And other men are always searching for beauty.

BELISA

And?

MOTHER (*Emotionally*)

Belisa, go to your room... There are certain things not fit for the ears of a young lady.

BELISA

Good afternoon.

(*She leaves.*)

MOTHER

She is like a lily. Have you noticed her face? (*She lowers her voice.*) Then you should see the rest!...Like sugar... But... pardon me... How could I speak of such things to such a competent and modern gentleman?

PERLIMPLÍN

Eh?

MOTHER

Yes... I meant no sarcasm.

PERLIMPLÍN

How can I express our gratitude?

MOTHER

"Our gratitude"... what delicacy! Your heart's gratitude as well as your own, of course... I understood immediately... immediately... despite the fact that I have not dealt with men in over twenty years.

MARCOLFA (*Aside*)

The wedding.

PERLIMPLÍN

The wedding...

MOTHER

Oh, as soon as you wish... though, naturally, (*Takes out a handkerchief and weeps*) for a mother... good evening.

(*Leaves.*)

MARCOLFA

At last.

PERLIMPLÍN

Marcolfa, what are you getting me into?

MARCOLFA

Marriage, of course.

PERLIMPLÍN

To be frank, I feel dreadfully parched. Why don't you fetch me some water?

(Marcolfa *approaches and whispers into his ear.*)

Really?

(*The piano is heard again. The theatre gradually grows dim.* Belisa *throws back her curtains, and begins to sing languidly. She is almost naked.*)

Love, love!
The sun swims like a fish
Between my legs.

MARCOLFA

Delightful girl.

PERLIMPLÍN

Like sugar... white inside. Can she strangle me?

MARCOLFA

Woman is weak if frightened in time.

BELISA

Love...
Cockrel, see, the night is leaving!
Don't let it leave! Don't!

PERLIMPLÍN

What is she saying, Marcolfa?

(Marcolfa *laughs*)

What is happening to me? What is this?

(*The piano plays on. A flock of paper blackbirds cross the balcony.*)

CURTAIN

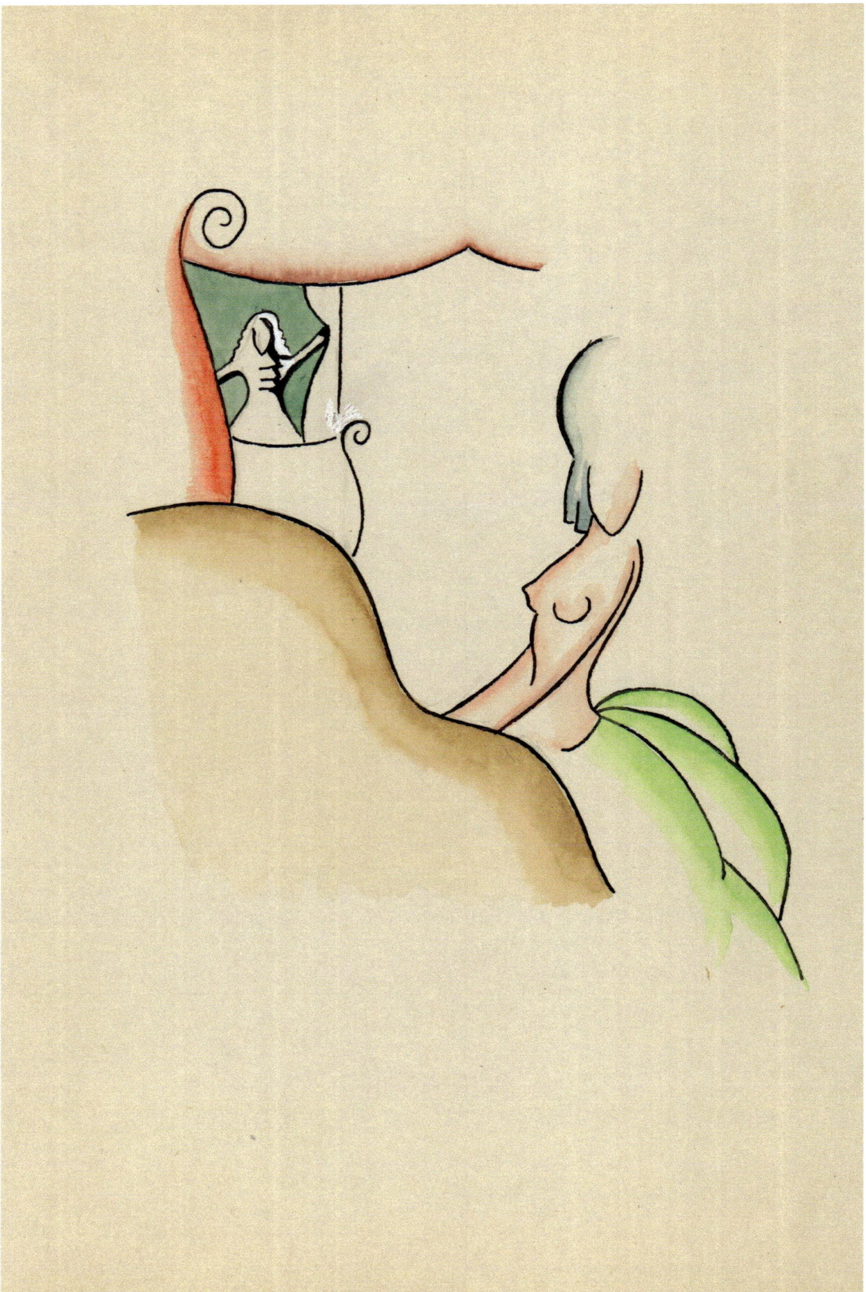

4.1 Fernando Zóbel, illustration for *Don Perlimplín in Love*.
Houghton Library, Harvard University.

SCENE I

Don Perlimplín's living-room. In the center stands a great canopied bed, adorned with flowers and feathers. There are six doors on the rear wall. The first one to the right is used by Perlimplín for his entries and exits. The scene takes place on the wedding night.

(Marcolfa, *holding a candlestick, stands before the first door to the left.*)

MARCOLFA

Good night.

BELISA (*From within*)

Good-bye, Marcolfa.

(Perlimplín *appears, magnificently dressed.*)

MARCOLFA

May you have a pleasant honeymoon, sir.

PERLIMPLÍN

Good-bye, Marcolfa.

(*She leaves.* Perlimplín *tiptoes towards the next room and peeps through the doorway.*)

PERLIMPLÍN

Belisa, in your lace you look like a wave. You frighten me in the same way the sea frightened me as a child. You have brought a strange secret restlessness into my house, and water grows warm in my tumblers before your presence. Alas! Perlimplín, where are you heading? Where are you heading, indeed, Perlimplín?

(*He tiptoes away.* Belisa *appears in a fantastic lace nightgown. Her hair falls loose about her shoulders and her arms are bare.*)[2]

BELISA

That woman has been spraying anisette instead of verbena, like I told her... (*goes towards the bed*)... and she hasn't spread the fine linen either.

(*At this moment we hear the soft music of a guitar.* Belisa *crosses her hands over her breasts.*)

---

2. The Ucelay text, p. 261 (U 261) adds information: "*Una cofia inmensa le cubre la cabeza y lanza una cascada de puntillas y entredoses hasta sus pies*" (A huge coif covers her head and sends a cascade of embroidered lace down to her very feet.)

BELISA

Aie! Search ardently and [you] will find me. My thirst is endless; endless like the thirst of gargoyles in fountains.

(*The music continues.*)

That music, oh Lord! That music! Warm like the feathers of the swan... Aie... is it me or the music?

(*She throws on a red velvet cloak and walks to and fro across the room. The music stops, followed by five whistles.*)

BELISA

Five!

(Perlimplín *appears*)

PERLIMPLÍN

Am I in the way?

BELISA

Heavens! Of course not.

PERLIMPLÍN

Are you sleepy?

BELISA

Sleepy?

PERLIMPLÍN

The night is growing cold.

(*Rubs his hands together. Pause in the conversation.*)

BELISA (*With decision*)

Perlimplín.

PERLIMPLÍN (*Trembling*)

What is it?

BELISA (*Vaguely*)

A nice name that, Perlimplín...

PERLIMPLÍN

Yours is much nicer, Belisa.

BELISA (*Laughing*)

Oh, thank you.

(*Short pause*)

PERLIMPLÍN

I want to tell you something.

BELISA

What?

PERLIMPLÍN

It took me some time to make up my mind. . .but now. . .

BELISA

Yes?

PERLIMPLÍN

Belisa. . . I love you!

BELISA

That is your duty, hubby!

PERLIMPLÍN

Yes?

BELISA

Yes.

PERLIMPLÍN

Why?

BELISA

Because

PERLIMPLÍN

But why "Because"?

BELISA (*Coyly*)

Because of course...

PERLIMPLÍN

No.

BELISA

Perlimplín!

PERLIMPLÍN

No, Belisa. I did not love you till I married you.

BELISA (*Jokingly*)

What are you saying?

PERLIMPLÍN

I married you in order to . . . well, never mind; but I didn't love you. I couldn't picture your body. When I saw you through the keyhole, trying on your bridal dress—then I knew I was in love! Then and only then! It was like a knife piercing my throat.

BELISA (*Intrigued*)

But. . . how about the other women.

PERLIMPLÍN

Other women?

BELISA

Yes; the women you've had before.

PERLIMPLÍN

But are there other women?

BELISA[3]

You surprise me.

PERLIMPLÍN

Hardly; I am the surprised one.

(*Pause. Five whistles are heard.*)

PERLIMPLÍN

What was that?

BELISA

The clock.

---

3. *U* 263: *Levantándose* (getting up)

PERLIMPLÍN

Can it be five?

BELISA

Time to go to sleep.

PERLIMPLÍN

May I remove my coat?

BELISA

Of course, (*yawns*) honey. Shut the light, please.

Perlimplín (*Shuts the light. Whispers.*)

Belisa.

BELISA (*Loudly*)

What, darling?

PERLIMPLÍN (*Whispers*)

I've shut the light.

BELISA (*Amused*)

So I notice.

PERLIMPLÍN (*Very low whisper*)

Belisa...

BELISA (*Loudly*)

What, my love?

PERLIMPLÍN

I adore you!

(*Two goblins appear from opposite ends of the stage and draw a grey curtain across it. The theater falls into a kind of twilight. Flutes play a dreamy air.* The goblins *should be played by little boys. They sit on the prompter's box, facing the audience.*)

GOBLIN 1

How goes it, friend

GOBLIN 2

So-so, cousin.

GOBLIN I

Well, here we are.

GOBLIN 2

Yes; and what do you think? Isn't it nice to cover up someone else's misfortune?

GOBLIN I

Of course. And the audience can have the fun of finding out later on.

GOBLIN 2

For if sins are not carefully hidden...

GOBLIN I

They can never be discovered.

GOBLIN 2

And what of the lower middle classes...

GOBLIN I

With nothing hidden to discover?

GOBLIN 2 (*Looking at the curtain*)

We mustn't leave a single crack.

GOBLIN I

Today's keyholes become tomorrow's mystery.

(*They laugh.*)

GOBLIN 2

When things are done out in the open...

GOBLIN I

Man never finds them worth his notice.

GOBLIN 2

And off he trots towards the mists, to find what he already knew.

GOBLIN I

That's why we are here. Nothing like Goblins!

GOBLIN 2

Did you know Perlimplín?

GOBLIN 1

From childhood.

GOBLIN 2

And Belisa?

GOBLIN 1

Oh, I know her very well. Her room was so thick with perfume that once I feel asleep and woke up between the paws of her cat.

(*They laugh.*)

GOBLIN 2

This whole business...

GOBLIN 1

It's very obvious, to say the least.

GOBLIN 2

Everyone saw it coming.

GOBLIN 1

Gossip might want to pick a more mysterious subject.

GOBLIN 2

When things are done out in the open...

GOBLIN 1

Man never finds them worth his notice.

GOBLIN 2

And off he trots towards the mists, to find out what he already knew.

GOBLIN 1

That's why we are here. Nothing like Goblins!

GOBLIN 2

Did you know Perlimplín?

GOBLIN 1

From childhood.

GOBLIN 2

And Belisa?

GOBLIN 1

Oh, I know her very well. Her room was so thick with perfume that once I fell asleep and woke up between the paws of her cat.

(They laugh.)

GOBLIN 2

True. We must keep it as dark as possible. The time hasn't come yet to roll back that efficient and most stimulating curtain.

GOBLIN 1

Yes, keep them guessing a little longer.

GOBLIN 2

Perlimplín's chicklike soul is being enlarged and enriched by the minute.

(They laugh)

GOBLIN 1

The audience is getting restless.

GOBLIN 2

Can't blame them. Shall we go?

GOBLIN 1

Let's. I can feel a breeze down my back.

GOBLIN 2

Five cold dawn-flowers have burst on the bedroom wall.

GOBLIN 1

Five balconies gaze out upon the city.

(They rise, wrapping large blue cloaks about themselves.)

GOBLIN 2

Don Perlimplín, have we hurt or helped you?

GOBLIN 1

We have helped him... it's never nice to show an audience the misfortunes of a noble man.

GOBLIN 2

Right, cousin. "They say" is never the same as "I have seen with my own eyes."

GOBLIN 1

And they'll know all about it by tomorrow, anyhow.

GOBLIN 2

That's what we want.

GOBLIN 1

Gossip keeps the world rolling.

GOBLIN 2

Shush.

(*The flutes begin to play*)

GOBLIN 1

Shall we go, Cousin?

GOBLIN 2

By all means, my friend.

GOBLIN 1

Now?

GOBLIN 2

Now.

(*As they leave they draw back the curtain.* Don Perlimplín *lies in bed.*
His head has sprouted a stupendous pair of gilded flowering horns.[4]
Belisa lies at his side.
The five balconies behind are open, the white rays of
the morning sun flood the stage.)

PERLIMPLÍN (*Awakening*)

Belisa, Belisa, wake up!

BELISA (*Pretending to awaken*)

Perlimpleeny, what is it?

---

4. In Zóbel's source text, the Losada (*L*) edition, Guillermo de Torre points out that the description of the cuckold's horns (*cuernos*) was crossed out by the government censor. Zóbel uses Torre's note, or perhaps the 1941 Graham Lujan and Richard O'Connell translation, to reconstruct the line. See *U* 269. The horns preserved in the Centro García Lorca, supposedly from the 1933 performance, are entwined with flowers but rather small.

PERLIMPLÍN

Tell me!

BELISA

What? I fell asleep before you?

(Perlimplín *jumps out of bed, fully dressed*)

PERLIMPLÍN

Why are the balconies open?

BELISA

The wind was strong last night.

PERLIMPLÍN

And why are there five ladders against the windows?

BELISA

It's a custom where we come from.

PERLIMPLÍN

And whose hats are those beside the ladders?

BELISA (*Jumping out of bed*)[5]

Why, they belong to drunkards, of course; drunkards who stagger about during the night, Perlimpleeny, my love!

(Perlimplín *looks at her and falls in[to] a kind of trance.*)

PERLIMPLÍN

Belisa! Belisa! And why not? You can explain everything. I am willing to believe you. Why not?

BELISA (*Coyly*)

I'm not a little liar.

PERLIMPLÍN

I love you more every minute!

BELISA

That's fine.

5. *U* 270 adds "en espléndida toilete" (presumably, "in a splendid dressing gown").

PERLIMPLÍN

I am happy for the first time in my life!

(He approaches and hugs her. Suddenly he draws back brusquely.)

Belisa. Who has kissed you? Don't lie now! I know!

BELISA *(Putting up her hair)*[6]

Of course you know! What a witty little husband I have! *(Whispers)* You have! You have kissed me!

PERLIMPLÍN

Yes. I have kissed you... But... what if someone else has too... what if someone else has... do you love me?

BELISA

(Putting out one of her bare arms to hug him)

Yes my little Perlimplín.

PERLIMPLÍN

In that case... What difference does it make?

(Hugs her.)

Are you really Belisa?

BELISA *(Whispers coyly)*

Yes! Yes! Yes!

PERLIMPLÍN

It seems like a dream!

BELISA *(Suddenly changing her tone)*

Look here, Perlimplín, close the windows. People will be passing by any moment now.

PERLIMPLÍN

Why close them? We have slept long enough. Don't you want to see the rise of dawn?

BELISA

Yes, but...

(She sits on the bed.)

6. *U* 270 adds "y echándolo por delante" (and moving it over her shoulders.)

PERLIMPLÍN

I have never really seen the dawn before. . .

(Belisa *falls back exhaustedly on the pillows.*)

PERLIMPLÍN

This view. . . strange. . .moves me! Don't you like it?

(*Turns around.*)

Belisa... are you sleeping?

BELISA (*Half asleep*)

Yes.

(Perlimplín, *on tiptoes, covers her with the scarlet cloak.*
A brilliant golden light comes in through the balconies.
Bells start ringing and a flock of paper birds flies across the windows.)
(Perlimplín *sits on the edge of the bed.*)

PERLIMPLÍN

Love, love,
[I'm] dying[7]
Dying because love is flying;
dying
dying of love!
Run out into the street crying,
"It was the nightingale above!"
A four-bladed knife slashed your throat.
Silence. Hear him sighing,
"Hold me tight my love.
Hold me, for I am lying
dying for the love that's flying
dying,
dying of love."

CURTAIN

7. *U* 272: estoy herido: literally, I'm wounded. Following the mistaken reading in Losada (está herido), Zóbel translated "you're dying."

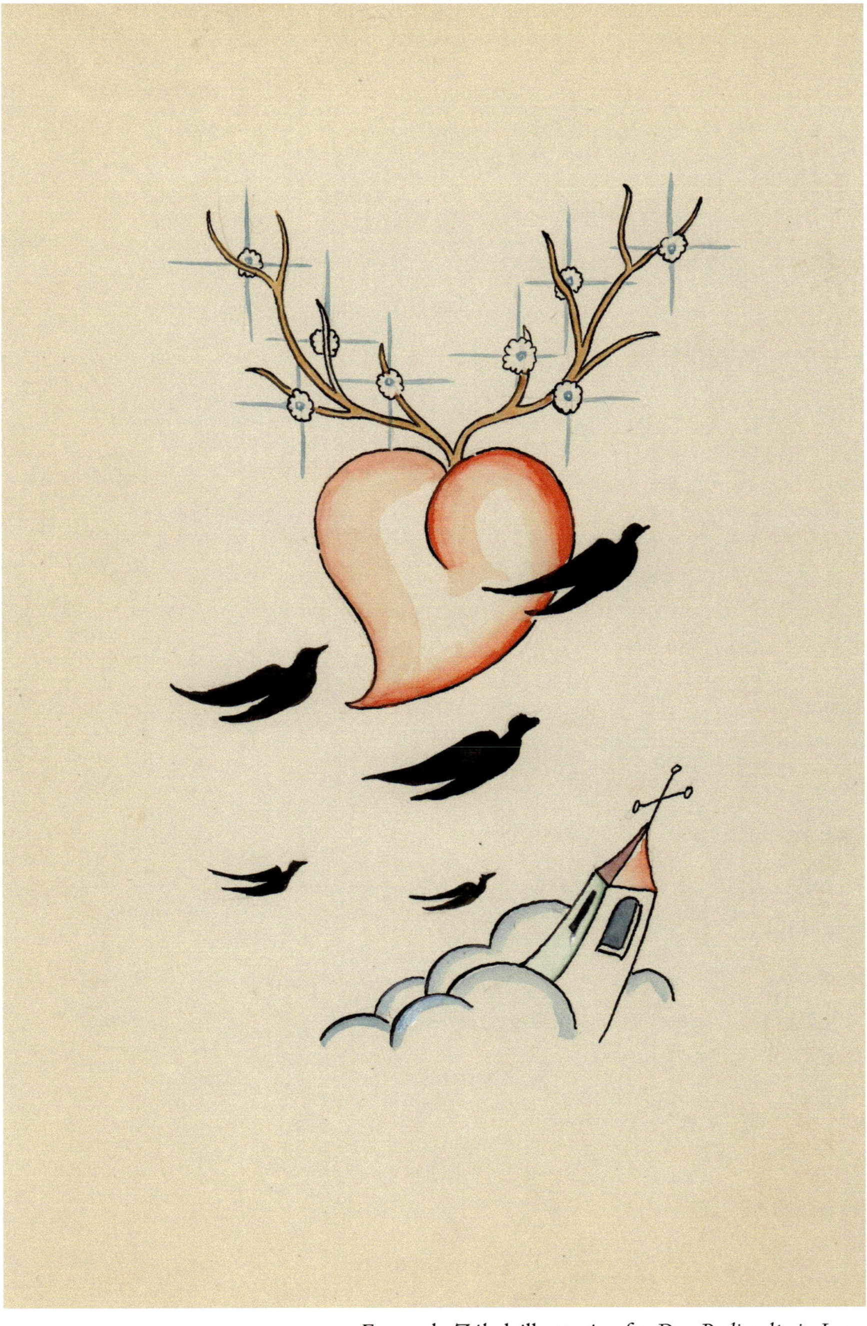

4.2 Fernando Zóbel, illustration for *Don Perlimplín in Love*.
Houghton Library, Harvard University.

SCENE II

Perlimplín's dining room. The perspective should be delightfully wrong, and the table should have all the objects painted on, as in a Primitive's "Last Supper."

PERLIMPLÍN

Will you do as I say?

MARCOLFA (*Weeping*)

You may trust me, sir.

PERLIMPLÍN

Marcolfa, why must you keep on crying?

MARCOLFA

Your lordship knows as well as I do. Five men came in through the balconies on your wedding night. Five! Representatives of the five races of man. A bearded European, an Indian, a Negro, an Oriental and a Yankee. And you don't give it the slightest importance.

PERLIMPLÍN

But it has no importance.

MARCOLFA

And yesterday she had another one.

PERLIMPLÍN

Eh?

MARCOLFA

What's more, she made no attempt to hide it.

PERLIMPLÍN

Just the same I feel quite happy, Marcolfa.

MARCOLFA

Your Lordship, really!

PERLIMPLÍN

Yes, you have no idea how happy. I have learned much and I can imagine more—that is even better.

MARCOLFA

I'm afraid your Lordship loves her much too much.

PERLIMPLÍN

Not half as much as she deserves.

MARCOLFA

Here she comes.

PERLIMPLÍN

You may go now.

(Marcolfa *leaves and* Perlimplín *hides in a corner.* Belisa *enters.*)

BELISA

I haven't as much as seen him. While I walked along the Promenade everyone followed but him. His skin must be the color of bronze; his kisses must burn and perfume like cloves or sassafras. Sometimes he walks under my balcony and waves his hand slowly towards me, causing my breasts to quiver...

PERLIMPLÍN

Harrumpf...

BELISA (*Turning*)

Oh! You've frightened me.

PERLIMPLÍN (*Approaching lovingly*)

I overheard you talking to yourself.

BELISA (*Disgusted*)

Go away!

PERLIMPLÍN

Shall we take a little stroll?

BELISA

No.

PERLIMPLÍN

Shall we go to the candy shop?

BELISA

I said "no" the first time!

PERLIMPLÍN

Sorry.

(A letter wrapped around a stone falls through the window. Perlimplín *picks it up.)*

BELISA

Give it to me!

PERLIMPLÍN

Why should I?

BELISA

It's for me.

PERLIMPLÍN *(Jokingly)*

How do you know?

BELISA

Perlimplín, don't read it!

PERLIMPLÍN *(With pretended gruffness)*

What do you mean?

BELISA *(Weeping)*

Give it to me!

PERLIMPLÍN *(Approaching her)*

Poor Belisa! I know just how you feel. That is why I am going to give you this precious letter...

(Belisa *takes it and hides it within her breast.)*

...Oh, I can see what goes on. I am sorry to say that you are living in a melodrama.

BELISA *(Tenderly)*

Perlimplín...

PERLIMPLÍN

I know that you have been unfaithful and that you will keep on being unfaithful...

BELISA *(Archly)*

You're the only man for me, Perlimplín.

PERLIMPLÍN

. . .and that is why I am going to help you, as every husband should when his wife is a Tower of Chastity. . . Look here.

(Closes the doors and speaks mysteriously.)

I know everything! I knew immediately. You are young and I am old. . . It can't be helped. And I can understand......

(Pause. Lowers his voice.)

Has he ever been around here?

BELISA

Twice.

PERLIMPLÍN

Did he make any signs?

BELISA

Yes. . . but rather carelessly. I was hurt!

PERLIMPLÍN

Don't worry. I met that same young man about two weeks ago. I was really struck by his beauty. I have never seen anyone so manly and yet so gentle.[8] When I first saw him—I don't know why—I immediately thought of you.

BELISA

I have never seen his face. . .but. . .

PERLIMPLÍN

Don't feel shy. . . I know that you are in love with him. . . I love you, yes, but like a father. . . my days are over. . . gone. . .

BELISA

He writes to me.

PERLIMPLÍN

I know.

BELISA

But he won't let me see him.

---

8. U 277: *Jamás he visto un hombre en que lo varonil y lo delicado se den de una manera más armónica.* Zóbel translates more literally in "Theme and Conflict" (12): "Never have I seen a man in whom the masculine and the delicate are found together so harmoniously."

PERLIMPLÍN

Strange.

BELISA

Sometimes I almost think that... he despises me.

PERLIMPLÍN

My, but you are naïve.

BELISA

What I do know is that he loves me as I wish to be loved...

PERLIMPLÍN

Eh?

BELISA

The other letters... I never bothered to answer them because I had you... The other letters spoke of foreign lands, of dreams, of bleeding hearts... but his letters!... look...

PERLIMPLÍN

Go on.

BELISA

He speaks of...my body...

Perlimplín (*Gently stroking her arms*)

Your body!

BELISA

"I don't want your soul," he writes. "The soul is for the weak, for the sick, for the have-beens. The best souls go with white hair and crinkled hands, and they live on the edge of eternity. But I don't want your soul, Belisa! I want your body! I want your quivering flesh!"[9]

PERLIMPLÍN

Hmm. Who might it be?

---

9. U 278: *¿Para qué quiero tu alma? Me dice. El alma es el patrimonio de los débiles, de los héroes tullidos, y las gentes enfermizas. Las almas hermosas están en los bordes de la muerte, reclinadas sobre cabelleras blanquísimas y manos macilentas. Belisa. ¡No es tu alma lo que yo deseo!, ¡sino tu blanco y mórbido cuerpo estremecido.* Zóbel translates the passage differently in "Theme and Conflict," 11: "Of what use is your soul to me? ... The soul is the refuge of the weak, of paralytic heroes and sickly folk. The truly beautiful souls are recognizable by their silvery hair and fleshless hands as they recline on the brink of death. Belisa, I don't want your soul; I want your white and tingling body."

BELISA

No one knows.

PERLIMPLÍN (*Inquisitively*)

No one?

BELISA

I have asked all my friends.

PERLIMPLÍN (*Decisively, yet with a touch of mystery*)

What if I told you that I know him quite well?

BELISA

It can't be!

PERLIMPLÍN

Wait a minute.

(*Goes to the window.*)

Look. There he goes.

BELISA

(*Runs*)

Where?

PERLIMPLÍN

What a shame. He has just turned that corner.

BELISA (*Breathless*)

Oh!

PERLIMPLÍN

Well, I suppose I am old enough to afford a sacrifice. What I am about to do has never been done before. However, I stand well above the world and its tiresome morality. Good-bye.

BELISA

Where are you going?

PERLIMPLÍN (*Grandiosely, standing by the door*)

You shall know soon enough! Soon enough!

CURTAIN

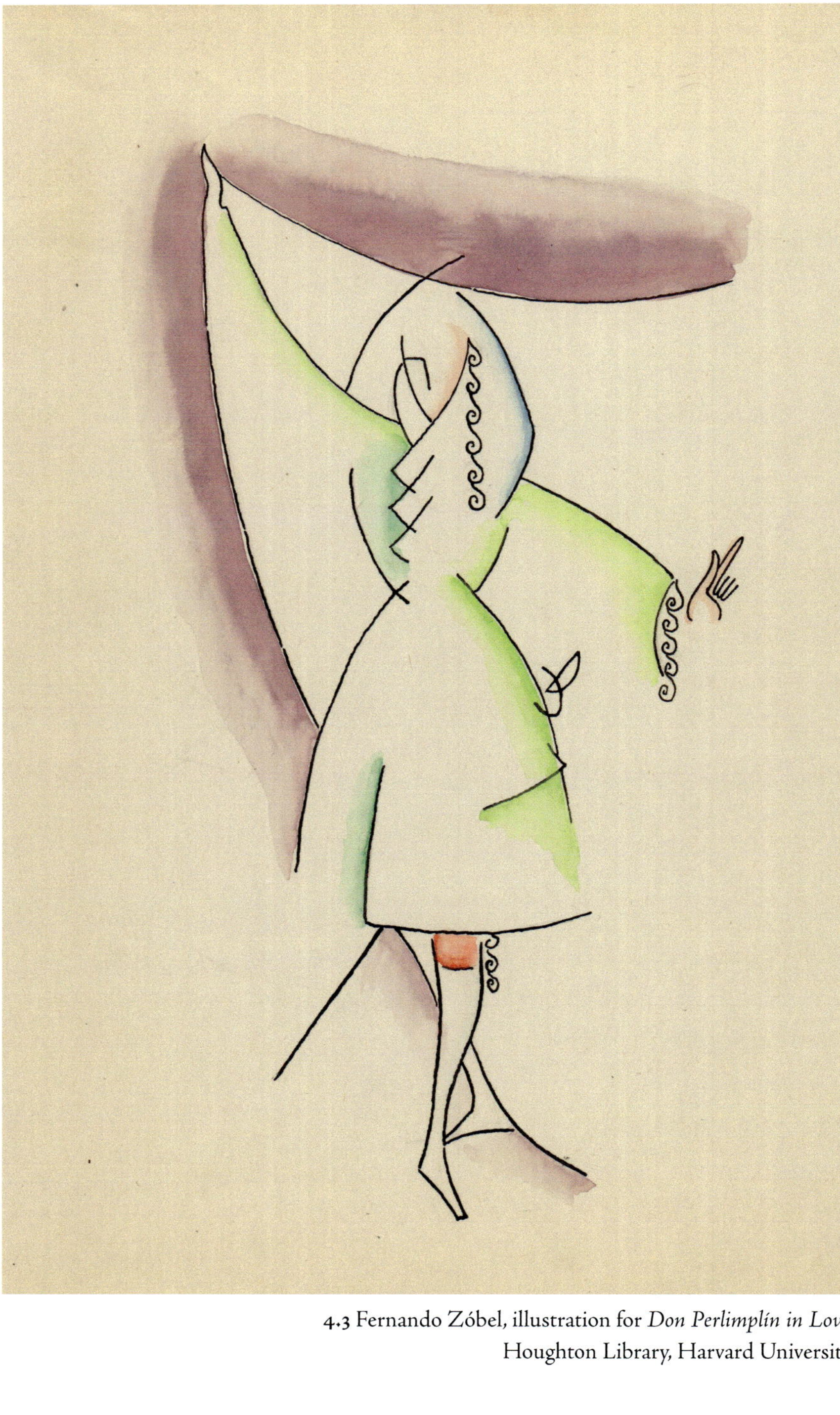

4.3 Fernando Zóbel, illustration for *Don Perlimplín in Love*.
Houghton Library, Harvard University.

SCENE III

Garden with olive trees and poplars. The curtain rises showing Perlimplín and Marcolfa in the garden.

MARCOLFA

Is it time?

PERLIMPLÍN

No, not yet.

MARCOLFA

Your Lordship, but what is this you're doing?

PERLIMPLÍN

I am doing what I never did before.

MARCOLFA (*Weeping*)

And it's all my fault!

PERLIMPLÍN

Marcolfa, if you only knew how grateful I am!

MARCOLFA

Everything went so smoothly before. Every morning I would serve your grapes and coffee...

PERLIMPLÍN

Yes... grapes... grapes! But... myself? I feel as if I have lived a hundred years. Once I never dreamt the world held so much richness and mystery. I never dared to go beyond the doorways... But now! Belisa's love has awakened me to my treasures... for instance, if I close my eyes I can see... anything I wish... there... my mother visited by friendly fairies... oh, you know what they're like... small, very small... marvelous, why, they can actually dance on my little finger.

MARCOLFA

Yes, fairies, fairies; ... what about this other business?

PERLIMPLÍN

Oh, the other business. (*Joyfully*) What did you tell my wife?

MARCOLFA

Well, you know I'm no good at this sort of thing, but I told her exactly as you said... that the young man... would meet her in the garden tonight, in his scarlet cloak, as usual.

PERLIMPLÍN

And she... ?

MARCOLFA

She blushed like a red geranium and clutched her heart; I left her kissing her beautiful tresses.

PERLIMPLÍN (*Delighted*)

... Like a red geranium?... And... what did she say?

BELISA

She just sighed... but how she sighed!

PERLIMPLÍN

Of course! Like no woman ever sighed before! Right?

MARCOLFA

She must be madly in love.

PERLIMPLÍN (*Vibrantly*)

That's it. She probably loves that man more than her own flesh! And she does love him.

MARCOLFA (*Weeping*)

I can't stand by and listen to this... Don Perlimplín, how can you? How can you? You are actually encouraging your wife to commit the worst sins!

PERLIMPLÍN

How can I?... Why, Don Perlimplín has lost his honor and wishes to be amused. Can't you understand? Tonight my fair Belisa is to have a new and unknown lover. How can I help singing?

(*Sings*)

Don Perlimplín has lost his honor!
Lost his honor!
Lost his honor!

MARCOLFA

Sir, I beg to inform you that this very moment I am giving notice. Even servants can sometimes feel ashamed.

PERLIMPLÍN

Oh my poor Marcolfa! Tomorrow you shall be as free as a bird… but wait till tomorrow. Go and do your duty now. Will you follow my orders?

(Marcolfa *departs, drying her tears*)

MARCOLFA

And what else can I do? What else?

PERLIMPLÍN

Good. That is sweet of you.

(*A soft serenade is heard.* Perlimplín *hides behind a clump of bushes.*)

BELISA (*Singing from within.*)

Night is bathing
along the river.

VOICES

Along the river.

BELISA

Within Belisa's breasts
the branches die of love.

VOICES

The branches die of love.

PERLIMPLÍN

The branches die of love!

BELISA

Upon the bridge of Spring
night sings nakedly.

VOICES

Night sings nakedly.

BELISA

Belisa bathes her skin
with reeds and fresh waters.

VOICES

With reeds and fresh waters.

PERLIMPLÍN

The branches die of love!

BELISA

See the silver glitter of the roofs
on a night of anisette.

VOICES

On a night of anisette.

BELISA

Anisette of snowy thighs,
silver brooks and mirrors.

VOICES

And the branches die of love!

(*Enter* Belisa *brilliantly dressed. Moonlight shines wanly on the stage.*)

BELISA

What voices fill this shred of night with gentle harmony? I can feel your weight and your warmth upon me, my beloved… Oh! The bushes are moving…!

(A man, *dressed in a scarlet cloak, appears and cautiously crosses the stage.*)

BELISA

Sssh…This way! Here!

(The man *motions his hand to show that he will soon return.*)

Oh yes! Yes! Come back soon, my love! It seems as if the sky—rootless field of lilies—is about to cave in upon me… Night! My night! Night of mint and sapphire…

(*Enter* Perlimplín)

PERLIMPLÍN (*Surprised*)

Why, what are you doing out here?

BELISA

I was just taking a walk.

PERLIMPLÍN

Just a walk?

BELISA

It's such a lovely night.

PERLIMPLÍN (*Energetically*)

Belisa, what are you doing here?

BELISA (*Surprised*)

But didn't you know?

PERLIMPLÍN

I don't know a thing.

BELISA

You sent me the message.

PERLIMPLÍN

Belisa . . . do you still want him to come?

BELISA

More than ever!

PERLIMPLÍN (*Sternly*)

Why?

BELISA

Because I love him.

PERLIMPLÍN

He will come.

BELISA

The odor of his body through his clothes. . . I love him! Perlimplín, I love him! I feel like another woman.

PERLIMPLÍN

Victory.

BELISA

What victory?

PERLIMPLÍN

The victory of my imagination!

BELISA

True, you helped me to love him.

PERLIMPLÍN

And I shall help you to mourn him.

BELISA (*Surprised*)

Perlimplín! What do you mean?

(*The clock strikes ten. A nightingale sings.*)

PERLIMPLÍN

The time has come!

BELISA

He should arrive any minute.

PERLIMPLÍN

He is jumping over my garden wall.

BELISA

In his scarlet cloak.

PERLIMPLÍN (*Unsheathing a dagger*)

Scarlet like his blood.

BELISA (*Gripping his arm*)

What are you going to do?

PERLIMPLÍN (*Embracing her*)

Do you love him?

BELISA

Yes!

PERLIMPLÍN

If you love him that much, I don't ever want him to leave you. I shall kill him with this knife. In that way he shall be yours forever. Are you happy?

BELISA

Perlimplín! For God's sake!

PERLIMPLÍN

Dead, he will be truly yours, handsomer and more desirable than ever. You shall love him without fear of his not loving you in return; for his love will be the boundless love of death, and I shall be freed from the nightmare of your body... never meant for me!!!

(*Turning towards the garden*)

Look, there he is! Let me go, Belisa!... Let me go!

(*He tears himself away and runs.*)

BELISA (*In despair*)

Marcolfa, bring me the sword over the mantlepiece. I am going to stab my husband in the throat.

(*Shouts are heard.*)

BELISA

Loathsome reptile!
Murder him and I
shall murder you,
Don Perlimplín!

(*A man, wrapped in a scarlet cloak, appears from the bushes. He staggers and is obviously wounded.*)

BELISA (*Embracing him*)[10]

Who slashed your veins, covering my garden with your blood? My love! Let me see your face, even if for a moment! Aie! Who has killed you, tell me... who?

PERLIMPLÍN (*Dropping his cloak*)

Your husband has just killed me with this emerald dagger.

(*He shows her the dagger stuck in his chest*)

BELISA (*Terrified*)

Perlimplín!

PERLIMPLÍN

He ran off to the woods; you will never see him again. He killed me because he knew that my love was greater than any other... While he stabbed me he shouted: "Now Belisa has a soul!" Come closer.

(*He lies against a bench.*)

10. *L* abrazándole (embracing him) does not appear in *U* 287.

BELISA

But. . . are you really wounded?

PERLIMPLÍN

Perlimplín has murdered me. Ah there, Don Perlimplín! You impotent puppet, you lecherous mummy, Belisa's body was not for the likes of you... Her body was for younger muscles and for burning lips. . . I, I was in love only with your body! So he murdered me. . . with this sparkling cross of jewels.

BELISA

What have you done!

PERLIMPLÍN (*Growing weaker*)

Don't you see? I am my soul and you are your body. . . Let me then, having loved it so long, die with my arms clasped about it.

(Belisa *sits next to him*[11] *and embraces him.*)

BELISA

Yes. . . but the man? Why have you fooled me?

PERLIMPLÍN

The man!

(*Shuts his eyes. The light turns logical.*[12] *Enter* Marcolfa.)

MARCOLFA

Madam!

BELISA (*Weeping*)

Don Perlimplín is dead!

MARCOLFA

I could see it coming. Now we shall dress him for burial. His winding-sheet shall be that scarlet cloak he used when he walked beneath your window.

BELISA (*Weeping*)

I never dreamt he could be so many men!

---

11. *U* 288: Se acerca medio desnuda y lo abraza (She draws near, half naked, and embraces him.)

12. *U* 288 La escena adquiere luz mágica (The stage acquires magical light).

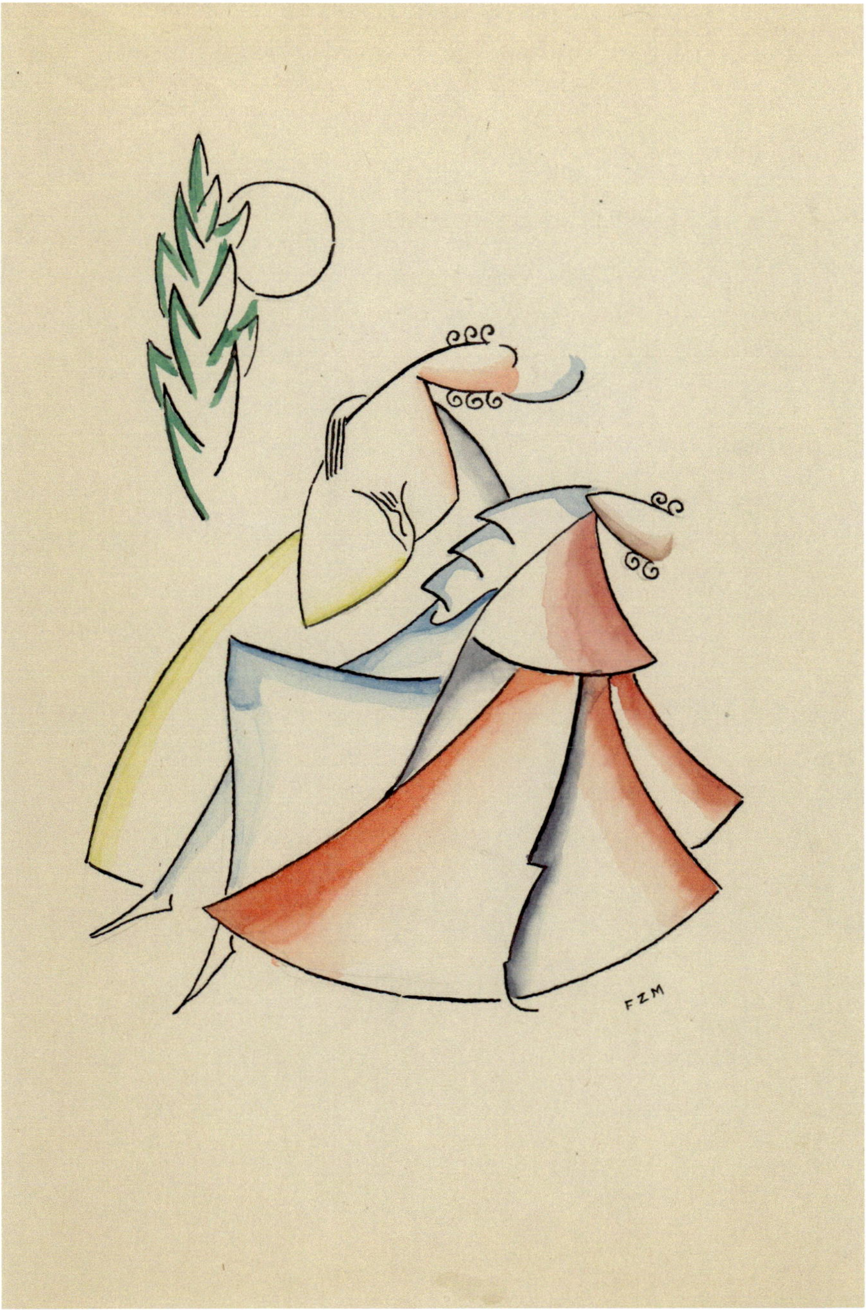

4.4 Fernando Zóbel, illustration for *Don Perlimplín in Love*.
Houghton Library, Harvard University.

MARCOLFA

You found out too late. I shall weave him a wreath of flowers like the noontide sun.

(Belisa, *absently, as if in another world.*)

BELISA

Perlimplín, what have you done, Perlimplín?

MARCOLFA

Belisa, you have become another woman. You have been sanctified by my Lordship's most precious blood.

BELISA

But that man... who was he?

MARCOLFA

He was that handsome youth, whose face you will never see.

BELISA

Yes, Marcolfa, I love him. I love him with all my body and soul. But where is the man with the scarlet cloak? Dear lord, where is he?

MARCOLFA

Don Perlimplín, can you hear her?... Can you hear?... Rest in peace, then, Don Perlimplín.

(*The morning bells begin to ring.*)

CURTAIN.

THE END.

FEDERICO GARCÍA LORCA
ARR. GUSTAVO PITTALUGA

MUSIC
AMOR DE DON PERLIMPLÍN CON BELISA EN SU JARDÍN

1 (p. 85)

Don Perlimplín's house. Green walls; chairs and furniture painted black. Backstage, an open balcony, from which Belisa's window may be seen.

Sonata

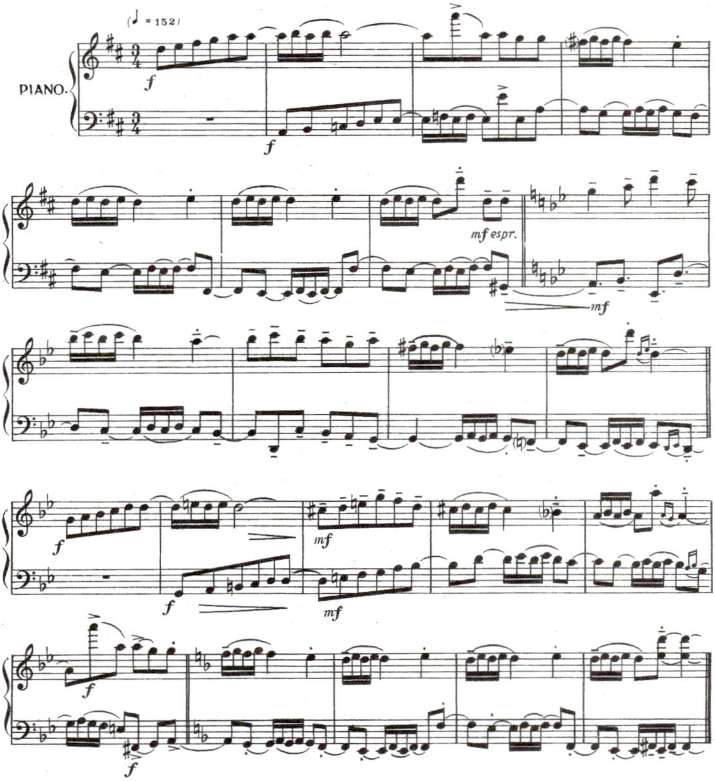

PERLIMPLIN: What?
MARCOLFA: I am blushing. (*Pause. A piano is heard. Then* BELISA'S *voice, from within, singing.*)

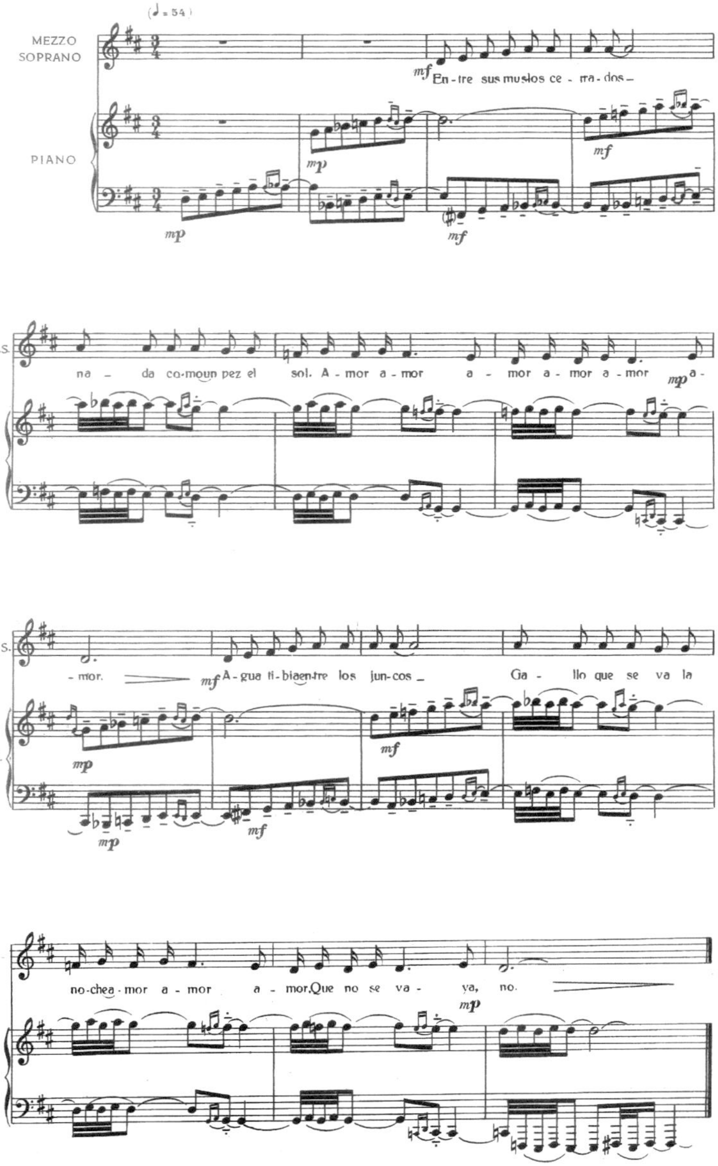

3 (p. 93)

BELISA: That woman has been spraying anisette instead of verbena, like I told her… and she hasn't spread the fine linen either. (*At this moment we hear the soft music of a guitar.*

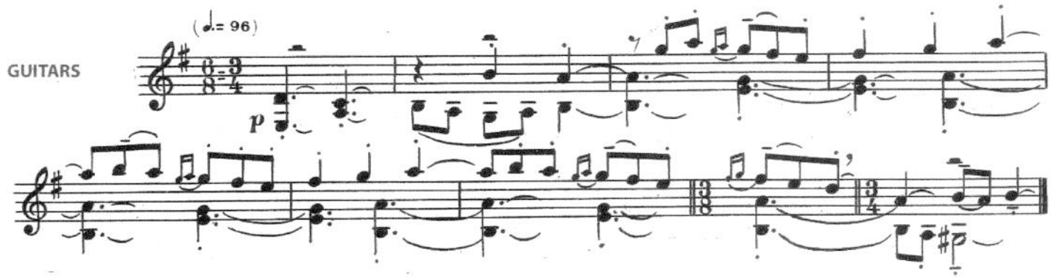

4 (p. 97)

PERLIMPLÍN: I adore you! (*Two goblins appear from opposite ends of the stage and draw a grey curtain across it. The theater falls into a kind of twilight. Flutes play a dreamy air.*)

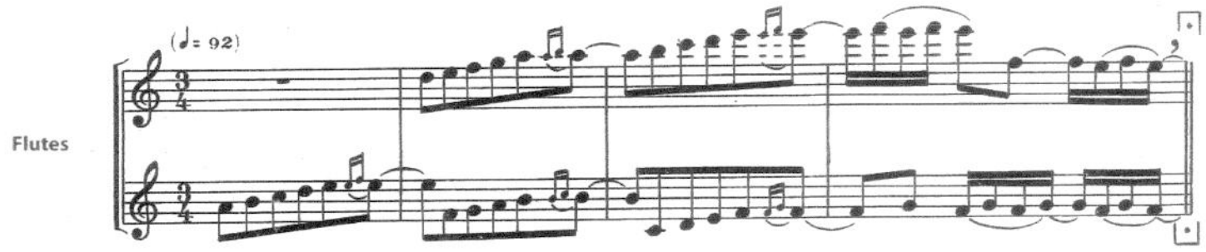

SECOND GOBLIN: Shush! *(The flutes begin to play.)*

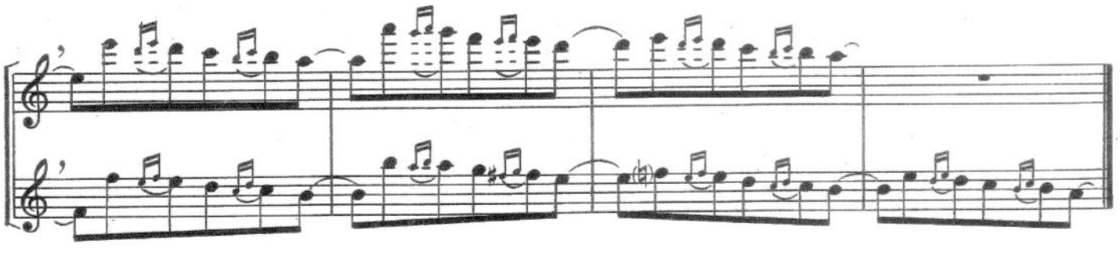

5 (p. 114)

PERLIMPLÍN: Why, Don Perlimplín has lost his honor and wishes to be amused. Can't you understand? Tonight my fair Belisa is to have a new and unknown lover. How can I help singing? (*Sings*)

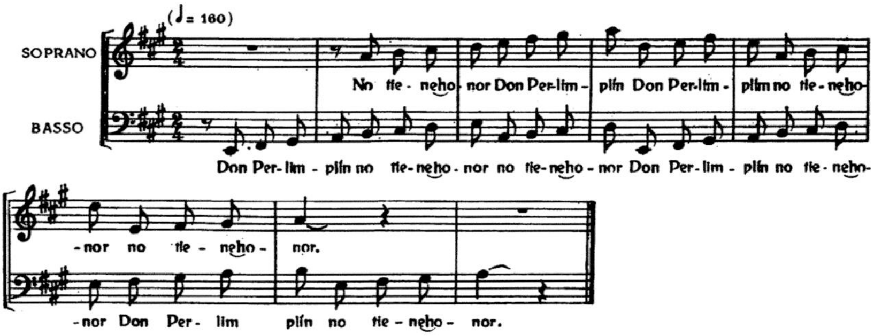

6 (p. 115)

PERLIMPLÍN: Good. That is sweet of you. (*A soft serenade is heard.*
PERLIMPLÍN: *hides behind a clump of bushes.*)
BELISA: (*Singing from within.*)

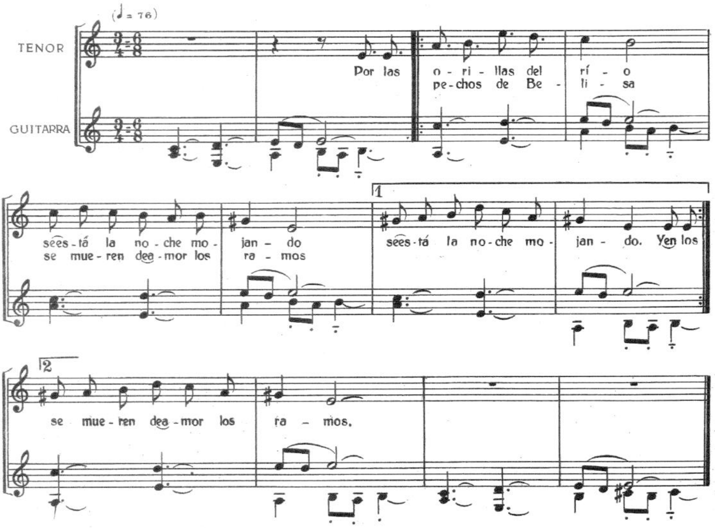

CHRISTOPHER MAURER AND LINCOLN SON CURRIE

FROM STAGE TO PAGE: A *PERLIMPLÍN* CHRONOLOGY

1924 Fernando Zóbel is born in Manila.

In a July 1924 letter, Lorca (1898-1936) asks his friend Melchor Fernández Almagro to tell theater director Cipriano Rivas Cherif about his farce *La zapatera prodigiosa* (*The Shoemaker's Prodigious Wife*) and ask him if he "wishes to collaborate with me on something else I'm preparing [*¿Don Perlimplín?*], which I'll tell him about soon" (FGL, *Epistolario completo* (Madrid, Cátedra, 1998): 242. (=*E* 242). All translations mine except as otherwise indicated.

APRIL 1925 Lorca writes to his parents that he will spend Holy Week with Salvador Dalí and his family in Cadaqués, where he will work on the final scene of *La zapatera prodigiosa* and "una nueva obra teatral que he comenzado" ("a new theatrical work which I've begun") (*E* 267).

SEPTEMBER 1925 "I'm working intensely. I have written a book of dialogues and another book of poems. A little natural history, a garland of fruits, covered in insects. And I'm now making a work of grotesque theater, *Amor de Don Perlimplín con Belisa en su jardín*. These are the *aleluyas* I explained to you in [the Café] Savoia, remember? You have no idea how idiotically enjoyable this is." Letter to Fernández Almagro (*E* 300).

JANUARY 1926

Lorca sends Fernández Almagro a sample (the second part of the fourth "Cuadro") of what he calls "my erotic *aleluya Amor de Don Perlimplín con Belisa en su jardín*" and his newly composed "Romance de la luna luna de los gitanos" (Ballad of the Gypsy Moon) (*E* 320-23).

SPRING 1926

In the bar of a Madrid hotel, Lorca offers to read *Amor de Don Perlimplín* to Luis Buñuel and Salvador Dalí, but gets no farther than Scene I. Buñuel remembered the incident many years later for the writer Max Aub: Federico "told me, 'You're an animal, and you don't understand a damned thing, but this guy [Dalí] can tell you about the piece I've just done.' And Dalí, with that Catalan accent of his that he's never lost, assures me that's true: 'Yes, of course, it's great, truly magnificent.' So we agree Federico will read us his *Don Perlimplín*... And after the first act of the play, a character, I forget who [a Goblin or Duende], comes out of the prompter's box, or something like that. And I tell him, 'This is really bad, Federico.' Federico gets up, really angry: 'Well, Dalí doesn't think so. And *you* don't deserve to be my friend.' 'Am I right?' he asks, turning to Dalí. And Dalí answers: "Well, no, it isn't very good, no." So Federico gets up angrily, gathers his papers, and goes off" (Ucelay, 131).

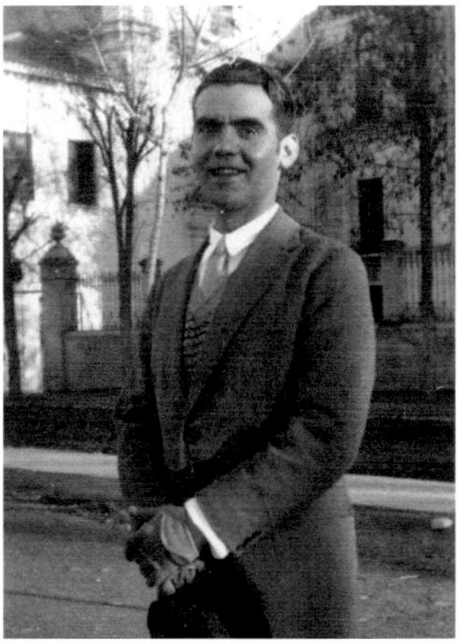

5.1 Federico García Lorca in Granada, 1927. Photograph by his English friend Campbell ('Colin') Hackforth-Jones. Archive of Andrew A. Anderson.

DECEMBER 1928 In an interview, Lorca says that he is preparing to publish a volume of theater including his puppet play *Los títeres de Cachiporra* (The Billyclub Puppets) and *Don Perlimplín* (*Palabra de Lorca,* 30). The volume never comes to fruition.

JANUARY 1929 Rivas Cherif's experimental theater company, El Caracol, rehearses the play, but for reasons never fully clarified—perhaps because theaters had been ordered closed for mourning over the death of the Queen Mother, or because of the "erotic" subject matter and wearing of cuckold's horns by an actor who was also a soldier, or because the play was taken to allude to the dictator Primo de Rivera—the production is shut down in rehearsals by the police chief of Madrid and the manuscript is sequestered as pornography in a government archive (Margarita Ucelay's introduction to her edition provides abundant details). Asked a few years later why his play had been shut down, Lorca answered, "I honestly don't know. It was a joyful farce, not a terrible one" (*Palabra de Lorca,* 50).

OCTOBER 1929 During a nine-month stay in New York, while also working on *Poet in New York,* Lorca rewrites the play and tells his parents in a letter: "Some English friends of mine in New York have begun to see what they can do to have my theater performed here [...] If something were performed, it would be *Perlimplín* and *The Billyclub Puppets,* translated into English and done with a nice set. There is avant-garde theater here, and it wouldn't be difficult. I don't want to get my hopes up; I'll just wait and see. It is the ladies who are taking an interest in all this. In fact, it is women who do everything in America. One of them [Irene Lewisohn] is a millionaire and there are also three or four Jewish women connected with the world of letters [probably Edith Isaacs, Aline Berstein, and Rita Wallach Morgenthau]. I haven't done anything, but we'll see. Naturally, I would love to be successful here. Not only would it advance my career, it would be beautiful to arrive in New York and have them perform what was shamefully banned in Spain or what no one wanted to put on 'because there's no public for it.' But as I said, I'm not getting my hopes up." See *E* 658 and *Poet in New York*, ed. C. Maurer (New York: Farrar, Straus and Giroux, third edition, 2013), 241-242; my translation.

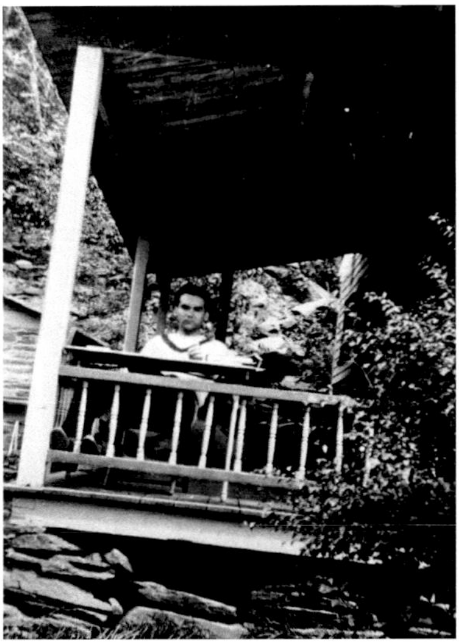

5.2 Federico García Lorca writing, at a cottage in Bushnellsville, in the Catskill Mountains, New York, while visiting Ángel del Río and his wife Amalia Agostini in August and September 1929. Centro Federico García Lorca. Del Río remembers that Lorca read them *Amor de Don Perlimplín*, which he had revised in New York.

On Wednesday October 30, Lorca's Mexican friend María Antonieta Rivas writes from New York to the painter Manuel Rodríguez Lozano: "Lorca has read us two of his theater pieces, which are stupendous. *The Billyclub Puppets* and *The Love of Don Perlimplín With Belisa in the Garden, An Erotic Alleluia* [and has] sung for us songs from all over Spain, in a curious, delightful geographical map that he serves up with the tunes. He has recited his ballads and the latest things he is writing." (Luis Mario Schneider, *García Lorca y México*, UNAM, 1998: 33; my translation.)

On Christmas Eve, Lorca reads the play at a gathering at the home of his New York friends Norma and Herschel Brickell. Also in attendance are his future biographer the journalist Mildred Adams and her friend Jack Carwithen Leacock, a linen merchant from Madeira. Lorca gives Adams the manuscript of the play to translate. She makes a partial attempt, but gives up: "The process of translation had proved impossible. In Spanish the play was delightful; in English it did not make theater sense. Also there was too much poetry in it for a journalist to cope with..." Adams, *García Lorca: Playwright and Poet* (New York: Braziller, 1977): 124.

JANUARY 26, 1932 Despite her misgivings, Adams sends her partial translation to Edith Isaacs, editor of *Theatre Arts Monthly*, who comments that "it does give a nice sense of [Lorca's] poetic quality. But it is not the kind of play I should recommend putting forward as an indication of the way the young moderns in Spain are going. I believe that is what you said you thought too. Thank you very much for letting me see it." (Letter from Isaacs, Mildred Adams papers, Hispanic Society of America)

APRIL 5, 1933 The Club Teatral de Cultura, an amateur group directed by Pura Maortua de Ucelay, who has retrieved a copy of Perlimplín from the censors' archives, gives the first public performance of *Perlimplín* together with *The Shoemaker's Prodigious Wife* in the Teatro Español, Madrid. Lorca is involved throughout the production process (Edwards, *New Theatre Quarterly* 23, no. 4: 304-316). The set was designed by Santiago Ontañón and the cast included Ontañon (Don Perlimplín), Pilar de Bascarán (Belisa), señora Domínguez (Marcolfa), Pilar García (Madre de Belisa), and Augusto and Andrés Higueras (the two Duendes). Punctuated by five sonatas of Domenico Scarlatti performed by the pianist Pura Lago, the production is described by Lorca as "a chamber version, exclusively for minorities," "a tremendous work which has been a lot of fun for me. A theater of human rag dolls [*monigotes*] which begins in jest and ends on a tragic note. The hero, or antihero, who is cuckolded, is Spanish and in the tradition of Calderón [de la Barca]; but he doesn't want to react in that vein, and that is what causes his struggle, the grotesque tragedy of his case. I am not sure how a chamber audience will receive my play, but I had great fun writing it and it makes me happier every time I read it or see it being rehearsed" (*Palabra de Lorca,* 98-99; translation mine). In another interview, Lorca calls *Don Perlimplín* "the sketch for a grand drama. I've put into it only the words necessary to sketch out the characters. I say 'chamber version' because later I'll try to develop the theme in all of its complexity. Don Perlimplín is the least cuckolded man in the world. His dormant imagination awakens with the tremendous cheating of his wife. But he manages to cuckold all the women in existence. What has interested me in *Don Perlimplin* is drawing out the contrast between the grotesque and the lyrical, and mixing them constantly. The work rests on music, as in a little chamber opera. The brief moments between acts are tied together by Scarlatti sonatas and the dialogue is constantly interrupted with chords and musical backgrounds." (*Palabra de Lorca,* 102; translation mine.)

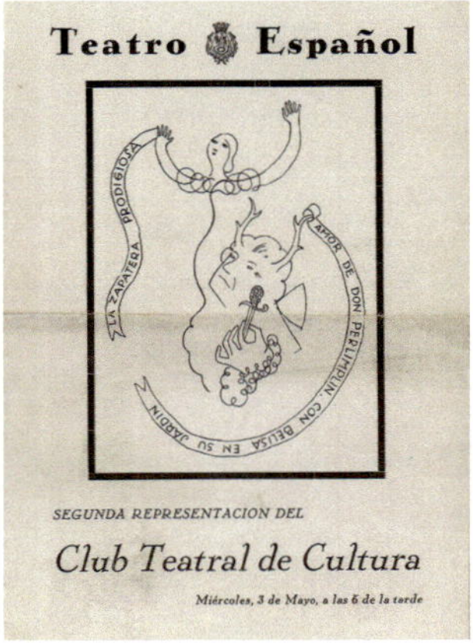

5.3 Program for the Madrid premiere of *Amor de Don Perlimplín,* with a drawing by Santiago Ontañón (1903-1989), who designed the set following Lorca's indications, and played Don Perlimplín.

NOVEMBER 1933 From Buenos Aires, where he has gone to direct his plays and deliver a series of lectures, Lorca tells his parents that there are "great expectations" for the staging of *The Shoemaker's Prodigious Wife* and *Don Perlimplín*, which are in rehearsal (*E* 782). But the performance of *Don Perlimplín* never materializes (cf. *E* 800).

1935 *Bodas de sangre (Blood Wedding)* is staged unsuccessfully at the Neighborhood Playhouse, New York in a florid translation by José Weissberger. Most of the reviews are devastating. *The New Yorker* (April 1, 1935) dismisses the play as a "Rococo Spanish peasant tragedy in which all the peasants talk like contributors of poetry to the women's magazines. A sad evening all around."

In an interview, Lorca calls *Perlimplín* his favorite work, "a small work whose true lyricism no professional company dares to put on." (*Palabra de Lorca*, pp. 363-64)

NOVEMBER 29, 1937 Mildred Adams, writing to Paul Willert of Oxford University Press, whom she hopes to interest in a biography of Lorca, mentions her copy of *Perlimplín*: "Lorca had it with him when he was in New York and left it for me to translate. I returned the original to him when I went back to Spain in... [1931] and I think it was put on in Madrid last season." In a letter (March 8, 1938) to Louise Silcox, secretary and treasurer of the Authors League of America, she adds: "Señor Lorca left two plays with me when he was in this country in 1930. I translated one and made a partial translation of the other, but have not up to the present time tried to interest anyone in production. Since Lorca's death at the hands of the Rebels he has become one of the heroes of the revolution, and there is at the present time some interest in putting on one of these two plays. It is also suggested that a third play [the historical drama *Mariana Pineda*], which was presented in Barcelona but has not, as far as I know, been translated, might be of interest to the American public. My chief interest in this matter is to safeguard these plays from being pirated and to make sure that any money which may accrue from their production goes to the proper sources. They have neither of them been copyrighted in the U.S. and I do not even know whether copyright is possible in their present condition." (Papers of Mildred Adams, Hispanic Society of America)

1938 Lorca's friend Guillermo de Torre, in exile in Buenos Aires, publishes *Amor de Don Perlimplín con Belisa en su jardín*, together with *Bodas de sangre* and *Retablillo de Don Cristóbal* in vol. I of his edition of Lorca's *Obras completas*—the source text for Zóbel's translation (Buenos Aires Losada).

On September 2, in the midst of the Spanish Civil War, the poet Rafael Alberti lectures on Lorca and presides over a performance of *Perlimplín* by the actors of the Alianza de Intelectuales para la Defensa de la Cultura. The cast includes María Teresa León and Santiago Ontañón, who designed the stage sets and played the leading role in the play's Madrid premiere in 1933. Manuel Aznar Soler, "Mª Teresa León y el teatro español durante la guerra civil," *Revista Stichomythia* no. 5 (2007): 58.

1941 In a volume titled *From Lorca's Theatre. Five Plays of Federico García*, published by the prestigious Charles Scribner's Sons (NY) and edited by Maxwell Perkins, Richard L. O'Connell and James Graham-Lujan offer their translation of *The Love of Don Perlimplín and Belisa in the Garden. An Erotic Alleluja in Four Scenes*. With a "Foreword Note" by theater critic Stark Young, who had met Lorca at the Residencia de Estudiantes, *From Lorca's Theatre* was the "first book-length translation of Lorca's dramatic pieces to appear in the English language." The plays are "rich in elements of painting, the dance and music. Above everything they are pure theater" (Lloyd Mallan, "Lorca's Poetic Drama," *New York Times*, March 29, 1942). In another review, Robert Whitehand points out that Lorca was previously known in the U.S. only through *Blood Wedding*, and that the plays published here, "strung together on the barest of plot skeletons," never hold "consistently to a mood. Fare and sentiment and tragedy mingle freely in the same piece, as in life." ("Slain Spaniard's Five Best Plays Lack Only Plot," *The Daily Oklahoman*, October 19, 1941).

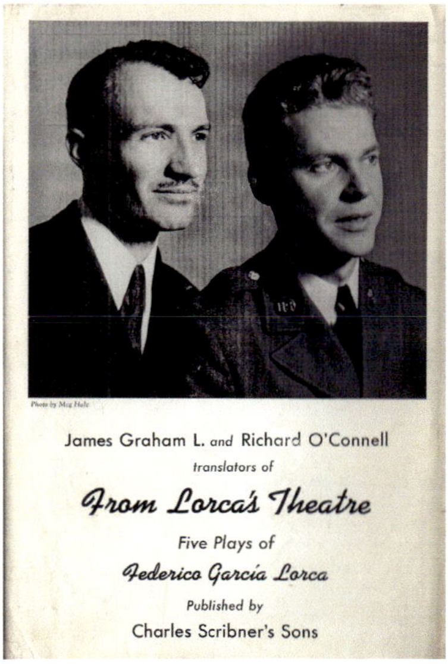

5.4
Richard L. O'Connell and James Graham Lujan, translators of *From Lorca's Theatre. Five Plays of Federico García Lorca* (1941). For decades, O'Connell and Graham Lujan had a contract with the Lorca Estate making them the only translators authorized to publish English translations of Lorca's plays, including *Amor de Don Perlimplín*.

The Harvard Dramatic Club puts on the first performance in Boston of *La zapatera prodigiosa* (The Shoemaker's Prodigious Wife). See "The Stage. Brattle Hall," Boston Globe, December 4, 1941.

1942 In a September 26, 1942 letter to Latin American historian Hubert Herring, Mildred Adams complains of a paucity of translators. "I wish I could find you another young translator [other than O'Connell and Graham-Lujan]. But, so far I have had no luck. People tell me about possibilities, but then I find that they have simply had Spanish courses and have done no English writing." (Mildred Adams Papers, Radcliffe Institute, 81-M49–81-M160)

1943 The Harvard Dramatic Club and the Radcliffe Idler stage the first American production of Lorca´s *Doña Rosita la soltera* (Doña Rosita the Spinster), translated by Graham-Luján and O'Connell (*Boston Globe* April 7, 1943). A *Boston Globe* review (April 29, 1943) praises the play´s language while criticizing "a tendency to ornateness in the translation."

Drama critic Francis Fergusson and Bennington College professor of theatre David Crewell stage a version of *Don Perlimplín and Belisa* in the Adams Memorial Theatre, Burlington, Vermont—perhaps the first performance in the U.S.—with a musical score by Carlos Buhler. See "College Plays Will Be Staged," *The Bennington Evening Banner*, June 30, 1943 and "Chilean Musician Composes for Play," *North Adams Transcript*, July 8, 1943. The experience will inform Fergusson's excellent essay, "'Don Perlimplín': Lorca's Theatre-Poetry" (1955).

1945 "'The newly formed Theatre Workshop (Manchester, England), with Joan Littlewood and Ewan MacColl at the helm, [go] on tour with …*The Love of Don Perlimplín for Belisa in His Garden*, performing it, along with other plays, over a period of six years." See Gwynne Edwards, "'Theatre Workshop and the Spanish Drama," *New Theatre Quarterly* 23 no. 4 (Nov. 2007), 304.

1946 On February 4, Zóbel arrives in Seattle after a two-week sea voyage from Manila. En route to Harvard, he buys his first box of paints (Francisco Calvo Serraller, *Zobel*, Madrid; Fundación Juan March, 1984, n.p.) In

Cambridge he translates Perlimplín and illustrates it with four pen and watercolor drawings, his "primeras obras plásticas conocidas" (first known graphic works). He paints *A las cinco de la tarde / At Five in the Afternoon,* "the second oil painting I did, and the first with an original composition. Subject matter suggested by the poem by García Lorca, *Lament for Ignacio Sánchez Mejías.*" Lorca is an enduring presence in Zóbel's aesthetics and work. In 1957 his *Saetas* series draws inspiration from *Poema del cante jondo* (Poem of the Deep Song), and in 1963, he would title one of his drawings using a line from Lorca's "Poema doble de Lago Eden" in *Poet in New York*: "Así hablaba yo cuando Saturno detuvo los trenes" (That's what I was saying when Saturn stopped the trains.) See Alfonso de la Torre, "Zóbel-Chillida: A Meeting," *Mayoral Magazine*, April 29, 2019. http://galeriamayoral.com/en/magazine/zobel-chillida-a-meeting-alfonso-de-la-torre/ and Ángeles Villalba Salvador, "Cronología–Fernando Zóbel."

1947 New Directions publishes the first edition of *Three Tragedies* in the "authorized" translation by O'Connell and Graham-Lujan, introducing Lorca to a wider English-speaking public. With the editorial help of Robert M. MacGregor, Francisco García Lorca contributes an excellent introduction. Zóbel spends part of the summer in Spain.

MARCH 1949 Although the Losada (Buenos Aires) edition of *Perlimplín* is found "in the best bookstores of Madrid," an informant to Franco's censors is ambivalent about its morality. Like Lorca's puppet play *Los títeres de Cachiporra* (The Billyclub Puppets), *Perlimplín* "attacks morals on almost every page," but it can be allowed to circulate because of its "literary quality and its sense of pure aesthetic play." See Juan Aguilera Sastre, "Dos Exilios...", *Archivum*, LXIII (2013), 22.

In his senior year at Harvard, Fernando Zóbel submits his undergraduate honors essay "Theme and Conflict in Lorcan Drama" to the Department of History and Literature.

JULY 24, 1949 Future Academy-Award nominated director Sidney Lumet directs a version of *Don Perlimplín* at Lucille Lortel´s White Barn Theatre in Westport, Connecticut. See Louis Calta, "Todd Seeks Talent," *New York Times,* July 23, 1949.

1954 With the cooperation of the García Lorca family, Arturo del Hoyo edits the first Spanish edition of Lorca's complete works, modifying the Losada edition of *Perlimplín* (the one followed by Zóbel) after consulting a manuscript in the family archives. *Obras completas* (Madrid: Aguilar, 1954): 887-926; 1633-34.

1955 Stella Adler directs *Don Perlimplín* at her Studio Theatre, New York, with the desire to transcend the "Chekhovian realism" at the root of her work. "García Lorca Play to Open," *New York Times,* March 3, 1955; Joanna Rotté and Stella Adler. "An Interview with Stella Adler." *Theatre Topics* 12, no. 2 (2002): 191-202. Project Muse.

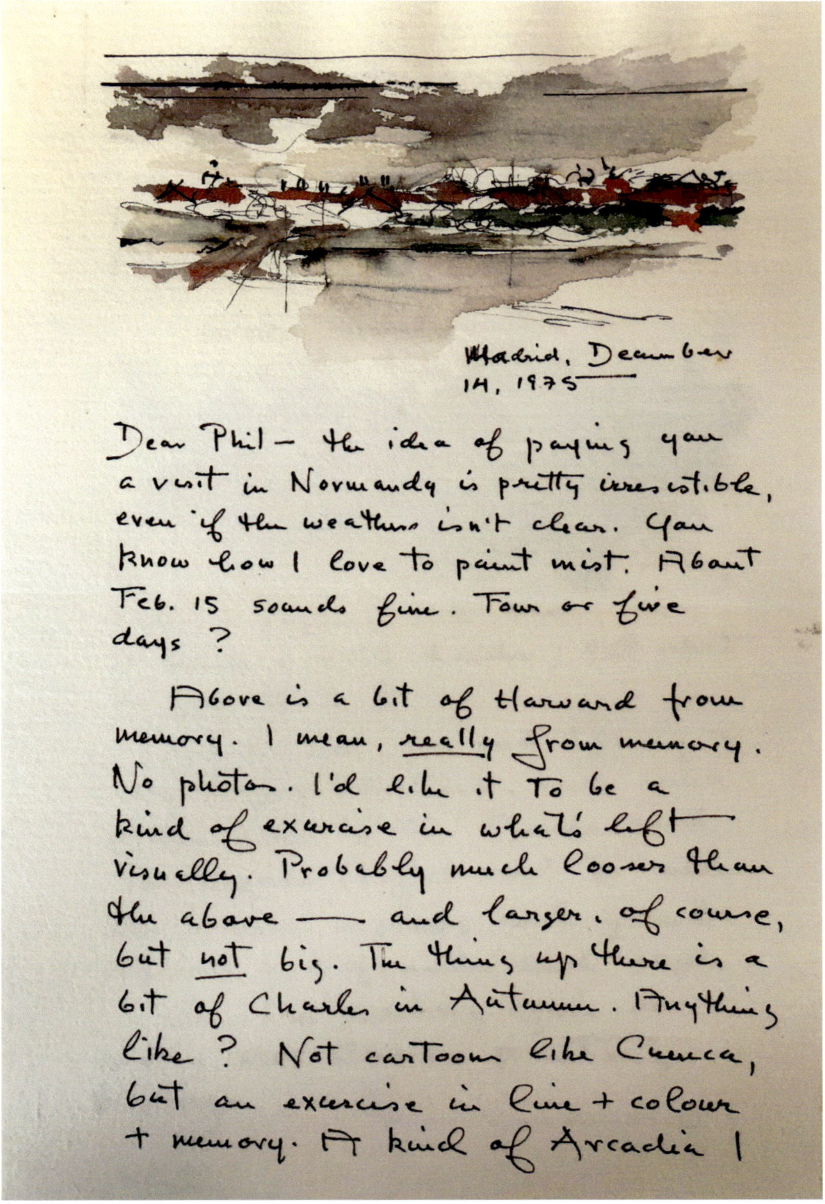

Madrid, December 14, 1975

Dear Phil – the idea of paying you a visit in Normandy is pretty irresistible, even if the weather isn't clear. You know how I love to paint mist. About Feb. 15 sounds fine. Four or five days?

Above is a bit of Harvard from memory. I mean, <u>really</u> from memory. No photos. I'd like it to be a kind of exercise in what's left visually. Probably much looser than the above — and larger, of course, but <u>not</u> big. The thing up there is a bit of Charles in Autumn. Anything like? Not cartoon like Cuenca, but an exercise in line + colour + memory. A kind of Arcadia I

6.1 Letter to Philip Hofer, December 14, 1975. In the 1970s, after he had been living for a while in Cuenca, Spain, Zóbel remembered the beauty of Harvard in a series of watercolors. Some he did from photographs (illustrations 2.1 and 2.6), but these two, in a letter to his old friend Phil Hofer, of Houghton Library, were "a bit of Harvard from memory. I mean *really* from memory. No photos. I'd like it to be a kind of exercise in what's left visually. […]

(Continued on next page)

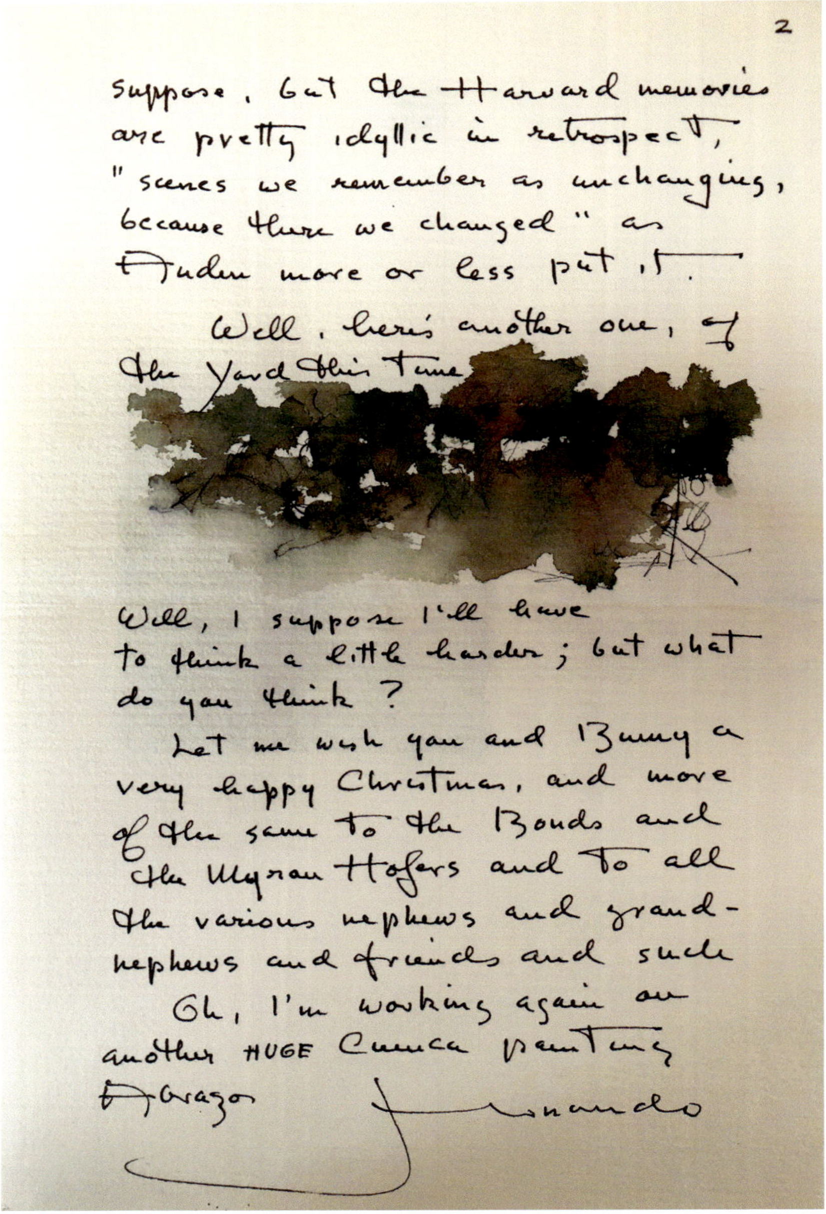

2

suppose, but the Harvard memories are pretty idyllic in retrospect, "scenes we remember as unchanging, because there we changed" as Auden more or less put it.

Well, here's another one, of the Yard this time

Well, I suppose I'll have to think a little harder; but what do you think?

Let me wish you and Bunny a very happy Christmas, and more of the same to the Bonds and the Myron Hofers and to all the various nephews and grand-nephews and friends and such

Oh, I'm working again on another HUGE Cuenca painting

Aragon

Fernando

The Harvard memories are pretty idyllic in retrospect. 'Scenes we remember as unchanging / because there we changed,' as Auden more or less put it." In the letter, Zóbel reminds Hofer that he likes to paint mists. And here were the mists of remembrance: "an exercise in line + color + memory. A kind of Arcadia, I suppose." Philip Hofer Papers, MS Typ 1229, Houghton Library, Harvard University.

ILLUSTRATIONS

Frontispiece

0.1 Fernando Zóbel at his easel, 1950s. Photo by Nicolás Muller. ©Fondo Nicolás Muller en el Archivo Regional de la CAM. Courtesy of Ana Muller.

Felipe Pereda, Zóbel Reads Lorca

1.1 Fernando Zóbel, Letter to Philip Hofer (Cuenca, July 8, 1978). Papers of Fernando Zóbel, Houghton Library, Harvard University. MSS Typ 687. Photo: author.

1.2 Fernando Zóbel, Undated print of Fox Club. Papers of Fernando Zóbel, MS Typ 688 (5). Photo: Harvard University.

1.3 Fernando Zóbel, Mural Paintings. Fox Club, Cambridge MA. Photo: author.

1.4 Fernando Zóbel and Fox Club mural. Fox Club. Photo: author

1.5 Fernando Zobel. *Ornitóptero*. Fundación Juan March. Photo: Fundación Juan March.

1.6 Fernando Zóbel, Sketchbook #56, 1965-66, fols. 1v-2. Fundación Juan March. Photo: Fundación Juan March.

1.7 Fernando Zóbel, Letter to Paul Haldeman, January 23, 1946. Papers of Fernando Zóbel, MS Typ 688 (5), Houghton Library. Photo: Harvard University.

1.8 Fernando Zóbel, Letter to Paul Haldeman, June 5, 1946. Papers of Fernando Zóbel, MS Typ 688 (5), Houghton Library. Photo: Harvard University.

1.9 Fernando Zóbel. Caricature. *Harvard Alumni Bulletin*, October 14, 1950. Photo: author.

1.10 Fernando Zóbel. Caricature. *Harvard Alumni Bulletin*, November 11, 1950. Photo: author.

1.11 Fernando Zóbel. Caricature. *Harvard Alumni Bulletin*, March 24, 1951. Photo: author.

1.12 Fernando Zóbel, Class notes, 1946. MS Typ 688, Houghton Library. Photo: author.

1.13 Jack Levine, *String Quartette*, 1937. Metropolitan Museum of Art. © Estate of Jack Levine / Licensed by VAGA at Artists Rights Society (ARS), N.Y.

1.14 Fernando Zóbel, *Letabundus Rediit, ex Carmina Burana*. Fundación Juan March. Photo: Fundación Juan March.

1.15 Fernando Zóbel, *Stultifera Navis* (frontis). Fundación Juan March. Photo: Fundación Juan March.

1.16 Fernando Zóbel, *El idiota del espejo* (The Mirror's Fool), in *Stultifera Navis*. Fundación Juan March. Photo: Fundación Juan March.

1.17 Georg Grosz, *A Little Yes and A Big No: The Autobiography of George Grosz* (New York: Dial Press, 1946) with Grosz's dedication to Fernando Zóbel. Fundación Juan March. Photo: Fundación Juan March.

1.18 Georg Grosz, *Uprooted. The Painter of the Hole*, 1948. Harvard Art Museums. Photo: Harvard Art Museums.

1.19 Fernando Zóbel, "El ojo crítico" ("The Critical Eye"), in "Stultifera Navis." Fundación Juan March. Photo: Fundación Juan March.

1.20 Federico García Lorca, illustration from *Poeta en Nueva York* (México: Séneca, 1940). Photo: author.

1.21 Walter Gropius and the members of TAC (The Architects Collaborative) on Richard Lippold's *World Tree*, 1950.

1.22 Fernando Zóbel. "A World Tree Almanac." *Harvard Alumni Bulletin*, January 12, 1952. Photo: author.

1.23 Fernando Zóbel. "June," from "A World Tree Almanac." *Harvard Alumni Bulletin*, January 12, 1952. Photo: author.

1.24 Fernando Zóbel. "October," from "A World Tree Almanac." *Harvard Alumni Bulletin*, January 12, 1952. Photo: author.

1.25 Fernando Zóbel, Diary #2 (August 6, 1950), fol. 12. Fundación Juan March, Madrid. Photo: Fundación Juan March.

1.26 Alfonso Ossorio, *Thomas Aquinas*, 1950. Ateneo Art Gallery, Manila. Photo: author.

1.27 Fernando Zóbel. Preparatory drawing for the portrait of Paul Haldeman. Fundación Juan March. Photo: Fundación Juan March.

1.28 Fernando Zóbel. "Road Map of Modern Art." In "Outlines for the Course Introduction to Contemporary Painting." Photo: Ateneo Art Gallery.

1.29 Fernando Zóbel. *Self Portrait in a Mirror* (1954). Private Collection. Photo: Ateneo Art Gallery.

Luis Fernández-Cifuentes, Zóbel's Harvard and the 1940s Crisis in Higher Education

2.1 Fernando Zóbel, "Las torres de Harvard en los años '40 desde el Lars Anderson Bridge", from Sketchbook 83 (1976). Zóbel was working "from a photo, ca. 1948," "before the new buildings changed the skyline." Fundación Juan March, Madrid.

2.2 Zóbel photographed by his friend Dave Perkins, 1947. Fundación Juan March.

2.3 Fernando Zóbel. Sketch of a professor lecturing at Harvard. Renato Poggioli? Sketchbook 6 (1951). Fundación Juan March, Madrid.

2.4 *General Education in a Free Society. Report of the Harvard Committee.* Harvard University Press, 1945.

2.5 Harry Levin and students. Harvard University. Radcliffe Archives.

2.6 Zóbel, View of Harvard Yard from Sketchbook 83 (1976). Fundación Juan March.

2.7 Harry Levin's report on Fernando Zóbel's senior honors thesis. Fundación Juan March, Madrid.

2.8 Fernando Zóbel, one of a series of studies of the Charles River. Sketchbook 13 (1954). Fundación Juan March.

2.9 *Class of 1949. Twenty-fifth Anniversary Report* (Cambridge, Harvard University Printing Office, 1974).

Christopher Maurer, American *Perlimplín*

3.1 "Historia de D. Perlimplín." Private collection.

3.2 "Vida de Don Perlimplín." University of New Mexico Center for Southwest Research and Special Collections.

3.3 "Historia de Perlimplín y Belisa en su jardín." Centro Federico García Lorca, Granada.

3.4 From the review of the premier of *Amor de Don Perlimplín. Luz* (Madrid), April 6, 1933

3.5 Cartoon by Del Arco accompanying a review of *Amor de Don Perlimplín. Heraldo de Madrid*, April 6, 1933.

García Lorca/Fernando Zóbel, *Don Perlimplín in Love*

4.1-4.4 Fernando Zóbel illustrations for *Don Perlimplín in Love*. Fernando Zóbel Papers, MS Typ 688 (2), Houghton Library, Harvard University.

Federico García Lorca/Gustavo Pittaluga, Music to *Amor de Don Perlimlín*

From *Canciones del teatro de García Lorca* (Madrid: Unión Musical Ediciones, 1960).

Christopher Maurer and Lincoln Son Currie, From Stage to Page: A *Perlimplín* Chronology

5.1 Federico García Lorca in Granada, 1926. Photo by Campbell ('Colin') Hackforth-Jones, courtesy of Andrew A. Anderson.

5.2 Federico García Lorca at Bushnellsville, New York, summer 1929, where he worked on revising *Amor de Don Perlimplín*. Centro Federico García Lorca, Granada.

5.3 Program for the Madrid performance of *Amor de Don Perlimplín* (1933). Centro Federico García Lorca, Granada.

5.4 James Graham-Lujan and Richard O'Connell, early translators of *Amor de Don Perlimplín*.

6.1 From a letter to Paul Haldeman, June 5, 1946. Papers of Fernando Zóbel, MS Typ 688, (5), Houghton Library, Harvard University.

NOTES

Marta Mateo, "Preface" (pp. vii-x)

1. For two brief but comprehensive biographies of the artist see the Art Gallery Diane de Polignac website, https://dianedepolignac.com/en/home-gb/artists-en/00-fernando-zobel-gb/ and John Seed, "Fernando Zóbel de Ayala. Brief Life of a Peripatetic Man of Arts: 1924-1984," *Harvard Magazine*, March-April 2009. Available at: https://www.harvardmagazine.com/2009/03/fernando-z-bel-de-ayala.

Felipe Pereda, "Zóbel Reads Lorca" (p. 1-40)

1. In English in the original.
2. Natalie Edgar, "Is There a New Spanish School?," *Art News* 59, no. 5 (1960): 44-45. See, more recently, María Dolores Jiménez-Blanco, "Spanishness and Difference. The Reception of Spanish Informalism in New York." *Contemporary Transatlantic Dialogues. Art History, Criticism, and Exhibition Practices in Spain and the United States* (New York: Center for Spain in America, 1960): 15-20. A more ambitious description within an analysis of the Regime's cultural politics, in Jorge Luis Marzo, *Arte Moderno y Franquismo. Los orígenes conservadores de la vanguardia y de la política artista en España*, 2006. https://www.soymenos.net/arte_franquismo.pdf
3. *Interview*, October 21, 1964.
4. Stuart Preston, "Art: From 3,000 B.C. to Andy Warhol," *The New York Times*, April 3, 1965.
5. Fernando Zóbel, "Si me pincharan mucho, mucho, me parece que vería obligado a decir que Rothko es el mejor pintor de los que conozco. Sus cosas, cuando son rotundas, lo son totalmente." Diary #7, New York, July 23, 1964.
6. Diary #8, March 16, 1965.
7. Diary #8, New York, April 8, 1965. Zóbel continues: "Glad I wasn't around. It would have felt like an examination; the kind of exam that really matters."
8. The letter is found with the correspondence with the rare books dealer Herman Cohen, of whom Zóbel was a friend and a client, for over thirty years. It is now at the Houghton Library, Harvard University.
9. *Interview*, October 21, 1964.
10. For two different analyses of Fernando Zóbel's heritage, see, Patrick D. Flores, "The Zóbel Nexus," *Kritika Kultura* 24 (2015), 182-205 and Florina H. Capistrano-

Baker, "Whither Art History in the Non-Western World: Exploring the Other('s) Art Histories, *The Art Bulletin* 97 (2005): 246-257.

11. "Greenberg cae en el error tan corriente en la crítica achantada [sic] por la ciencia moderna. El error de creer que la excelencia artística consiste en abrirse nuevos caminos visuales. Para mi esa novedad no tiene más que un interés bien relativo. No pretendo saber en qué consiste la sorpresa que nos causa la obra de arte. Lo que sí sé es que esa sorpresa no tiene absolutamente [his emphasis] nada que ver con asuntos de técnica. Absolutamente nada. El creador usa (y usa bien) la técnica que le sirve y nada más." (Greenberg falls into the error, which is so common in criticism stunted by modern science: the error of believing that artistic excellence consists in opening new visual paths. For me that novelty has only a relative interest. I don't pretend to explain the surprise given to us by a work of art. What I do know is that that surprise has absolutely nothing [his emphasis] to do with technical matters. Absolutely nothing. The creator uses (and uses well) the technique he finds useful, and that's that.) The above comes from a long commentary on Clement Greenberg, "The Crisis of Abstract Art," *Arts Yearbook* 7 (1964), written in Zóbel's diary (*Diario* #7) between September 13 and 17 of the same year.

12. George Kubler, *The Shape of Time*, (New Haven: Yale University Press, 1962), 40, cited in F. Zóbel, *Sketchbook* 56 [1965-66], f.1.

13. Kubler, *The Shape of Time*, 19.

14. A biography of Fernando Zóbel is still waiting to be written. In the meantime, I have profited from Peter Soriano, "A Biographical Sketch of Zóbel's Formative Years," in *Zóbel*, 200: 258-263. Also, Ángeles Villalba Salvador, "Cronología Fernando Zóbel," *ibid.*: 205-236. I would also like to thank Soriano for attending to my questions when preparing the current article.

15. See Luis Fernández Cifuentes' chapter in this volume for more on the classes he took.

16. The description of the class in the list of *Courses of Instruction*, 1945-46, reads: "Art of the Twentieth Century. From Post-Impressionism to the present. Emphasis on painting of this century."

17. Andrew McClellan and Sally Ann Duncan, *The Art of Curating. Paul J. Sachs and the Museum Course at Harvard*, (Los Angeles: Getty Research Institute, 2018).

18. Frederick S. Wright, *Milestones of American Painting* (Boston: Institute of Contemporary Art, 1949): 7.

19. Rowland described it as "surprisingly pleasant," and gave it an A-.

20. Fernando Zóbel, "El verdadero arte plástico de nuestra civilización es la caricatura." *Diario* #2, August 1950.

21. Sketchbook #2, signed and dated on the last folio: *Inv. et pinxit, Cantavrigiae MDCCCL*, Fundación Juan March, Madrid.

22. Arno Werner was responsible for bindings of rare books in Houghton Library, and had been recommended to him by Phil Hofer. See on his work the exhibition catalogue, *Arno Werner, Master Bookbinder: An Exhibition at the Houghton Library,* Cambridge, 1981. Lisa Callaway and Carolyn Coman, *Arno Werner on Book-binding,* (Lancaster, N.H.: Stinehour Press, 1981).

23. Zóbel very much admired Froben's edition of Erasmus' *Encomium Moriae,* in which Erasmus famously included a similar caricature.

24. Esther da Costa Meyer,"George Grosz, *The American Scene,*" *Yale University Art Gallery Bulletin,* 37 (1980): 4-7. Juerg M. Judin, ed., *George Grosz. The Years in America 1933-1958* New York: Hatje Cantz, 2009); Brigit Möckel, *George Grosz in Amerika 1932-1959* (Frankfurt am Main, Germany and New York: Peter Lang, 1997).

25. George Grosz, *An Autobiography,* trans. Nora Hodges (Berkley, CA: University of California Press, 1998): 296-297.

26. The exhibition included 22 watercolors and opened in April 1948 in the Associated American Artists Galleries, NY. That year, *Look* included him in the list of the ten most important American artists. Birgit Möckel, *George Grosz in Amerika, 1932-1959* (Berlin: Peter Lang, 1996): 163-184.

27. *Busch-Reisinger Museum. History and Holdings* (Cambridge, 1991) includes a list of the exhibitions organized by the museum, including: *George Grosz. Watercolors and Drawings* (1935); *George Grosz* (1942), traveling from the MOMA, and the 1949 show.

28. Letter of Charles Kuhn to the editor of the *Christian Science Monitor,* November 7, 1949. Harvard Archives, Exhibition Records, 1931-1950, HUAM Records, 2008.184, Carton, 37.

29. On loan from the Associated American Artists. A full list of the works exhibited, oils and watercolors, is kept in the exhibition files: Harvard Archives, Exhibition Records, 1931-1950, HUAM Records, 2008.184, Carton, 37.

30. BR49.711

31. Zóbel's absolute lack of interest in painting's iconography is itself telling. During his time at Harvard, Erwin Panofsky not only gave the Charles Eliot Norton Lectures (1947-48), but also taught two seminars at the History of Art Department, which his diaries do not even mention.

32. "Si se perdiera la Pintura, quizás con estos tres tomos se podría volver a descubrir" (Diary #3). Zóbel had read Malraux's book in the French edition (*Psychologie de l'art*), although already translated in 1949-50 (Bollingen Series, 3 vols).

33. Renato Poggioli's *The Theory of the Avant-Garde* (New York and London: Icon Editions, 1968) would later become an influential text among Spanish art critics as they addressed the work of Zóbel's generation of painters.

34. The most complete study and most complete catalogue is Mario Hernández, *Libro de los dibujos de Federico García Lorca* (Madrid: Tabapress/Fundación Federico García Lorca, 1990). English translation: *Line of Light and Shadow. The Drawings of Federico García Lorca*, trans. Christopher Maurer, Durham and London: Duke University Press/Duke University Museum of Art, 1991. There are now several studies on this aspect of his work. See Cecelia J. Cavanaugh, SSJ, *Lorca's Drawings and Poems. Forming the Eye of the Reader* (Lewisburg and London: Bucknell University Press, 1995): 27-35 for a short history of the drawings in Lorca's scholarship.

35. A facsimile of the catalogue, including a list of the works exhibited, is included in Laura Muir, ed., *Object Lessons. The Bauhaus and Harvard* (New Haven and London: Yale University Press, 2021). See, L. Muir, "'The Center for Bauhaus Material in America'. Exhibiting the Bauhaus at Harvard 1930-2019," *ibid.*: 37-64. See also Gregor Langfeld, *German Art in New York. The Canonization of Modern Art, 1904-1957* (Amsterdam University Press, 2015): 68-70.

36. Robert Wiesenberger, "The Bauhaus and Harvard," https://harvardartmuseums.org/tour/the-bauhaus/slide/6339. See also Sybil Gordon Kantor, *Alfred H. Barr, Jr. and the Intellectual Origins of the Museum of Modern Art* (Cambridge, Mass.: MIT Press, 2002): 197-210.

37. See for the negotiations Margret Kentgens-Craig, *The Bauhaus and America. First Contacts 1919-1936* (Cambridge, Mass.: MIT Press, 1999): 194-198.

38. For a full list of these exhibitions, see Peter Nisbet and Emilie Norris, *The Busch-Reisinger Museum: History and Holdings* (Cambridge, Mass: Harvard University Art Museums, 1991).

39. The recording of his speech at the opening is now available: https://sds.lib.harvard.edu/sds/video/434741882

40. Miro's mural was installed slightly later, but before October 27, 1951, when it was announced in the *Harvard Alumni Bulletin*.

41. Martin Duberman, *Black Mountain. An Exploration in Community* (New York: E.P. Dutton, 1972): 281-282.

42. An interesting document of their friendship comes from the testimony the Pfeufers' son Eric recorded on the occasion of the sale of their estate, in a documentary written by John Seed (2015): https://www.geringerart.com/works-by-fernando-zobel-from-the-estate-of-jim-and-reed-pfeufer/.

43. Fernando Zóbel *Diary* #2.

44. *Diary* #2, August 6, 1950, f. 12.

45. "Vi a Gordon Binkerd que está de vuelta escribiendo su tesis. Cené con ellos. Le interesa la idea de componer una ópera. Discutimos como librito magnífico las 'Bodas de Sangre': No solo tenemos una gran obra literaria, sino que es un melodrama magnífico, hecho a medida. Lo único que le falta es música. Claro que sería una pena traducirlo al inglés." (I saw Gordon Binkerd, who is back, writing his thesis. I ate

dinner with them. He's interested in composing an opera. We talked about *Bodas de sangre* as a magnificent libretto. Not only do we have a great work, it's also a magnificent melodrama, made to order. The only thing it lacks is music." Diary #2, October 7, 1950, f. 41.

46. "La gente no habla de Corea: es marca de mala educación; como hablar de muerte, o de enfermedades o de actos sexuales o escatológicos. Estamos hartos de guerra y copiamos al avestruz. El mundo se nos vuelve líquido ante los ojos, y nos pudrimos de desesperación lenta, puesto que el futuro se nos niega como base de construcción." (People do not talk about Korea, it would show a lack of politeness, like talking about death, or illnesses or sexual or scatalogical acts. We are sick of war and we copy the ostrich. The world has become liquid before our eyes, and we are slowly rotting with despair, because the future is denied to us as a basis for construction.) *Diary* #2, October 10, 1950, f. 42.

47. "Hoy, a casa de Alfonso Ossorio para recoger mi cuadrito de Sto. Tomás de Aquino. Cuadrito monumental, muy bonito, se ve que ha estado pintando murales Alfonso. Jackson Pollock, el pintor, y su mujer ocupan la casa, ahora llena de pinturas abstractas. Pollock muy serio, algo calvo, como sus cuadros, un poco pelmazo. Aspecto de arquitecto avanzado. La mujer fea y simpática. Tercera persona: un tal Smith de aspecto muy fin de siècle," (Today, to Alfonso Ossorio's house to pick up my little picture of St. Thomas Aquinas. A monumental little picture, very pretty; one can tell he has been painting murals. Alfonso, Jackson Pollock the painter and his wife occupy the house, which is now full of abstract paintings. Pollock, very serious, a bit bald, like his paintings a bit dull. The look of an advanced architect. His wife ugly and nice. A third person: a certain Smith with a fin de siècle look.) (Diary #3, December 28, 1950). Later, he also mentions a fourth person, the architect Charles Strickland as being in the house.

48. Deborah Solomon, *Jackson Pollock. A Biography* (New York: Simon and Schuster, 1987), 196. For Jackson Pollock and Lee Krasner's friendship with Ossorio, see Gail Levin, *Lee Krasner, a biography* (New York: HarperCollins, 2011), 256-262; and Gail Levin, "The Extraordinary Interventions of Alfonso Ossorio, Patron and Collector of Jackson Pollock and Lee Krasner," *Archives of American Art Journal*, 50 (2011): 5-19.

49. *15 Americans*, (New York: MoMA, 1952), 15-16, exhibition catalog.

50. Deborah Solomon, *Jackson Pollock*, 196-205.

51. Diary #3, December 29, 1950.

52. "Birthplace: City built by my ancestors in a country invented by them and in which I am a yearly fingerprinted alien. The contradictions bruise minutely." Diary #6, Manila, March 4, 1963.

53. "Puede que sea algo importante: este reconocimiento del hogar. Si hay que perderse en algún sitio, que sea en éste. Pese a todos los ornamentos, pese a la comodidad

de la prosa inglesa me reconozco como español" (Manila, December, 1959). (Perhaps it's something important, this recognition of home. If one must get lost someplace, let it be in this one. In spite of all of the ornaments, in spite of my ease with English prose, I recognize myself as Spanish." Quoted in Ángeles Villalba, "Cronología de Fernando Zóbel," 214.

54. Zóbel began to do this extensive work in Manila in the early 1950s. The most important result is the book, *Philippine Religious Imagery* (Manila: Ateneo de Manila, 1963).

55. Zóbel wrote in his Diary: "Jean Bratton turned up with Alfred Barr from the Museum of Modern Art and his wife. Quiet, elderly, very charming and intelligent [...] Barr saw the place slowly, taking notes, drinking it all in. At the end he asked if he had time for a second round. He did, so he started again at the beginning and repeated the whole tour. Lunch at Semperés. Barr leaned over and whispered that he and his wife thought it the most beautiful museum he had ever seen. I asked him if he would repeat that. He said yes, and repeated it aloud. The crowd cheered and we made him an honorary curator on the spot. More singing, dancing, etc. The Barrs are obviously enthralled." Diary #8, January 1, 1967. See now on the early history of the museum, *La ciudad abstracta. 1966. El Nacimiento del Museo de Arte Abstracto Español* (Cuenca: Fundación Juan March, 2006).

56. "So all in all the spirit shrinks a bit and I keep it alive by shutting myself and painting. I find I cannot paint those careful multi-textured things I used to do in emulation of Reed and Hyman Bloom. I paint big, bright, simple and flashy. It gives me a boost. Something like pulling myself up, Münchaussen-like, by the hair. Perhaps you would like these rather aggressive pictures of mine. I think that the enjoyment I have in making them somewhat remains in the finished product and in this neurotic age this simple pleasure may perhaps strike some as being a meritorious originality. Hein? Say yes. On the other hand, I have now been painting seriously for 8 years and I do not have very much to show for it. It is only during the last year that I have been able to produce something respectable in a respectable quantity. About 6 paintings, some 30 drawings and about 200 sketches worth keeping. I [sic] makes me feel good to put it down in black and white. It also does me good to tell you about it. I hesitate to tell or to write Reed about painting. I have never known why. The Pfeufers, after all these years, remain for me profoundly mysterious in many ways and this makes me love them all the better." Letter to Paul Haldeman, Manila, February, 17, 1953, Houghton Library.

57. See on the artist now, Erica E. Hirschler, *Hyman Bloom. Matters of Life and Death* (Boston: Museum of Fine Arts: 2019).

58. Fernando Zóbel, "Se me ocurre: qué buena idea seguir no ganando nada este verano y convencerle a Hyman Bloom que me enseñe a pintar. Creo que me tomaría por estudiante."(It occurs to me—what a good idea—to go on earning nothing this

summer and to convince Hyman Bloom to teach me to paint. I believe he would take me as a student.) Diary #3, March, 3, 1551. In December of the previous year, 1950, Zóbel had shown three of his paintings at a collective exhibition at the Hyman Swetzoff gallery.

59. On February 18, 1951, he writes: "Estoy pintando mejor que nunca. Me atrevo a usar colores fuertes pero también me convenzo que aún no me es posible pintar sin negro;" (I'm painting better than ever. I'm daring to use strong colors, but I'm also convinced that I still cannot paint without black.) And on February 15, 1951: "Si me descuido un día de estos voy a resultar pintor, y el alma del pobre tío Ataulfo (ese tío Ataulfo que todos tenemos y que fue guardia civil) se volverá a morir." (If I let down my guard one of these days I'm going to turn into a painter, and the soul of poor Uncle Ataulfo (that Uncle Ataulfo we all have and who was a Civil Guard) will die all over again.)

60. "Of painting: I am suddenly painting very well. I don't know if I told you that. Probably did. It is mildly miraculous how one goes by spurts and explosions. I painted badly during my vacation. Why? It worried me at the time. And now I am pouring out paintings, stealing time where I can, going to bed early and getting up early, even waking up in the middle of the night to nail down an idea. And my technique has suddenly improved by itself. I can do pictorial acrobatics that were completely beyond my means a mere six months ago; beyond my understanding in fact. You must have had similar experiences. It makes one happy to be alive and also makes one hideously impatient with that rattling of stones in a tin can that people try to force on one under the label of 'activity.' And yet (this is my own learned lesson) what effective background the rattling provides. Hermits need an audience to which not to speak, and the hermit's cave is in the desert but not too much further that a stone's throw from the City limits. Not that I'm a hermit, ye gods. I'm much more likely to be elected 'Businessman of 1956'. What strange costumes one assumes. If you send me a picture of you in uniform I'll retaliate with one of me behind my huge, clean (efficient) desk, complete with dictaphone. Then we can snigger in unison like kids snigger between themselves when they latch onto something the old don't know." Letter to Dave Perkins, December 6, 1955, Houghton Library.

61. Kept in the Archive of the Ateneo Museum, Manila (unpublished).

Luis Fernández-Cifuentes, "Zóbel's Harvard and the 1940s Crisis in Higher Education" (pp. 41-61)

1. All courses in the College were divided into three categories: Humanities (roughly equivalent to the medieval *trivium*), Natural Sciences or simply Sciences (the *quadrivium*) and a new and much debated category, the Social Sciences, which included sociology, psychology, anthropology, etc. "There is a great battle in progress between the old good disciplines, like History, Classics, Literature and the like, and

sociology, social anthropology, psychology, etc., in which one cannot but be on the side of the former," wrote Isaac Berlin to a friend in 1949, when he was teaching at Harvard. He lamented that in the Social Sciences "so much is spoken, so little said, still less demonstrated or rendered plausible, so many old, trite truths come masquerading as new discoveries." See Berlin, *Enlightening. Letters 1946-1960* (London: Chatto & Windus, 2009), 85 and 751. In some colleges, history was a social science; in others, it was part of the humanities. Regarding the natural sciences, Zóbel rectified many years later (Diary, December 1981): "Physics and mathematics, which have always been a total mystery, long hated, now a source of helpless admiration."

2. Isaac Berlin, in his 1949 assessment of Harvard students, had these words of praise for a "curiosity" that was not interested in practical or *useful* gains: "Once a community automatically begins to consider disinterested curiosity as being idle, time-wasting, self-indulgent and, therefore, immoral, it is in a very bad way." (Berlin, 755).

3. An English composition course required of all freshmen, a stepping stone to more advanced courses in English provided one passed it with high grades. It was taught by the poet and novelist Theodore Morrison, who must have given Zóbel a good grade: it allowed him to move on to Advanced Composition with the poet and short-story writer Delmore Schwartz (whom Zóbel calls a "socialistic poet"). Schwartz gave Zóbel an A- (Diary of July 2, 1946).

4. Howard Mumford Jones was a renowned professor in the department of English, a specialist in 19th and 20th century literature who won a Pulitzer prize in 1965 for his book *O Strange New World*, on 20th century American culture. In the Spring of 1949 he taught two undergraduate courses: American Literature From 1850 to 1901 and American Literature Since 1890. Benjamin Rowland was a specialist in Western Art. In the Spring of 1949 he taught an undergraduate course on American Art From the Revolution to the Present Day, a graduate seminar on Methods of Research in Oriental Art, and a course in the Core Humanities: Types of Art: the Representation of Nature in European and Asiatic Art. Zóbel, a devoted collector of Chinese scrolls, probably chose the third.

5. Prescott, Peter. *A Darkening Green. Notes on Harvard, the 1950s and the End of Innocence* (New Brunswick: Transaction Publishers, 2009): 173.

6. *Harvard University Catalog* (Cambridge: Harvard University Press, [1945-1949]).

7. Barrett Wendell (1855-1921), a celebrated professor of literature at Harvard, had been the founder and first chairman of the Committee on Degrees in History and Literature in 1906.

8. "Wendell Prize in History and Literature, to Schlesinger," *The Harvard Crimson*, June 3, 1936.

9. *The 1949 Harvard Album* (Cambridge: Harvard University Press, 1949). It

may be worth noting that in the *Harvard Album* most of Zóbel's classmates recorded above all their accomplishments in sports. But Zóbel was an oddity in several regards. In 1945, only 3% of all Harvard freshmen came "from the Territories and from foreign countries" (Harvard University 1949,184). "Territories" was a euphemism for colonies. Thus, Zóbel was part of a tiny minority within a minority. Zóbel's identity seems to have been always in flux, pulled apart by tensions between his very wealthy origins in the colonies (the Philippines became independent from the US precisely in 1946), his overwhelming preference for Spain, and his intellectual dependence on the United States; or, in other words, his adamant but never-quite-effective rejection of Manila, his definitive settlement in Madrid, and his regular returns to New York. A triangular conundrum.

10. In 1949-1950, during his first and only year at Harvard Law School, Zóbel found that the strenuous coursework prevented him from painting at all and he dropped out.

11. Prescott, *A Darkening Green*, 109.

12. Louis Menand, *The Free World. Art and Thought in the Cold War* (New York: Farrar, Straus and Giroux, 2021): 455.

13. Louis Menand, *The Marketplace of Ideas. Reform and Resistance in the American University* (New York: Norton and Company, 2010): 28.

14. Gerald Graff, *Professing Literature. An Institutional History* (Chicago: University of Chicago Press, 1987): 162.

15. Harvard University. *General Education in a Free Society. The Report of the Harvard Committee* [the *Redbook*]. Cambridge: Harvard University Press, 1946. "General Education" was part of the Cold War effort to fight "radical doctrines of the nineteenth-century based on the notion of class struggle," as President Conant put it in 1948 (Graff, 167).

16. *General Education*, 108. Predictably, some intellectuals criticized this notion of "unity" from the start and more so during the 1960s: it was considered authoritarian and antidemocratic (Graff, 165 and 173). In 1966, when the hippy movement was well underway, a new book took stock of a new crisis: Daniel Bell's *The Reforming of General Education.*

17. The same unencumbered, self-conscious disarray can be recognized in Zóbel's choice of readings at any given time or place. One example: "Tedium. I gorge on books, pell-mell. Two or three books a day. Philosophy, poetry, religion, China, history, science-fiction, sociology, pornography" (entry for August 24, 1966 in Diary #8 (1964-67).

18. *General Education*, 5.

19. *General Education*, 50.

20. *General Education*, 40.

21. *General Education*, 100.

22. *General Education*, 196.

23. Graff, *Professing Literature*, 164.

24. Menand, *The Marketplace of Ideas*, 32.

25. Curiously, the *Redbook* understood General Education to mean "spending four years in the study of approximately one hundred great books of the Western tradition, supplemented by ancient and modern languages, mathematics and laboratory sciences." *General Education*, 182.

26. Menand, *The Marketplace of Ideas*, 42.

27. *General Education*, 207.

28. Humanities 3a also included, at least for a while, another Spanish text: Ortega y Gasset's *The Revolt of the Masses*. "My favorite course, Humanities 3, was modestly called 'Crisis and the Individual' [...]. After Homer, in rapid-fire succession, came Thucydides, Ibsen, Shaw, Shakespeare, Marx, Ortega y Gasset, Plutarch, Stendhal, Sophocles—and that was only the first term" (Prescott, *A Darkening Green*, 65). Things are somewhat different at Harvard in the 21st century. Cervantes has been taken off the reading list of Humanities 10. Literature in Spanish is now represented by Sor Juana Inés de la Cruz, García Márquez, and Valeria Luiselli. Starting in the 1940s (if not earlier) Latin American literature and culture increasingly prevailed over Peninsular literature and culture (including the Golden Age masters) in most departments of Spanish. See Estellita Hart's compilations, *Courses on Latin America in Institutions of Higher Education in the United States* (Pan American Union, Division of Education, 1946-1947, 1948-1949, etc.) In the 1940s Harvard offered numerous courses on Latin America in the departments of History, Anthropology, Economics and RLL. The *Harvard Educational Review* devoted its October 1943 issue to Latin America: the articles had just been read at a Harvard Workshop on "Latin American Studies in New England Schools." The phenomenal North American success of the writers of the Boom in the late 60s and the 70s (García Márquez, Vargas Llosa, etc.) accelerated a process that modified substantially the status of Spanish sections in all colleges, including Harvard. Zóbel does not show at any point any interest in Latin American culture.

29. Berlin, *Enlightening. Letters*, 750.

30. One more conjecture. Zóbel probably took a course with Renato Poggioli, eventually the second reader of his thesis and, in Claudio Guillén's opinion, a great professor. The course may have been Comp. Lit. 151, European Romanticism: Its Origins and Development, in the Spring of 1947 (after all, Zóbel declared "Nineteenth Century, with emphasis in the Romantics" his specialization.) The course "presumed [...] a good reading knowledge of French, German, Italian or Spanish" and was cross-listed with RLL.

31. Zóbel differs from the likes of Lionel Trilling, who acknowledges *Don Quixote*

as the fundamental pivot of the modern novel from *Tom Jones* to *Ulysses*. See, for example, *Sincerity and Authenticity*, the book that collects his 1969-1970 Norton Lectures at Harvard, in which he summed up his Great Books classes. Cervantes was the only Spanish author mentioned in Trilling's lectures. A well-established US academic tradition justified the exclusion of everybody else. In the 1920s, an officer of New York State's Department of Education declared: "he is a bold man who will claim that Spain ranks with England, France, América or Germany in any element of greatness. Its literature is far inferior to that of Italy. The average educated Englishman, American, German or Frenchman credits Spain with only one great author—Cervantes—and one great book—*Don Quixote*—." But this was already an old axiom and I have traced it elsewhere. Luis Fernández Cifuentes, "La literatura española en los Estados Unidos: historia de sus historias." In *Historia literaria / historia de la literatura*, ed. Leonardo Romero (Zaragoza: Prensas Universitarias, 2004): 259.

32. *General Education*, 205.

33. I.A. Richards, *Practical Criticism* (New York: Harcourt, Brace and Company, 1929): 171.

34. *General Education*, 119-120.

35. *General Education*, 124.

36. *General Education*, 121.

37. *General Education*, 123, reiterated on 126.

38 *General Education*, 126. Because of these shortsighted discriminations, the *Redbook* was not always well received, especially in literary journals that paid some attention to the relegated foreign languages. Just one example. In his review for the *Modern Language Journal*, a very disappointed and even shocked Theodore Huebener, director of Foreign Languages for the New York school system, calls attention to some of the *Redbook* statements quoted above (vol. 29, n. 8, December 1947, p. 677).

39. Morton and Phyllis Keller, *Making Harvard Modern. The Rise of America's University* (Oxford: Oxford University Press, 2001): 430.

40. Donald Allen, *The New American Poetry, 1945-1960* (New York: Grove Press, 1960).

41. *Poetics of the New American Poetry* (New York: Grove Press, 1973).

42. A cursory look at literary journals devoted in all or in part to literature in Spanish, like *Hispanic Review* (University of Pennsylvania), *Hispania* (the American Association of Teachers of Spanish and Portuguese with Johns Hopkins University), and *Romanic Review* (Columbia University), confirms such predominance. The exception may be *Revista Hispánica Moderna*, where Federico de Onís and Ángel del Río, both friends of Lorca, maintained a more ecumenical perspective. In 1941 del Río coordinated a special issue of *Revista Hispánica Moderna* devoted to García Lorca, with an impressive bibliography. Zóbel wrote in his thesis that it was "the richest and most interesting single volume ever published about Lorca." If Lorca had a sanctuary

in the US, it was the *Casa Hispánica* at Columbia University, the headquarters of *Revista Hispánica Moderna*.

43. *Syllabi, course outlines and reading lists in Spanish, 1927-1979*.

44. Grases, López Morillas, Regalado and Lorca were all distinguished Spanish exiles. The histories of Spanish intellectual exiles in the US have failed so far to account for one of the darker sides of their experience at American universities. The exiles' letters to one another speak more often than not of too much work, too little pay and difficulties in publishing their work. What is worse: many were eminent scholars in Spain, but most of them came to the US equipped at best with only a traditional philological training that no longer had much currency in their new academic environments. They were also too old or too proud to pick up the new tools of the trade. As a result, they remained in general isolated (sometimes bitterly so) in the Spanish sections of their universities, second class citizens unable to converse with their counterparts in English, Comparative Literature, Slavic, etc.

45. Claudio Guillén, *De leyendas y lecciones* (Barcelona: Crítica, 2007): 283-287.

46. Keller, *Making Harvard Modern*, 245.

47. Amado Alonso, *Materia y forma en poesía* (Madrid: Gredos, 1960): 81.

48. Information drawn from *Papers of Amado Alonso*, Harvard University Archives.

49. Prescott, *A Darkening Green*, 174.

50. Richards, *Practical Criticism*, 340.

51. Richards, 314.

52. Christopher Maurer read this paper meticulously and suggested decisive improvements. He has all my gratitude.

Christopher Maurer, "American *Perlimplín*" (pp. 62-80).

1. Zóbel and Desmond Morris: see Mario Hernández, Fernando Zóbel. *El misterio de lo transparente* (Madrid: Ediciones Rayuela, 1977): 31. For Lorca's comments on Perlimplín see Federico García Lorca, *Palabra de Lorca. Declaraciones y entrevistas completas*, ed. Rafael Inglada (Barcelona: Malpaso, 2017): 99; translation mine. Lorca describes the play as a "teatro de monigotes humanos, que empieza en burla y acaba en trágico." On the word *monigote*, which Zóbel translates as "puppet," see Paul McDermid, *Love, Desire and Identity in the Theatre of Federico García Lorca* (London: Tamesis, 2007): 74. For an excellent overview of interpretations of the play, with its "unresolved, and perhaps unresolvable, ambiguities, discontinuities, and unknowns," see Andrew A. Anderson, "Undecidability in Lorca's *Amor de Don Perlimplín con Belisa en su jardín*," *Hispanic Studies Review* 3, no. 1 (2018): 1-13.

2. Sketchbook #18 (October 1958 to September 1959; Fundación Juan March) offers translations of Miguel Hernández, Rafael Alberti, and Paul Valéry, and poems from the flamenco repertoire.

3. "Probablemente letras solas, pero qué letras! Tienen que desbordarse, correr

por la página, agarrar al lector por el pescuezo. Para un experimento como este lo que mejor pega es verso; sobre todo un verso lleno de colorido como lo es el de Lorca.'El Diván de la Tamarit' [sic]. El nombre solo ya es un poema. Se escribe solo." August 25, 1940, Sketchbook #2 (May-November 1950), Fundación Juan March.

4. *From Lorca's Theatre. Five Plays of Federico García Lorca*, trans. Richard L. O'Connell and James Graham L. (New York: Charles Scribner's Sons, 1941): 47-71. Gwynne Edwards points out that the "translations by [these two] were for over forty years the only ones allowed in published form by the Lorca Estate. In many cases their literal character, combined with Americanisms, made them virtually unspeakable in performance. The translation of *Don Perlimplín* is one of the better ones in this respect." See "Theatre Workshop's Translations of Three Spanish Plays," *New Theatre Quarterly* 25, no. 1 (2009): 62, note 11. In *Lorca in English*, Andrew Samuel Walsh lists translations by O'Connell and Graham-Luján (1941, revised 1963), David Johnston (1990), Gwynne Edwards (1990) and Caridad Svich (2000).

5. Zóbel, "Theme and Conflict in Lorcan Drama." Undergraduate Honors essay submitted to The Department of History and Literature, Harvard College, March 1949: 10. The Library of Fernando Zóbel. Fundación Juan March (Madrid).

6. "Theme and Conflict," 10. The earliest performance of *Amor de Don Perlimplín* at Harvard seems to have been the Poets' Theatre production, directed by the Puerto Rican actor Victor Gabriel Junquera in March 31, 1959, coupled with James Broughton's *The Last Word* See Melvin Maddocks, "'Love of Don Perlimplín' by Poets' Theatre Group," *The Christian Science Monitor*, April 1, 1959 and the review by Julius Novick in *The Harvard Crimson*, April 7, 1959, online at https://www.thecrimson.com/article/1959/4/7/the-love-of-don-perlimplin-and/)

7. "Theme and Conflict," 27, note 1. See note 38 below.

8. Francisco García Lorca, *In the Green Morning: Memories of Federico*, trans. Christopher Maurer (New York: New Directions, 1980): 182.

9. "Theme and Conflict," 10.

10. Gwynne Edwards, "Theatre Workshop and the Spanish Drama," *New Theatre Quarterly* 23, no. 4 (Nov. 2007): 312.

11. Zóbel offers the following succinct and accurate definition: "An illustrated broadsheet, somewhat similar to a comic strip, in which the usually anonymous author comments in doggerel verse on human foibles, the political situation, current morals or any other appropriate subject. These are traditionally sold during Holy Week." "Theme and Conflict," 10, note 1.

12. Francisco García Lorca, *In the Green Morning*, 182. See also Helen Grant, "Una aleluya erótica de Federico García Lorca y las aleluyas populares del siglo XIX," *Actas del Primer Congreso de la Asociación Internacional de Hispanistas celebrado en Oxford del 6 al 11 de septiembre de 1962* (Oxford: The Dolphin Book Company, 1964): 310. Online at https://cudl.lib.cam.ac.uk/view/PR-TAB-B-00721-00003/1.

13. In May 1920 the librettist and journalist Juan Gómez Renovales, writing in a children's magazine, evokes the world of Perlimplín and other characters from the *aleluya*, cut into pieces and tossed from a balcony: "Dancing through the air came Don Perlimplín, an agile dancer and an expert with a fencing sword, in love with doña Sempronia. The Little Rascal [pilluelo] of Madrid, on the loose from his orphanage, stealing handkerchiefs and beating dead dogs. The illustrious Periquín, born inside an egg, trapped by a harrier, bitten by a dog and swallowed by a shark. Singular, immortal characters printed on sheets of a thousand colors, the *aleluyas* that children cut up and toss from balconies." "Origen de la procesión del Corpus," *Mi Revista* X , no. 15 (May 30, 1920): 3. Translation mine.

14. To my knowledge, the most complete compilation of *aleluyas* is J. Amades, J. Colominas and Pau Vila, *Les auques. Imatgeria popular catalana*, 2 vols. (Barcelona: Editorial Orbis, 1931 and 1933). "Historia de D. Perlimplín" is reproduced in facsimile in Vol. II, plate lxxxii (see p. 66, below). Helen Grant reproduces the only other known version, "Vida de Don Perlimplín" in "Una aleluya erótica," p. 310, found here on p. 67 and online at https://cudl.lib.cam.ac.uk/view/PR-TAB-B-00721-00003/1

15. "Señor Perlimplín, / dressed as emperor / was declaiming *Il Trovatore* / in a theater in Peking." "These four verses can keep the same meaning and be combined in different ways. How many ways? Which ones?" "Entretenimientos," *La Hormiga de Oro. Ilustración Católica* (Madrid) 27, no. 39 (Sept. 24, 1910): 23.

16. See the rendering of typical figures from Europe, Asia, Africa and the Americas in plate LXXIX in *Les Auques*, vol. 2.

17. Francisco García Lorca, *In the Green Morning*, 186.

18. On Lorca's mix of heterogeneous elements, see Cecilia Vega Martín, "Aspectos del juego y de la tragedia en *Amor de Don Perlimplín con Belisa en su jardín*" in Cristóbal Cuevas García, ed., *El teatro de Lorca: tragedia, drama y farsa* (Madrid: Publicaciones del Congreso de Literatura Española Contemporánea, 1995): 258 ff.

19. Quoted in J.M. Pedrosa, "De *Perlinpinpin* a *Perlimplín. Féerie* francesa, *Cyrano*, cuentos de Calleja…y Lorca," *Liburna* 8 (November 2015): 119. Luis Fernández Cifuentes, *García Lorca en el teatro: La norma y la diferencia* (Prensas Universitarias de Zaragoza, 1986): 115-131.

20. As in the 1923 Twelfth-Night performance organized by Lorca and his friend and mentor the composer Manuel de Falla at Lorca's family home in Granada of the *Misterio de los Reyes Magos* (Mystery of the Three Kings), which used dozens of figures cut out of heavy cardboard and painted by Hermenegildo Lanz. Falla would use the same technique in his *Retablo de Maese Pedro*. See Mónica Hurtado Hernández, *Los Cristobitas en Lorca. Tradición y vanguardia en los "puntales del teatro"* (Vigo: Editorial Academia del Hispanismo, 2019): 159 and—on that performance and on the esthetics of "planismo"—Andrew A. Anderson, "Títeres bidimensionales: Lagar, Barradas, Lorca, Lanz," *Acotaciones* 48 (Jan.-June 2022): 297-329. Lorca's friend

José Mora Guarnido spoke of the "planista repertoire" of Lorca's "Teatro Cachiporra Andaluz" (Andalusian Billyclub Puppets). Hurtado Hernández, 160.

21. See Margarita Ucelay, ed., *Amor de Don Perlimplín con Belisa en su jardín* (Madrid: Cátedra 1990): 88-93, and Paul McDermid, who interprets Lorca's "planar" theater as "an animation of the two-dimensional, whether a plastic image or a written verse." *Love, Desire and Identity in the Theatre of Federico García Lorca* (Woodbridge: Tamesis, 2007): 70, 74. In the introduction to her edition, Ucelay (133) recalls Lorca's 1926 letter to Melchor Fernández Almagro speaking of a play "whose characters are photographic blow-ups." A fragment has been printed by Marie Laffranque, ed., FGL, *Teatro inconcluso: fragmentos y proyectos inacabados* (Granada: Universidad de Granada, 1987): 170-175.

22. "*Teatro de aleluyas*" in Ucelay, p. 37 and Federico García Lorca, *Obras completas*, ed. Miguel García-Posada, vol. 2, *Teatro* (Barcelona: Galaxia Gutenberg/Círculo de Lectores, 1997): 850. The rest of the note shows Lorca's original intention to imitate the *aleluya*—often printed on brightly colored paper—onstage: "Framed in a dark border, the scenes [will have] green, yellow, and white backgrounds. The figures will always be dressed in black, with their hands and faces the same color as the background, and their features sketched in black. A supreme inexpressiveness and coldness are the characteristics of this theater, and there is thus a tragic, almost sublime expression in the words and actions of its figures. The scene, the characters and the verses will have their masks. Transcendent things of the world—love, death—will be stripped bare, come onstage and leave with the same importance and vacuity as any sort of trivial action. At times a vulgar act, or one with no transcendence at all, will vibrate in the most intense damatic manner, alongside an intense and universal one which will pass tamely by. The voices of the characters will maintain a monotone and will have a childish ring to them" (my translation).

23. García Lorca, *Collected Poems*, ed. Christopher Maurer (New York: Farrar, Straus and Giroux, 2002): xliii. The original may be found in "[Apuntes sobre la escenificación de los romances"], in *Obras completas*, vol. 3, *Prosa*, ed. Miguel García-Posada (Barcelona: Galaxia Gutenberg/Círculo de Lectores, 1997): 324.

24. Fernández Cifuentes, 120-21.

25. Ed. Margarita Ucelay, 37-41.

26. Gwynne Edwards translates Lorca's subtitle as "An Erotic Print in Four Scenes." For dates and titles of recent translations and productions, see "Out of the Wings," http://www.outofthewings.org/db/play/amor-de-don-perlimplin-con-belisa-en-su-jardin/translations.html A translation not listed there, by Anne Ketcham Blodgett and Marion Lipscomb Miller and preserved in the New Directions Publishing Corp. Records, Houghton Library (bMS AM 2077 5940) subtitles the play "An Erotic Easter Card in Four Scenes and a Prologue," a subtitle inaccurate but suggestive, given the play's unmistakable allusions to Christ and the Eucharist. José

Ignacio Badenes convincingly relates Perlimplín's struggle to the "passion, death, and resurrection of Jesus Christ," and the allegorical religious drama of Calderón de la Barca. See "'This Is My Body Which Will Be Given Up For You': Federico García Lorca's *Amor de Dom Perlimplín* and the *Auto Sacramental* Tradition," *Hispania* 92, no. 4 (December 2009): 688-695.

27. *From Lorcas's Theatre*, xxvi. The translators applied a similarly misleading expression—"A finely wrought Victorian Valentine" with "punctured paper lace" to the farewell scene at the end of Act One in *Doña Rosita la Soltera*; see xxviii-xxix.

28. Kevin Kelly, "*Love of Don Perlimplin*. Small Play by Federico Lorca Well-Suited to Poet's Theater," *The Boston Daily Globe*, April 1, 1959; Italics mine.

29. "Don Perlimplín: Lorca's Theatre-Poetry." *The Kenyon Review* XVII, no. 3 (Summer 1955): 342.

30. On the "intricate network of influences" detectable in *Perlimplín*, "from the Italian *commedia dell'arte* to the short theater of the Spanish Golden Age, to French Symbolism" and beyond, see Emilio Peral Vega, "Morir y matar amando: *Amor de Don Perlimplín con Belisa en su jardín*," *Arbor* (Madrid) CLXXVII, nos. 699-700 (March-April 2004): 691-702 and Peral Vega *Pierrot/Lorca. White Carnival of Black Desire* (Woodbridge: Tamesis, 2015).

31. Zóbel, "Theme and Conflict," 10.

32. *Heraldo de Madrid*, 10 de marzo de 1933.

33. *Palabra de Lorca*, 98, from an interview in April 1933.

34. "Introduction," *Five Plays: Tragedies and Tragicomedies* (New York: New Directions, 1963): 10.

35. Alberto Marín Alcalde, "Dos farsas de García Lorca, en el Español, *Ahora*, April 6, 1933. In another review, Juan Chabás remarks that the piece has "el mismo elegante ritmo de un minué del XVIII" (the same elegant rhythm as an eighteenth-century minuet). "Función de gala en honor de García Lorca," *Luz* (Madrid, April 6, 1933.

36. Nelson R. Orringer, *Lorca in Tune With Falla* (University of Toronto Press, 2014): 224, note 40, with detailed elaboration in "Falla's *Harpsichord Concerto* and Lorca's *Don Perlimplín*" in Irene Gómez Castillo and Aurélie Vialette, eds., *Dissonances of Modernity: Music, Text, and Performance in Modern Spain* (North Carolina Studies in the Romance Languages and Literatures, 2021): 225-240. Luis T. González del Valle, "La concepción musical de *Amor de Don Perlimplín con Belisa en su jardín*." *El teatro de Federico García Lorca y otros ensayos* (Lincoln, NE: Society of Spanish and Spanish American Studies, 1980): 61-79. Describing "El teatro musical de Federico García Lorca" in 1933, the poet and pianist Gerardo Diego wrote that *Perlimplín* "comes close to perfection thanks to the studied contrast of its four scenes, its tonal relations and counterpoints, the nostalgic, ironic, anguished, gallant or grotesque rhythm with which each scene unfolds, like the slow-moving tableaux of

a Baroque 'ballet,' partly Italian and partly Versaillesque, not to mention the obvious reminiscences of our minor, courtly classical theater." Quoted in Marco Antonio de la Ossa, Ángel, musa y duende: Federico García Lorca y la música (Madrid: Alpuerto/ Ediciones de la Universidad de Castilla-La Mancha,2014): 151 (translation mine).

37. First published by Gustavo Pittaluga in 1962 (see p. 00) and reproduced in Margarita Ucelay's edition, 293-96.

38. "Greatly admired"—and played—"by Falla and Lorca alike". Nelson R. Orringer, *Lorca in Tune with Falla*, 224, note 40. To my knowledge, no one has identified the five Scarlatti sonatas played by Lago, but among those in her repertoire was the Sonata in D major K. 29 L 461; see *La Libertad* (Madrid), January 17, 1923. An account in *Heraldo de Madrid*, April 5, 1933 mentions "cinco sonatinas."

39. Years earlier, in November 1926, she had collaborated with Cipriano Rivas Cherif—who had tried to stage *Perlimplín* in 1929—on a combined recital of poetry and music. In a review of that event, at the Círculo de Bellas Artes, Madrid, the critic Enrique Díez-Canedo comments on the musical affinities of modern poets. "Información teatral," *El Sol*, December 1, 1926.

40. Gwynne Edwards, "Theatre Workshop and the Spanish Drama," *New Theatre Quarterly* 23, no. 4 (2007): 312. See also, by the same critic, "Theatre Workshop's Translations of Three Spanish Plays," 57.

41. "He's interested in composing an opera. We talked about *Bodas de sangre* as a magnificent libretto. Not only do we have a great work, it's also a magnificent melodrama, made to order. The only thing it lacks is music." Diary #2, October 7, 1950, f. 41.

42. Robert M. MacGregor to Richard O'Connell, August 1, 1958, New Directions Publishing Corp. Records, bMS Am2077.1 (731d).

43. Note from MacGregor, "Printers Copy–Manuscripts of Five Plays by García Lorca" in New Directions Publishing Corp. Records, bMS AM2077.1 (732), Houghton Library, Harvard University.

44. *Five Plays*, 108.

45. As early as 1945 John Crow, who lived in Lorca's dormitory at Columbia University, writes that both *The Shoemaker's Prodigious Wife* and *Don Perlimplín* "have in them the seeds of a great ballet. With folksongs, dances, and great possibilities for dramatic tableaux, they surpass *The Three-Cornered Hat* [by Manuel de Falla] as choreographical material, and in their Spanish presentations, the most was made of this intuitive and rhythmic body-mindedness of the author." John Crow, *Federico García Lorca* (Los Angeles, UCLA, 1945): 61. On musical adaptations, see Roger D. Tinnell, *Federico Garcïa Lorca y la música* (Madrid, Fundación Juan March, 1993): 12-17. María Isabel de Vicente-Yagüe Jara provides a list of musical adaptations through 2019, including those of Xavier Montsalvatge and Federico Mompou, Luigi Nono, Heitor Villa-Lobos, Michel Saltet, Harold Gramatge, Jorge Peixinho, Claude Arrieu,

György Behár, Albert Biales, Miguel Ángel Coria, Arnold Elston, Eduardo Feldman, Wolfgang Fortner, Bruno Maderna, Vittorio Rieti, Balduin Sulzer, and Conrad Susa. See "Federico García a través de la mùsica. Selección y análisis didáctico de un repertorio musical con hipotexto teatral", *Bellaterra Journal of Teaching & Learning Language & Literature* 12, no. 4 (November-December 2019).

46. *Don Perlimplín ovvero il trionfo dell'amore e dell'immaginazione.* In a subtle analysis of the rhythm of certain scenes of his brother's drama, Francisco García Lorca observes that "If the actors place even the slightest emphasis on the tonal and rhythmic qualities, the words turn into a dialogue between musical instruments" (*In the Green Morning*, 184). See also Andrés Soria Olmedo's introduction to Federico García Lorca, *Obras completas*, vol. 2, *Teatro* (Madrid: Biblioteca Castro/Fundación José Antonio Castro, 2021): lxv; and his "Don Perlimplín en Venecia: Nono y Maderna," *Rassegna Iberistica*, 40, no. 107 (June 2017): 23-40.

47. "Frank Eng," *Daily News* (Los Angeles), November 10, 1947.

48. Eric Bentley, *The Playwright as Thinker: A Study of Drama in Modern Times* (New York: Reynal & Hitchcock, 1946). Quoted from the fourth edition (University of Minnesota Press, 1987): 223.

49. E.F.M., "*Doña Rosita* in Cambridge," *The Christian Science Monitor*, April 29, 1943.

50. Francisco García Lorca, *In the Green Morning*, 188.

51. Theresa Loeb, "Interplayers Start on Repertoire," *Oakland Tribune*, August 26, 1947.

52. "Frank Eng" in *Daily News* (Los Angeles), November 28, 1947.

53. Eng in *Daily News* (Los Angeles), Nov. 20, 1947.

54. "A group of prominent theater executives representing the Theatre Guild and other producing organizations visited the Coronet for the purpose of gauging the possibilities of the García Lorca play for Broadway." See "Coronet Play May Be Seen on Broadway," *Los Angeles Times*, Nov. 30, 1947 and "Frank Eng", *Daily News*, June 10, 1947, where Eng declares that the Pelican production of *Bernarda Alba* will be "the first time a García Lorca play has been offered by a professional company in this country." It had been performed a few months earlier—July 1947—at Mills College where Milhaud had written the score (Opus 280) for clarinet, oboe, bassoon and percussion ("Spanish Drama to Aid Fund," *Oakland Triubune*, July 23, 1947).

55. "Studio Briefs," *Los Angeles Times*, May 5 and September 3, 1948.

56. Luis Fernández Cifuentes brilliantly reconstructs audience expectations and Lorca's divergence from them in *García Lorca en el teatro: La norma y la diferencia*.

57. *Christian Science Monitor*, June 18, 1949.

58. Eng in *Daily News* (Los Angeles), Nov. 20, 1947.

59. Fernández Cifuentes, *García Lorca en el teatro*, 116-117.

60. *Trenton Evening Times*, Dec. 13, 1979. Of his puppetry Lenton remarks, "I'd

never try to do Richard III, but there are things that can be done better with things than with people. You can do fantasy things better. You can get a human reaction from an audience doing things with puppets that seem awkward when real people do them. Like with *Don Perlimplín*." William Speers, "The World on a String," *The Philadelphia Inquirer*, December 16, 1979.

61. "Life, Love and Comedy Along the Río Grande", *The Morning Herald* (Hagerstown, Maryland), October 6, 1944. The playwright Lynn Butler won a statewide competition to write a companion piece for *Perlimplín*, with *The Santero's Dream Woman*. Sharing Perlimplín's "theme of love and intimacy" and stretching cultural companionship to the limits, Butler's play "is about an aging Chimayo *santero* who falls in love with the most beautiful of his statues after it magically comes to life." *The Morning Herald*, June 26, 1944.

62. William A. Henry 3rd, "'Don Perlimplin' Chilling Tale Cloaked in Deceptive Beauty," *The Boston Globe*, February 14, 1972.

63. Kevin Kelly, "*Love of Don Perlimplín*," *The Boston Daily Globe*, April 1, 1959.

64. R.G.J., "Library Theatre 'Summer Fare,'" *The Guardian* (London), September 13, 1949.

65. Gwynne Edwards, "Theatre Workshop's Translations of Three Spanish Plays," 56. A reviewer in the *Manchester Evening News* reports that "Somehow Lorca's [play], described as an 'erotic alleluia,' seems to misfire. Or is it just that English audiences faced with this kind of thing communicate their discomfort to the actors?" ("Summer Fare," 13 Sept. 1949). See also the amusing accounts of *Perlimplín* performances in Joan Littlewood, *Joan's Book*, 4th edition, Bloomsbury Publishing, 2018. An earlier performance (1946) had been panned in Liverpool: "As a play, *The Love of Don Perlimplín and Belisa in the Garden*, to this phlegmatic and coughy clime, appears trivial and senile." W.R.B., "Don Perlimplin's Love," *Liverpool Echo*, January 12, 1946. The play got a "coughy" reception, also, in England's Lake District, where the "suitably young and voluptuous" Swedish actress Kerstin Lind played Belisa (Edwards, "Theatre Workshop.") Luis Meana, who had formed part of Lorca's theater troupe La Barraca, joined Littlewood for the premiere in Kendal and was curious to see "how [the audience] would take its first taste of Theatre Workshop eroticism." "There wasn't a sound out front when Kerstin finished her first aria. Was the hall empty? No, there was plenty of coughing. It was the same all the way through, and at the end? Silence. Silence, followed by a few hisses and cluckings, till one or two began to clap wildly."

66. Letter to the editor, *The Manchester Guardian*, September 19, 1949.

67. *In the Green Morning*, 185. He adds that "Perhaps the 'Erotic Aleluya' was Federico's attempt to write an opera libretto on his own terms [and not those of Manuel de Falla] and perhaps this is the source (aside from the poet's temperament and personal background) of the musical and rhythmic nature of its language." 188.

68. Howard Taubman, "New Bowles Score Gets First Hearing," *New York Times*, March 31, 1943.

69. "Tar, GI Swipe Applause in Ballet Russe," *Daily News* (New York), April 11, 1944. The work had been performed in the U.S. at least since 1938. See "Ballet to Mark Academy Bill," *The Philadelphia Inquirer*, April 10, 1938.

70. Lorca's brother Francisco had assented to the production and had consulted with Rieti.

71. See Walter van de Leur, *Something to Live For: The Music of Billy Strayhorn* (New York: Oxford University Press, 2002), 121; Jonathan Mayhew, *Lorca's Legacy. Essays in Interpretation* (London and New York: Routledge, 2018): 114-118; and Lisa Barg, "Queer Encounters in the Music of Billy Strayhorn," *Journal of the American Musicological Society* 66, no. 3 (2013): 780.

72. Robert M. MacGregor to Francisco García Lorca, September 10, 1974, New Directions Publishing Corp. Records, bMS Am2077 (5792). See also Else Albrecht-Carrie, Permissions Editor, to Michael Jeffrey Shapiro, March 3, 1977: "Many composers have wanted to use this lovely play as a libretto over the years, but so far the Lorca Estate, whom we represent, has not been willing to permit anybody to do so (except under very limited circumstances, if any)." New Directions Publishing Corp. Records, bMS aM 2077 (5792 [12]-(5795 [4], Box 816. In August 1979 Albrecht-Carrié writes Manuel Fernández-Montesinos: "We ourselves have for close to twenty years consistently turned down all requests for permission to use *Don Perlimplín* for an operatic setting; and we have had more requests for this particular play than for any other" letter of August 23, 1979, New Directions Publishing Corp. Records). Albrecht-Carrie consulted with Jack Beeson, "head of the Music Department at Columbia University, a friend of mine and himself a composer of several operas" who confirmed her thinking that "the rights [to Lorca plays] should be protected and not be given freely until a really outstanding composer came around and wanted them. If we permitted second-rate composers to use the plays, outstanding composers would no longer bother." The request from Shapiro was later granted by Manuel Fernández-Montesinos.

BIBLIOGRAPHY

Adams, Mildred. *García Lorca: Playwright and Poet*. New York: Braziller, 1977.
___. Papers. Hispanic Society of America.
___. Papers. 1936-1963. Schlesinger Library, Radcliffe Institute.
Aguilera Sastre, Juan. "Entre dos exilios: Rivas Cherif y García Lorca." *Archivum* LXIII (2013): 7-58.
Allen, Donald. *The New American Poetry, 1945-1960*. New York: Grove Press, 1960.
___. *Poetics of the New American Poetry*. New York: Grove Press, 1973.
Alonso, Amado. *Materia y forma en poesía*. Madrid: Gredos, 1960.
___. Papers. Harvard University Archives.
Amades, J., J. Colominas and Pau Vila. *Les auques. Imatgeria popular catalana*. 2 vols. Barcelona: Editorial Orbis, 1931 and 1933.
Anderson, Andrew A. "Títeres bidimensionales: Lagar, Barradas, Lorca, Lanz," *Acotaciones* 48 (Jan.-June 2022): 297-329.
___. "Undecidability in Lorca's *Amor de Don Perlimplín con Belisa en su jardín*." *Hispanic Studies Review* 3, no. 1 (2018): 1-13.
Aznar Soler, Manuel. "Mª Teresa León y el teatro español durante la guerra civil." *Revista Stichomythia* no. 5 (2007): 37-54.
Barg, Lisa. "Queer Encounters in the Music of Billy Strayhorn." *Journal of the American Musicological Society* 66, no. 3 (2013): 771-824.
Bentley, Eric. *The Playwright as Thinker: A Study of Drama in Modern Times*. New York: Reynal & Hitchcock, 1946.
Berlin, Isaac, *Enlightening. Letters 1946-1960*. London: Chatto & Windus, 2009.
Busch-Reisenger Museum. *Busch-Reisinger Museum. History and Holdings*. Cambridge, MA: Harvard University Art Museums, 1991.
Callaway, Lisa and Carolyn Coman. *Arno Werner on Book-binding*. Lancaster, NH: Stinehour Press, 1981.
Calvo Serraller, Francisco. *Zobel*. Madrid: Fundación Juan March, 1984.
Capistrano-Baker, Florina H. "Whither Art History in the Non-Western World: Exploring the Other('s) Art Histories." *The Art Bulletin* 97 (2005): 246-257.
Cavanaugh, Cecelia J., SSJ. *Lorca's Drawings and Poems. Forming the Eye of the Reader*. Lewisburg-London: Bucknell University Press, 1995.

Crow, John. *Federico García Lorca*. Los Angeles: UCLA, 1945.
Duberman, Martin. *Black Mountain. An Exploration in Community*. New York: E.P. Dutton, 1972.
Edgar, Natalie, "Is There a New Spanish School?," *Art News* 59, no. 5 (1960): 44-45
Edwards, Gwynne. "Theatre Workshop and the Spanish Drama." *New Theatre* Quarterly 23 no. 4 (Nov. 2007): 304-16.
___. "Theatre Workshop's Translations of Three Spanish Plays." *New Theatre Quarterly* 25, no. 1 (2009): 52-62.
Fergusson, Francis. "'Don Perlimplín': Lorca's Theatre-Poetry." *The Kenyon Review* XVII, no. 3 (Summer 1955): 337-48.
Fernández Cifuentes, Luis. *García Lorca en el teatro: La norma y la diferencia*. Zaragoza: Prensas Universitarias, 1986.
___. "La literatura española en los Estados Unidos: historia de sus historias." In *Historia literaria / historia de la literatura*, edited by Leonardo Romero. Zaragoza: Prensas Universitarias, 2004: 253-272.
Flores, Patrick D. "The Zóbel Nexus." *Kritika Kultura* 24 (2015): 182-205.
Fontán del Junco, Manuel, Celina Quintas and Daniel Sepúlveda, "A Life Lived Through Drawings: The Sketchbooks of Fernando Zóbel." *Master Drawings* 50, no. 1 (spring 2013): 87-104.
García Lorca, Federico. *Amor de Don Perlimplín con Belisa en su jardín*. Ed. Margarita Ucelay. Madrid: Cátedra, 1990.
___. *Collected Poems*. Ed. Christopher Maurer. New York: Farrar, Straus and Giroux, 2002.
___. *Epistolario completo*. Ed. Andrew A. Anderson and Christopher Maurer. Madrid: Cátedra, 1998.
___. *Five Plays. Comedies and Tragicomedies*. Trans. Richard L. O'Connell and James Graham Luján. Intro. Francisco García Lorca. New York: New Directions, 1963.
___. *From Lorca's Theatre. Five Plays of Federico García Lorca*. Trans. Richard L. O'Connell and James Graham L. New York: Charles Scribner's Sons, 1941.
___. *Obras completas*. Vol. I (*Amor de Don Perlimplín con Belisa en su jardín, Bodas de sangre, Retablillo de Don Cristóbal*). Buenos Aires: Losada, 1944 (1st edition 1938).
___. *Obras completas*. Ed. Arturo del Hoyo. Madrid: Aguilar, 1954.
___. *Obras completas*. Ed. Miguel García-Posada. Vol. 2, *Teatro*, Vol. 3, *Prosa*. Barcelona: Galaxia Gutenberg/Círculo de Lectores, 1997.
___. *Obras completas*. Vol. 2, *Teatro*. Ed. and intro. Andrés Soria Olmedo. Madrid: Biblioteca Castro/Fundación José Antonio Castro, 2021.
___. *Palabra de Lorca. Declaraciones y entrevistas completas*. Ed. Rafael Inglada. Barcelona: Malpaso, 2017.

____. *Poet in New York*. Ed. C. Maurer. Trans. Greg Simon and Steven F. White. Third edition. New York: Farrar, Straus and Giroux, 2013.

____. *Teatro inconcluso: fragmentos y proyectos inacabados*. Ed. Marie Laffranque. Granada: Universidad de Granada, 1987.

____. *Three Tragedies*. Trans. Richard L. O'Connell and James Graham Luján. New York: New Directions, 1963.

García Lorca, Francisco. *In the Green Morning*. Trans. Christopher Maurer. New York: New Directions, 1986.

____. *Federico y su mundo*. Ed. Mario Hernández. Madrid: Alianza, 1980.

González del Valle, Luis T. "La concepción musical de *Amor de Don Perlimplín con Belisa en su jardín*." *El teatro de Federico García Lorca y otros ensayos*. Lincoln, NE: Society of Spanish and Spanish American Studies, 1980: 61-79.

Graff, Gerald. *Professing Literature. An Institutional History*. Chicago: University of Chicago Press, 1987.

Grant, Helen. "Una aleluya erótica de Federico García Lorca y las aleluyas populares del siglo XIX." *Actas del Primer Congreso de la Asociación Internacional de Hispanistas celebrado en Oxford del 6 al 11 de septiembre de 1962* (Oxford: The Dolphin Book Company, 1964). Https://cudl.lib.cam.ac.uk/view/PR-TAB-B-00721-00003/1.

Grosz, George. *An Autobiography*. Trans. Nora Hodges. Berkeley, CA: University of California Press, 1998.

Guillén, Claudio. *De leyendas y lecciones*. Barcelona: Crítica, 2007.

Hart, Estellita. *Courses on Latin America in Institutions of Higher Education in the United States*. Washington, D.C.: Pan American Union, 1946-1947, 1948-1949, etc.

Harvard University. *Courses of Instruction*, 1945-46.

____. *General Education in a Free Society. The Report of the Harvard Committee* [*The Redbook*]. Cambridge: Harvard University Press, 1946.

____. *Harvard University Catalog*. Cambridge: Harvard University Press, [1945-1949].

____. *Official Register of Harvard University. Final Announcement of the Courses of Instruction Offered by the Faculty of Arts and Sciences for the Academic Year [1945-1949]*. Cambridge: Harvard University Press, [1945-1949].

Harvard University Archives. *Syllabi, course outlines and reading lists in Spanish, 1927-1979*.

____. *Exhibition Records, 1931-1950*, HUAM Records, 2008.184.

____. *Syllabi, course outlines and reading lists in Comparative Literature, 1909-1979*.

____. *Papers of Amado Alonso*.

____. *Harvard Class Reports and Class Directories 1916-1999*. Harvard College, Class Report Offices.

____. *The 1949 Harvard Album*. Cambridge: Harvard University Press, 1949.

Hernández, Mario. *Fernando Zóbel. El misterio de lo transparente.* Madrid: Rayuela, 1977.

____. *Libro de los dibujos de Federico García Lorca.* Madrid: Tabapress/Fundación Federico García Lorca, 1990.

____. *Line of Light and Shadow. The Drawings of Federico García Lorca.* Trans. Christopher Maurer. Madrid: Tabapress/Fundación Federico García Lorca, 1991.

Hirschler, Erica E. *Hyman Bloom. Matters of Life and Death.* Boston: Museum of Fine Arts, 2019.

Houghton Library, Harvard University. *Arno Werner, Master Bookbinder: An Exhibition at the Houghton Library.* Cambridge: Houghton Library, 1981.

Hurtado Hernández, Mónica. *Los Cristobitas en Lorca. Tradición y vanguardia en los "puntales del teatro."* Vigo: Editorial Academia del Hispanismo, 2019.

Jiménez-Blanco, María Dolores. "Spanishness and Difference. The Reception of Spanish Informalism in New York." *Contemporary Transatlantic Dialogues. Art History, Criticism, and Exhibition Practices in Spain and the United States.* New York: Center for Spain in America, 1960: 15-20.

Judin, Juerg M. ed. *George Grosz. The Years in America 1933-1958.* New York: Hatje Cantz, 2009.

Kantor, Sybil Gordon. *Alfred H. Barr, Jr. and the Intellectual Origins of the Museum of Modern Art.* Cambridge, MA: MIT Press, 2002.

Keller, Morton and Phyllis. *Making Harvard Modern. The Rise of America's University.* Oxford: Oxford University Press, 2001.

Kentgens-Craig, Margret. *The Bauhaus and America. First Contacts 1919-1936.* Cambridge, MA: MIT Press, 1999

Kubler, George. *The Shape of Time.* New Haven: Yale University Press, 1962.

Langfeld, Gregor. *German Art in New York. The Canonization of Modern Art, 1904-1957.* Amsterdam University Press, 2015.

Levin, Gail. *Lee Krasner, A Biography.* New York: HarperCollins, 2011.

____. "The Extraordinary Interventions of Alfonso Ossorio, Patron and Collector of Jackson Pollock and Lee Krasner." *Archives of American Art Journal* 50 (2011): 5-19.

Littlewood, Joan. *Joan's Book. The Autobiography of Joan Littlewood.* 4th ed. London: Bloomsbury Publishing, 2016.

McClellan, Andrew and Sally Ann Duncan. *The Art of Curating. Paul J. Sachs and the Museum Course at Harvard.* Los Angeles: Getty Research Institute, 2018.

McDermid, Paul. *Love, Desire and Identity in the Theatre of Federico García Lorca.* London: Tamesis, 2007.

Marzo, Jorge Luis. *Arte Moderno y Franquismo. Los orígenes conservadores de la vanguardia y de la política artista en España.* 2006. https://www.soymenos.net/arte_franquismo.pdf

Mayhew, Jonathan. *Lorca's Legacy. Essays in Interpretation*. London and New York: Routledge, 2018.
Menand, Louis. *The Marketplace of Ideas. Reform and Resistance in the American University*. New York: Norton and Company, 2010.
____. *The Free World. Art and Thought in the Cold War*. New York: Farrar, Straus and Giroux, 2021.
Meyer, Esther da Costa. "George Grosz, *The American Scene*." *Yale University Art Gallery Bulletin* 37 (1980): 4-7.
Möckel, Brigit. *George Grosz in Amerika 1932-1959*. Frankfurt am Main, Germany and New York, NY: Peter Lang, 1997.
Muir, Laura, ed. *Object Lessons. The Bauhaus and Harvard*. New Haven and London: Yale University Press, 2021.
New Directions Publishing Corp. Records, Houghton Library, Harvard University.
Nisbet, Peter and Emilie Norris. *The Busch-Reisinger Museum: History and Holdings*. Cambridge, MA: Harvard University Art Museums, 1991.
Orringer, Nelson R. "Falla's *Harpsichord Concerto* and Lorca's *Don Perlimplín*." Eds. Irene Gómez Castillo and Aurélie Vialette. *Dissonances of Modernity: Music, Text, and Performance in Modern Spain*. Durham: North Carolina Studies in the Romance Languages and Literatures, 2021: 225-240.
____. *Lorca in Tune With Falla*. University of Toronto Press, 2014.
Pedrosa, J.M. "De *Perlinpinpin* a *Perlimplín*. *Féerie* francesa, *Cyrano*, cuentos de Calleja…y Lorca." *Liburna* 8 (November 2015): 117-63.
Peral Vega, Emilio. "Morir y matar amando: *Amor de Don Perlimplín con Belisa en su jardín*," *Arbor* (Madrid) CLXXVII nos. 699-700 (March-April 2004): 691-702.
____. *Pierrot/Lorca. White Carnaval of Black Desire*. Woodbridge: Tamesis, 2015.
Poggioli, Renato. *The Theory of the Avant-Garde*. New York-London: Icon Editions, 1968.
Polignac, Diane de. "Fernando Zóbel." https://dianedepolignac.com/en/home-gb/artists-en/00-fernando-zobel-gb/
Prescott, Peter. *A Darkening Green. Notes on Harvard, the 1950s and the End of Innocence*. New Brunswick: Transaction Publishers, 2009.
Richards, I. A. *Practical Criticism*. New York: Harcourt, Brace and Company, 1929.
Rotté, Joanna and Stella Adler. "An Interview with Stella Adler." *Theatre Topics* 12, no. 2 (2002): 191-202.
Schneider, Luis Mario. *García Lorca y México*. Mexico City: UNAM, 1998.
Seed, John. "Fernando Zóbel de Ayala. Brief Life of a Peripatetic Man of Arts: 1924-1984." *Harvard Magazine*, March-April 2009. https://www.harvardmagazine.com/2009/03/fernando-z-bel-de-ayala
____. *Zóbel and the Pfeufers: A Friendship in Art and Letters*. 2015. https://www.geringerart.com/works-by-fernando-zobel-from-the-estate-of-jim-and-reed-pfeufer/.

Solomon, Deborah. *Jackson Pollock. A Biography*. New York: Simon and Schuster, 1987.
Soria Olmedo, Andrés. "Don Perlimplín en Venecia: Nono y Maderna." *Rassegna Iberistica* 40, no. 107 (June 2017): 23-40.
Soriano, Peter. "A Biographical Sketch of Zóbel's Formative Years," in *Zóbel. Madrid: Aldeasa*, 2003: 258-263.
Tinnell, Roger D. *Federico García Lorca y la música*. Madrid: Fundación Juan March, 1993.
Torre, Alfonso de la. "Zóbel-Chillida: A Meeting." *Mayoral Magazine*, April 29, 2019. Http://galeriamayoral.com/en/magazine/zobel-chillida-a-meeting-alfonso-de-la-torre/
Trilling, Lionel. *Sincerity and Authenticity*. Cambridge: Harvard University Press, 1972.
Van de Leur, Walter. *Something to Live For: The Music of Billy Strayhorn*. New York: Oxford University Press, 2002.
Vega Martín, Cecilia. "Aspectos del juego y de la tragedia en *Amor de Don Perlimplín con Belisa en un jardín*." *El teatro de Lorca. Tragedia, drama y farsa. Actas del IV Congreso de Literatura Española Contemporánea*. Universidad de Málaga, 1996.
Vicente-Yagüe Jara, María Isabel de. "Federico García Lorca a través de la música. Selección y análisis didáctico de un repertorio musical con hipotexto teatral." *Bellaterra Journal of Teaching & Learning Language & Literature* 12, no. 4 (Nov.-Dic. 2019): 81-101.
Villalba Salvador, Ángeles. "Cronología Fernando Zóbel." In *Zóbel*. Madrid: Aldeasa, 2003: 205-36.
Walsh, Andrew Samuel. Lorca in English. *A History of Manipulation Through Translation*. New York: Routledge, 2020.
Wiesenberger, Robert. "The Bauhaus and Harvard." https://harvardartmuseums.org/tour/the-bauhaus/slide/6339.
Wright, Frederick S. *Milestones of American Painting*. Boston: Institute of Contemporary Art, 1949.
Zóbel, Fernando. *Diarios*. Fundación Juan March, *Archivo Fenando Zóbel*, ES.28006.BFJM.AFZ
___. Letters to Paul Haldeman. Fernando Zóbel Papers, 1945-1983. Ms Typ 688, Houghton Library, Harvard University.
___ and Nap C. Jamir. *Philippine Religious Imagery*. Manila: Ateneo de Manila, 1963.
___. "Theme and Conflict in Lorcan Drama." Fundación Juan March, *The Library of Fernando Zóbel*.

ACKNOWLEDGMENTS

A book, whether by a single author or several, is not possible without the support ofothers. The essayists are deeply grateful for the help, encouragement, support, and permission of Georgina Padilla-Zóbel and Alejandro Padilla Zóbel, and the estate of Fernando Zóbel; Laura García Lorca, Fundación Federico García Lorca, and Centro Federico García Lorca; Ana Muller, and the estate of Nicolás Muller; the staff of the Harvard University Archives; the Fundación Juan March; Peter Accardo and the Houghton Library; Laura Peimar of the Schlesinger Library (Harvard/Radcliffe Institute); Nancy Brown-Martínez of the University of New Mexico Center for Southwest Research and Special Collections; Charles Kronauer of the Fox Club; Peter Soriano; John Seed; Andrew A. Anderson; Instituto Cervantes at Harvard University-Observatorio de la Lengua Española y las Culturas Hispánicas en los Estados Unidos, and its Executive Director Marta Mateo; the Boston University Center for the Humanities, and Boston University UROP; the Faculty of Arts and Sciences, Harvard University; and to all those colleagues, friends, and those who have in various ways supported the publication of this book. Special thanks to designer Marianne Jankowski and to David Rade of Swan Isle Press.